Relaying Cinema in Midcentury Iran

CINEMA CULTURES IN CONTACT

Richard Abel, Giorgio Bertellini, and Matthew Solomon, Series Editors

Relaying Cinema in Midcentury Iran

Material Cultures in Transit

Kaveh Askari

UNIVERSITY OF CALIFORNIA PRESS

University of California Press
Oakland, California

Library of Congress Cataloging-in-Publication Data

Names: Askari, Kaveh, author.
Title: Relaying cinema in midcentury Iran : material cultures in
    transit / Kaveh Askari.
Other titles: Cinema cultures in contact ; 2.
Description: Oakland, California : University of California Press,
    [2022] | Series: Cinema Cultures in Contact ; 2 | Includes
    bibliographical references and index.
Identifiers: LCCN 2021033097 (print) | LCCN 2021033098 (ebook) |
    ISBN 9780520329751 (cloth) | ISBN 9780520329768 (paperback) |
    ISBN 9780520974357 (epub)
Subjects: LCSH: Motion pictures—Iran—History. | Motion picture
    industry—Iran—History. | BISAC: PERFORMING ARTS / Film /
    History & Criticism | HISTORY / World
Classification: LCC PN1993.5.I846 A84 2022 (print) |
    LCC PN1993.5.I846 (ebook) | DDC 791.430955—dc23
LC record available at https://lccn.loc.gov/2021033097
LC ebook record available at https://lccn.loc.gov/2021033098

Manufactured in the United States of America

31 30 29 28 27 26 25 24 23 22
10 9 8 7 6 5 4 3 2 1

Contents

Illustrations

Acknowledgments

I guess it was inevitable that my effort to recognize some of the colleagues and kin who have made this book possible would take the form of a travel record. It is a book on circulation written during a peripatetic twelve-year period. I began writing the first sections of this book while on a Mellon postdoctoral fellowship at UC Berkeley, where I was fortunate to have support from the Townsend Center for the Humanities and access to the university's special collections holdings of bound hardcopies of *Ettela'at*. Conversations there with Kathy Geritz, Michael Kunichika, Jaleh Pirnazar, Jon Shibata, Navid Sinaki, and Linda Williams set this project on course. Mike has made my life better in immeasurable ways since then. It was also during this time that, having just missed him in Chicago, Hamid Naficy mentored me through early stages of research while making sure that I finished my first book first. In the decade since, my debt to him has greatly increased.

In the Pacific Northwest, I had the supportive department chairs Marc Geisler and Kathryn Vulić, and a campus community that included Rich Brown, Joshua Cerretti, Kendall Dodd, Tiana Kahakauwila, Brenda Miller, Lysa Rivera, and Theresa Warburton. Andrew Ritchey made time to visit and helped me to understand what was so exciting about the soundtracks of the films I was watching. Thanks to the engaged students in my seminars on cinemas of Iran and the Middle East, including Nathaniel Barr (who labored to make spreadsheets out of my pile of material from the United Artists archive), Zachary Furste, Matthew

Holtmeier, Christopher Melton, Amos Stailey-Young, and Chelsea Wessels. It has been a pleasure to follow their careers after our time working together. Michael Falter at the Pickford Film Center was always available for collaborative projects and film banter—on camera and off. I was especially fortunate to be a short drive away from Jennifer Bean, who welcomed me in Seattle. Jennifer, along with Anupama Kapse and Laura Horak, spent significant time with my first chapter when a version of it was being prepared for *Silent Cinema and the Politics of Space*. Alyssa Gabbay also offered precise and thoughtful notes on that chapter, and the project as a whole, during this time.

At Northwestern University in Qatar, I was able to conduct the final research for the project thanks to my proximity to Tehran and grants from the Qatar Foundation. The foundation also contributed to the Tehran Noir program at Il Cinema Ritrovato. My wonderful media colleagues in Doha included Sami Hermez, Joe Khalil, Iman Khamis, Hasan Mahmud, Justin Martin, Jocelyn Mitchell, Anto Mohsin, Kirsten Pike, Ann Woodworth, and Zachary Wright. The students in seminars at NUQ helped me to develop many of ideas presented in this book. I am particularly grateful to Maysam Al-Ani, Urooj Azmi, Bohao Liu, and Sarhan Khan (for his research assistance as well as his academic work). A colleague at the campus next door, Firat Oruc has offered guidance and a collaborative energy that has brought me back to Doha multiple times since I left. Scott Curtis and I had known each other for a while, but we had the opportunity to become friends in Doha. His careful consideration of this project is most evident in the fifth chapter, a version of which was published in *Cinema Journal* at that time. I know I am not alone in saying that I also benefitted from his professional advice, administrative IQ, and precise attention to everyday aesthetic details.

At Michigan State University grants from the Humanities and Arts Research Program and the Muslim Studies Program made it possible to complete the chapters during an accelerated stage of this project. Presenting this material in courses and workshops with students including Liz Deegan, Jacob Eddy, Amrutha Kunapulli, and Fabrizzio Torero helped me to hit the ground running. I am indebted to colleagues working with or within the Film Studies Program, including David Bering-Porter, Marc Bernstein, Parisa Ghaderi, Juliet Guzzetta, Kenneth Harrow, Salah Hassan, Peter Johnston, Yelena Kalinsky, Mikki Kressbach, Ellen McCallum, Mihaela Mihailova, Justus Nieland, Swarnavel Pillai, Jordan Schonig, Daniel Smith, Kuhu Tanvir, William Vincent, Lily Woodruff, Jeff Wray, and Joshua Yumibe. Ellen, Lily, Ken,

Josh, and Justus provided lively feedback on the second chapter during one of our living-room research workshops. Justus ignored my hesitations about sending him multiple chapters and helped me to work through the fourth chapter and the introduction as well. This book would not have come together in the way that it did without the culture of generosity here. The film and media faculty made me realize, by example, that I was rarely as tired as I thought I was. The move to MSU has also put me a short walk from one of my oldest friends. I thank Joshua Yumibe for his empathy and unwavering confidence in the people around him. As a coworker, he is an aspirational model of persistence and effective problem solving.

I tested and reworked portions of this book at various institutions thanks to warm invitations from colleagues. A talk at the Moving Images research seminar at the University of Washington allowed formative conversations with Sudhir Mahadevan and James Tweedie. During a sabbatical in Los Angeles, I was welcomed by Joseph Bristow and Ali Behdad. Nasrin Rahimieh organized a lecture at the Samuel Jordan Center for Persian Studies at UC Irvine. Samhita Sunya invited me to present at the University of Virginia in connection to the Global South initiative of the Institute of the Humanities and Global Cultures. Since then, she has been a dear collaborator and fellow enthusiast for film ephemera. I would work with her again in a second. Michael Allan brought me to the University of Oregon to present a chapter in a forum where I received insight from faculty there, including Michael Aronson, Sangita Gopal, and Janet Wasko. Hamid Naficy, in his characteristic support of junior scholars, invited me to Northwestern twice. A talk in Qatar on my way to Iran helped to focus questions for my time in archives, and it gave me the idea that I might want to work at NUQ. Proximity to Toronto has been a perk during the past four years. Thanks to Jovanna Scorsone and Theresa Scandiffio for inviting me to present elements of this research at the Aga Khan Museum and TIFF. It was during trips like these, in conversation with Canan Balan, Nilo Couret, Cloé Drieu, Hatim El-Hibri, Nezih Erdogan, Laura Fish, Mania Gregorian, Sarah Keller, Peter Limbrick, Ross Melnick, Sara Saljoughi, and Babak Tabarraee, that I was able to get a better sense of what was meaningful in this project. Out of these conversations I accepted the generous offers to read a chapter from Claire Cooley, Cloé Drieu, Jean Ma, Nolwenn Mingant, and Daniel Steinhart. Blake Atwood and Golbarg Rekabtalaei read the draft manuscript from start to finish, offering it the insights of model scholars in the field.

The core work of this book has been cross-archival. I am indebted to archivists at several institutions for their knowledge of their collections' esoteric threads. Not only did they guide me through their collections during multiple visits, but they fielded follow-up questions every time I discovered an item abroad that linked back to a collection I had already visited. My communication history is dense with helpful messages from archivists at the Harry Ransom Center, the University of Southern California, the Margaret Herrick Library, the Wisconsin Center for Film and Theater Research, the National Film Archive of Iran, the National Library of Iran, the House of Cinema in Tehran, and the Museum of Cinema in Tehran. I am particularly grateful to Barbara Hall, Gholam Heydari, Mary Huelsbeck, Kit Hughes, Brett Service, and Ladan Taheri. Mo Taei assisted with some follow-up research at the National Library of Iran. My friend Masoud has spent many hours online with me discussing objects from these collections. Ramin Sadegh Khanjani has lived with this project for years as a researcher, interlocutor, and longtime friend. He has maintained his curiosity and enthusiasm for it despite being the one person besides me who has fallen deepest into its vortex of spreadsheets. Ramin also introduced me to Ehsan Khoshbakht, who has become a friend and collaborator over the past few years. This book would be much thinner if not for Ehsan's generosity in sharing his private collection of ephemera and his knowledgeable attention to every page of the manuscript.

At the University of California Press, Raina Polivka has been a dream to work with. She was confident about the project from its beginnings (when she was still in Indiana), and this same confidence helped to persuade me to finally let go of the manuscript. Her work, along with that of Madison Wetzell, Teresa Iafolla, Sarah Hudgens, and Dena Afrasiabi, assured me that the manuscript was in good hands. The press sent samples of the project to two advance reviewers and the complete manuscript to two final reviewers. Their perspectives helped me to broaden the scope of the book, and their attention to detail helped me to sharpen specific arguments in every chapter. It was a treat to have the opportunity to work again with series editors Richard Abel, Giorgio Bertellini, and Matthew Solomon. The timing of their series presented a lucky opportunity to draw from their expertise as I adapted my training in early cinema studies for this new material.

The work of completing a book is isolating, and acknowledging all the ways that writing is inherently social offers little to distract from that feeling. What did help in my case was a group of friends ready to work together in cafés and after-hours on campus. During the COVID-19 lockdown, we moved our informal writing group to a socially distant café and roastery in my East Lansing backyard. I am grateful to Tamara Butler, Delia Fernández, Yomaira Figueroa, Lyn Goeringer, and Tacuma Peters for showing up regularly with work timers and forms of sustenance. They motivated me, they helped me to work through frustrating setbacks, and they gave me the practice I needed before I could confidently pull a fine shot of espresso. I cannot imagine what 2020 would have been like without all the days when they dropped by unannounced.

The research for this book coincided with the time when I began to return to Iran every couple of years. As an adult, I maintained two active passports and increased my own movement to the place where I could find archival material and also the extended family that helped me in that access. This kinship formation, for almost all of my life, had been sustained only through electronic signals sent through undersea cables and satellite transmissions. Aunts, uncles, and cousins in Iran showed me around, put me up, and put up with me for months at a time. My aunt Marjan helped to open doors for me, and she found time to travel with me to museums or explore buildings where old cinema spaces had been converted to storerooms. I thank her for her wit and unstoppable energy. She patiently let me turn her dining room table into a magazine scanning operation and was standing behind the camera with me when I took some of the photographs that illustrate this book.

Midcentury Hollywood films were often playing at home while I was growing up in the United States, but I learned about them from my father, Amir Askari, who saw many of these films in Tehran in his youth. It took me a while to come to *filmfarsi* as a subject of research, perhaps in part because of assumptions—still widely held—that there was little value in films made in Iran in the 1950s and 1960s. But discussions about 1950s and 1960s Hollywood in my parents' home usually had something to do with Iran as well. I learned that Travis, my middle name, apparently came to my father's attention when he saw Lawrence Harvey's rendition of Colonel Travis in *The Alamo* (Wayne, 1960) in Tehran more than a decade before I was born. I was named both Kaveh, from the *Shahnameh*, and Travis, after a Tehran screening of a Hollywood film starring a Lithuanian-South African-British actor as a figure of American national mythology. This disclosure indicates something about the continuation of themes from this book into the cultural climate of the 1970s and my own position in that history. These curiosities of an instance of diasporic naming resurfaced as I began working on this project, particularly when I was working with one of the largest collections of documents about the circulation of Hollywood films in Iran, in the state where we and much of our extended family moved after leaving Iran. During my visits to Travis County, Texas, to do research at the Harry Ransom Center, I treasured the hospitality of the many Texas Askaris, especially my dear uncle Majid. He answered many phone calls to discuss obscure parts of this project.

I am thankful that Brian Whitener and I have never lost our ability to comfortably cohabit any place. We have received mail together at seven different addresses and have lived through a lot in those spaces. My mother, Linda Askari, has always appreciated my need to be in motion despite the distances it has created. One measure of those distances is that the route from Michigan to Miami, along which I can see her and my three brothers, feels to us like a short trip across town. My gratitude for living the better part of my life with Kristin Mahoney continues. She is alive to what is possible, in our work and in our not-work, be we in Paris or in Lansing.

Note on Transliteration and Titles

For the transliteration of Persian words, in consultation with the University of California Press, I have followed the *Iranian Studies* transliteration scheme with a few changes made in the interest of simplicity and readability within cinema and media studies. I do not use diacritics, and I drop silent consonants at the ends of words followed by hyphens. I also transliterate field-specific cognates using their English spellings. For example, instead of "*Setareh-ye Sinama,*" I use "*Setare-ye Cinema.*" This also applies to Persian-French cognates when the French term is commonly used in English in cinema and media studies (e.g., auteur, découpage, Moulin Rouge). I have made an effort to use the preferred, or the most searchable, spelling of Iranian names. For proper names of fictional characters, the spelling conforms to the standard scheme. "Behruz," a character in a film, is spelled differently throughout the text than a living actor who has chosen "Behrouz" as the spelling of his first name. I have dropped apostrophes from some names that would create double apostrophes in possessive constructions. For Iranian film titles, both Persian and English titles are used in the first instance in each chapter. For readability, the English title is used throughout the remainder of the chapter. Captions include both titles throughout each chapter.

Introduction

Midcentury   Film companies in Iran in the early 1960s did not always pay careful attention to their design elements, but Azhir Film had the ambition to bring its films, and especially its new release *Zarbat* (*The Strike*, Khachikian, 1964), into the world of midcentury cinema with a memorable design scheme. The film's creators did not realistically expect it to produce revenues outside of Iran, although they teased this possibility in the press as the project moved through various stages of its production.[1] The primary aim, rather, was to create a certain kind of cinematic experience when the film was released. The release called upon modern design's global ambitions at a time when packing movie houses in Tehran still typically meant securing a well-traveled film print.

A stubborn disagreement between filmmakers had left a lot riding on this particular crime thriller. Film studios in Iran tried to avoid competing releases, but this time, during a coveted release slot after the start of spring and the Iranian New Year, two producers refused to compromise. *The Strike*, produced by Josef Vaezian and directed by Samuel Khachikian, each of whom was coming off of a string of successful films, would be released the same week as the rival producer and former Khachikian collaborator Mehdi Missaghieh's *Ensan-ha* (*Human Beings*, Aghamaliyan). Industry professionals debated the ethics of this in the press, but neither producer would move aside.[2] *The Strike*'s distributor, Nureddin Ashtiany, pulled out all the stops with an extensive

FIGURE 1. Premiere of *Zarbat / The Strike* (Samuel Khachikian, 1964). Private collection.

publicity campaign and a premiere that drew a large street crowd and high-ranking special guests (figure 1).[3] The spectacular premiere motivated by a business feud, while not an unfamiliar occupational hazard in any film industry, marks a point of orientation in the topography of Iranian popular cinema of the time. It opens onto a moment when films circulated with great momentum but without the later-established transparency that would allow any one producer to really understand where and how their images and sound recordings traveled. Given the difficulty in tracking the large-scale phenomena of film culture in transit during a period of limited transparency, it helps to begin small. Consider, to start, the ephemera of this premiere and the modest labors of a billboard painter.

The 3D billboard above the marquee, the posters, and the title sequence, all created by the graphic artist Abbas Mazaheri, follow the design principles of compressing the experience of a film into streamlined graphic forms. At the start of the first reel, the audience encountered a pretitle sequence, something of a rarity for local productions, and a modernist animated graphic in simple white shapes. Diagonal

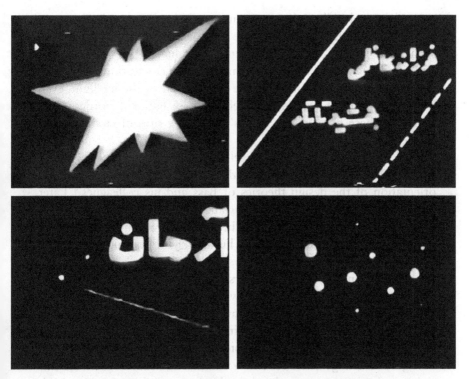

FIGURES 2A–2D. Title sequence from *Zarbat / The Strike* (Samuel Khachikian, 1964).

solid and dotted lines cut across the screen, rectilinear shapes expand and contract, and clusters of white dots blink in random patterns as the credits feature the members of the cast and crew in bold fonts (figures 2a–2d). The titles make use of a graphic motif that ran through much of the film's publicity material. A shattering blow (the "strike" of the film's title) was an iconic form on the billboard, and an abstract graphic of this strike opens the animated title sequence alongside the sounds of shattering glass and heavy percussion. When the sequence concludes, a lightning strike accompanies the first establishing shot. Had it been possible for Saul Bass to see this marketing campaign (the industry at the time depended on this impossibility) he might have felt vindicated that the design principles he proposed were being put to work successfully in an industry with dramatically fewer resources than the one in which he worked. The nearly invisible labor of a freshman designer who employed modernist design elements brought a film into the commercial sphere for a highly visible premiere. Azhir Film wanted to make films that announced, "This is cinema." The company continued these kinds of title sequences with subsequent films, such as the thriller *Sarsam* (*Delirium*), a product of the same director and title designer the following year. Part of the ambition of productions like these was to imagine the world orbit of the medium, even if their circulation was largely delimited by national borders. The design of these productions marks one of the sites of circulation in midcentury Iran.

The stylistic influence of a well-known midcentury designer in smaller film industries has remained largely unseen despite the global orientation of the design theories of Bass and his colleagues.[4] Later histories of film graphics in Iran are beginning to receive some consideration.[5] Abbas Kiarostami, the best-known Iranian director in the world, began his career by putting his art-school training to work on title sequences for films such as *Qeysar* (Kimiai, 1969).[6] To track stylistic influences in earlier film graphics in Iran, we could compare Bass's most recognizable work, like the swirl in *Vertigo*, with iterations elsewhere, including several Iranian movie posters, film magazine designs, and redesigned advertisements for imported films. The poster for *Tars va Tariki* (*Fear and Darkness*, Motevasselani, 1963) makes use of a *Vertigo*-like orange swirl around a character's head. Variants of this swirl appear in posters for local productions and imports alike. Midcentury film magazines make use of design schemes championed by Bass. We can see this in operation in a 1957 issue of *Film va Zendegi* (*Film and Life*): a young Sadegh Barirani designed the cover in a way that recalls the titles of sequences like those in *The Man with the Golden Arm* (Preminger, 1955). Barirani would go on to a celebrated design career that included posters for the Tehran International Film Festival and an invitation by Milton Glazer to the International Design Conference in Aspen.[7] Midcentury stylistic influence can offer some practical iterations of the global orientation of the design theories of Bass and his colleagues. It can also offer design-specific vectors of what Iain Robert Smith has termed "the Hollywood meme."[8] Parts of this book provide some resources for a discussion of stylistic influence in midcentury design.

My primary approach is slightly different, however, in its attention to circulating elements, modular components of cinema, including film scores and title design elements, as found *media objects*. The way distributors bundled publicity material with the films, and the way exhibitors and periodicals reassembled them, created a foundation for

FIGURE 3. Partial translation of William P. McGivern's serial *The Big Heat* (1952–1953, billed as *Zarbe-ye Bozorg / The Big Hit*) printed over an orange monochrome image from the poster, *Setare-ye Cinema*, December 8, 1957.

their stylistic currency. Browsing the layout in film magazines from this period, even relatively elaborate and well-funded ones such as *Setare-ye Cinema* (*Cinema Star*), one finds a particularly high concentration of design material reassembled from multiple sources of conspicuous provenance. A big film like *The Big Heat* warranted laying a translation of its original *Saturday Evening Post* story over a monochromatic orange reprint of the poster. The new title, *Zarbe-ye Bozorg* (*The Big Hit*), is printed in blue directly on top of the English title graphic from the poster (figure 3). Alongside discussions of Iranian actors imitating the styles of foreign stars, one finds thick eyebrows and almond-shaped eye makeup (popularized by Iranian stars) hand-painted over a colorized

FIGURE 4. Detail of cover image of Lana Turner, *Setare-ye Cinema*, Nowruz Special Issue, 1959.

portrait of Lana Turner on the cover of the 1338 (1959) Iranian New Year special issue of the magazine (figure 4).[9] The May 5, 1957, issue features *The Man with the Golden Arm* prominently. Its cover features a publicity portrait of Kim Novak, and the issue contains two articles about the film, one primarily from Preminger's perspective and the other from Novak's. The cover image, like the one of Lana Turner, is a color pinup of circuitous provenance. The half-tone images of Novak and Preminger inside are cut and pasted, with jagged edges still visible in the final layout. The film magazines that emerged in the 1950s, whether prominent or peripheral, have a collage quality to them. This quality, while not radically distinct from print operations elsewhere, is noticeable and significant to a history of circulation. The rough edges evident in layout highlight the publications' cut-and-paste practices of sourcing, editing, and translating found material.

If we look and listen closely, the title sequence for *The Strike* reveals something about the object lives of its found elements. It is perhaps closer to Len Lye than to Bass in its construction. Mazaheri, whose employment with Azhir Film began his fifty-year career, has described this period before the formalization of the profession as one dependent on found objects. Training in calligraphy helped, but he notes that design education in the early days of his industry came not through apprenticeships or formal programs but through imported print media that provided material templates.[10] Khachikian, too, was known to borrow compositions, and even footage, in his films. Lightning strikes are frequent enough in Khachikian films to be a kind of signature motif, and his first lightning strikes were made from footage cut from Hindi films found in the vaults of the Diana Film studio in Tehran (the company also exhibited and dubbed films).[11] The arrangement of music and effects in *The Strike*, credited to the director himself, is a collage of found sound. We first hear a police siren with the name of the production company (*azhir* means "siren"). Then a fragment of strings from a melodrama score accompany Khachikian's personal message about the film's social message, which is followed by the quivering organ of a mystery thriller. As the animated sequence begins, so does the modern pared percussion with the pulse of a proper midcentury thriller.[12] The film itself switches among codes of family melodrama, gothic horror, policier, and film noir. Its soundtrack, starting with the title sequence, is a collage of found material pulled directly from representative films in each of these genres. This was not an isolated experiment. The music for Mazaheri's title sequence and Khachikian's next title sequence for *Delirium* samples Henry Mancini's opening credit music for *Touch of Evil* (Welles, 1958). Its animations include a disembodied hand--not as minimalist as Bass's arm graphic for Preminger's film, but the resemblance is clear. Twenty years before Orson Welles would make his final films with funding from Iran, or before he would work as a voice actor for *Foroogh-e Javidan* (*The Flame of Persia*, Golestan, 1971) and an Agatha Christie adaptation shot in Isfahan, a sonic fragment that had branded his classic noir accompanied Persian titles designed in affinity with, if not as a direct citation of, *The Man with the Golden Arm*.[13] The soundtracks and print publicity, not to mention the films' plots, announced that they were assemblages.

From the perspective of the history of stylistic influence of global design trends, the fragmented and palimpsestic quality of the design of sequences like the opening of *The Strike* create a form of aesthetic friction that might have worried design theorists interested in a seamless consumer experience.[14] This strange combination of commercial practicality and experimental reassembly affirms the dream of global expansion of modern design while also calling attention to the frictions of its movement. It demonstrates enthusiasm for the commercial modernism of the international style while also calling attention to unexpected juxtapositions, to objects that bear the traces of their circulation, and to the labor involved in these objects' transport and reuse. Media archaeology can help to account for these phenomena, which extend into multiple forms, from the Persian text of the story for *The Big Heat* printed over the original poster in a film magazine to the magnetic audio tracks that were redubbed or sometimes manually glued over the original optical tracks of imported prints.

Relaying Cinema   To give focused attention to the way we conceive of the history of cinema's geographic vectors, I have structured this book around a conception of relay. The metaphors embedded in the term's usage span two relevant domains: mediated communication and physical movement. In its modern form, *relay* comes to everyday usage from wired and wireless communication networks. A relay point extends the range of a signal that has become weak and amplifies it. Relay technologies can be found at the limits of a signal's range. The relay point is at once dependent on the received signal and semiautonomous in its retransmission. Such a conception of relay can foreground the movement of media while also accounting for decentralized forms of agency in this movement. This decentered agency is especially evident in relay networks where little practical hope for top-down management of the network exists. In its second common usage, as a term of physical movement, *relay* refers to a race (archaically, to a hunt) that requires multiple animals (human or otherwise) who each hasten to a point of exchange. In athletics, the carriers of a baton in the first segments of a relay race cannot act upon, or sometimes even see, the actions of the latter segments. An object crosses a long distance through a sequence of individual races. Obstructions in the sequence are not failures of organization; they are defining features of a relay's cooperative movement. *Relay* thus highlights two dimensions of cinema's movements that this history prioritizes. The first suggests amplification in sequence: it directs attention to the transformations that take place in networks. The second draws attention to objects in transit, to the potentially beneficial obfuscations and obstructions at each stage of a relay. *Relay* evokes circulation but with an emphasis on sequence, interruption, and incremental agency over top-down or seamless transparency. A study of relayed cinema presents film culture, in Bernhard Siegert's terms, as "a gift of interception."[15] It stresses the juncture of circulation studies and media archaeology.

Studies of recycled global cinema and informal circulation in the Middle East and beyond have expanded in recent years. Amplification and transformation are threads that run through this work, and their insights about cinema's creative recontextualizations across borders and national cinema cultures have informed much of *Relaying Cinema in Midcentury Iran*. My interest lies in the celluloid prehistory of the contemporary states of circulation. Whereas many of these studies, including recent books by Ramon Lobato and Brian Edwards, tend to focus on the accelerated circulation of recent digital media environments, this book traces repurposed cinema back to the technologies of scissors, contact printers, and mag-stripe sound.[16] Compared with the small-scale affordability of digital storage and transmission formats, of the informal trade of VCDs and flash memory or lateral exchange of streams and torrents, heavy and expensive celluloid intended for theatrical runs might seem to leave far less significant opportunities to escape top-down control of the relayed item. But the obstructions inherent in relaying these bulky and costly objects invite one to consider comparable patterns of recontextualization. There is a kindred history of possibility, of long before digitization enabled audiovisual appropriation, in flat-fee sales of junk prints, unlicensed printing, and partial reproductions of film components. The ongoing scholarship on digital appropriations, such as the amateur dubbing of *Shrek* or small-scale VCD trading, can help to sharpen not only our understanding of global media environments looking forward but also the historiography of global media environments nearly a century in the past.[17]

Writing a history of celluloid and imaging machines as a history of relay foregrounds types of exchange that have stubbornly escaped notice. As chapters 1 and 2 reveal, in the late silent era and the early postwar era, markets in the Middle East were frequently seen as too difficult and as failed opportunities by US distributors. Studies of these periods in the history of film distribution carry scant references to the Middle East, and for good reason.[18] The distributors themselves understood these channels for prints as dead ends. Many understood that they were passing along objects that could continue to run through projectors for years, but without a reliable way to capture those screenings, their record-keeping system ended at these relay points. They were the final mark in the accountant's ledger. For more than a decade after WWII, exporters from United Artists could scarcely see Iran. They could see Baghdad, which supplied prints to Iran, but they could not see how the larger network of cinemas in Iran used the prints sourced from the smaller market in Baghdad. With the last profitable relay point, except for occasional clues, the archives of Hollywood exporters go dark. And despite laments about the lack of access to these markets, this darkness also provided benefits. It externalized risk and offloaded fragile prints as their maintenance and storage costs crept above their declining exhibition value. The inability of distributors to see and account for Iran, partly due to their own choices about acceptable burdens of risk and maintenance, has also meant that this history has gone unnoticed.

The gaps in studio archives mark dead ends in parts of the Middle East, but those gaps paired with archival material from the films' destinations reveal animated segments in the relay of cinema. To consider global cinema history only through the visible official screenings of exported films is like trying to imagine the unfolding of a relay race from only its first leg. Tracking at the material level these earlier forms of relay, from small-scale informal circulation of celluloid to ambitious collaborations with foreign filmmakers, means developing methods to work with archives that are dispersed, incomplete, and sometimes inaccessible. Researching local film exhibition, production, and the structure of intellectual cinema in locations like Iran requires a historiography that attends to their continued variability (a more durable form of what Rick Altman has described as crisis historiography), to the interarchival investigations they demand, and to the asynchronous and overlapping chronologies they produced. For these challenges and others, a disciplinary commitment to cinema history can offer useful tools.

To address this history of fortuitous obstruction, I have conducted archival research with collections in Iran and North America. Such comparative archival work makes it possible to track the amortization and provenance of actual prints, posters, sound recordings, and devices as they moved, say, from New York, through Rome and Cairo, to Tehran. Because structures of prestige were inevitably reframed in transit, with genre films recast as classic or art cinema, these relay networks can help film studies to challenge assumptions about the distinctions between classics and ephemeral films in the region. They indicate how enmeshed the Tehran film scene was with key distributors in Baghdad and Baku. They provide much-needed context for the interpretation of midcentury films made in Iran, which have been neglected (or dismissed as unserious) in part because their collages of found soundtracks and visual references that span adventure serials, film noir, and 1960s art cinema have made them difficult to classify within existing scholarly frameworks. The films' collages have trouble holding still. These challenges speak not only to scholarship on local reception but also to the way we form the canons of the well-known films (those that circulated into as well as from the Middle East) that have shaped the discipline of film studies.

While this is not a book on early cinema, its methods are informed by my training in the field. Early cinema studies might seem like an odd place to look for insight into traditions that move from the 1920s to the 1960s, but methods need not belong to periods. In adapting some of them, I seek to challenge a potential bottleneck in the historiography of cinema in Iran (with resonances elsewhere) around familiar archives, national industries, and their groundbreaking films. The field of early cinema studies has challenged, from its beginnings, a narrowed historiography around the classical film oligopoly, around a standardized formal system, and around a centripetal definition of cinema as a coherent medium. Early cinema scholars have emphasized the unevenness of cinema's textual address over a stable image of the movie spectator and exhibitor control over hierarchies of circulation that would otherwise privilege production centers. They have valued traditions that might seem too early or too late and have succeeded at reading myths of origin as allegories rather than as truths or falsehoods. Faced with received ideas steeped in a cult of invention, they have sought out moments of media volatility or plurality with the goal not of delimiting failures and crosscurrents but of exploring the ways these failures lay bare the fissures within traditions ordinarily understood as seamless or as heroic inventions.[19] Wary of privileging films over cinema, of imagining the individual film as something separate from the often-contradictory forces that bring it into view, the field has helped frame cinematic prestige in structural rather than textual terms.[20]

Early cinema scholars, a community that overlaps significantly with those of archivists and curators, regularly confront questions of ethics and accuracy that arise when working within the realities of severely limited access to material. These questions proliferate if one's primary focus is not Europe or North America. These kinds of challenges are familiar to media historians working on regions where the oligopoly encountered serious obstacles, where exhibitors dismantled hierarchies of distribution, where film texts often did not address a stable spectator, and where it remains difficult to avoid painful shortages, blockages, and imbalances of archival evidence. They have been pursued by scholars who have written extensively on silent cinema, such as Sudhir Mahadevan, Ana Lopez, and Anupama Kapse.[21] While the period of early cinema in Iran ended long before the postwar era discussed in chapters 2 through 5, a reader familiar with these methodological interventions and research challenges will see similar strategies for widening historiography in each chapter of this book.

Drawing from these intellectual traditions, *Relaying Cinema in Mid-century Iran* also expands their recent work with canonical accounts of cinema's role in the cultures of modernity, which have been foundationally focused on subjective experience (distraction, astonishment) and on time (acceleration, the new). *Relay* emphasizes physical objects and spatial configurations. It thus aligns with concerns over what Jennifer Bean has referred to as an "underspatialized historicism" in some studies of global silent cinema.[22] It affirms, alongside Ravi Vasudevan, that media objects need to be understood in their spatial dispersal while recognizing, alongside Hatim El-Hibri, that such media is itself involved in the production of space.[23] These are points that archivists and postcolonial scholars have long recognized, but there is much more work to do in ascertaining their relevance for film studies.

From Iranian studies, Golbarg Rekabtalaei demonstrates how a proper spatial account, defined for her in terms of the organization of the multiethnic city and its situated cosmopolitan imaginary, reinvigorates and relocates our understanding of cinema's position in urban modernity. As cultural histories of the space of the city become more fine grained, object-focused approaches might also extend those film histories that have considered modernity in terms of experience and sensory-reflexivity. A cosmopolitan fascination with items of trade, for example, could be better understood by tracking these items and identifying the ways that they were reused. The transporting, recutting, and reshaping of moving-image material are not unknown phenomena, but their persistence in global media history is much more significant than the discipline of film studies has taken into consideration.

This is not to say that reflection on modern experience and communication of that experience are not foundational for this study. Material objects center the methods of this book's inquiry, but often as a means to reconstruct aspects of the experience of cinema that might otherwise remain obscured. Discussions of cinema as a form of vernacular modernism, set into motion by Miriam Hansen, have informed this book since its inception, and so has the conviction that the provenance of prints, including junk prints and informal circulation, shapes the kinds of reflection that are possible. Put in terms that will bear repeating in case studies spanning from the 1920s to the 1960s, this book encounters cinema's cultural translation by attending to its physical translation. If Hansen's account has influenced studies of global cinema aesthetics with its verbal analogies of vernacularity, rhetorical topoi, and idioms, then perhaps it is worth adding that to relay can also mean to speak.[24] Those working on transcultural cinemas over the past twenty years have found value in using the analogy of rhetorical topoi to consider how an element of modern design or performance style in cinema enabled a reflexive experience of modernity in cities far from Los Angeles. The conception of classical Hollywood cinema as a robust and portable idiom has helped to foreground the everyday dialects of filmmakers and fans who made use of this idiom around the world. The verbal inflection of relay calls back to the utility of these analogies as transcultural cinema histories have expanded over the past twenty years.[25] To relay an idea is to speak, but also to be located.

In Iran   Why this particular location, and to which of this cinema's attributes is a study of relay attuned? Because of its natural resources, strategic geographical position, and the fact that it was never colonized by a single Western power, modern Iran experienced particular frictions of influence within and across its borders. Some of this competition manifested in the often-complex geopolitical lives of circulating film prints. Film trade was less tied to a primary administrative network than were many other markets of this size. It happened along several channels of distribution, involving multiple intermediaries in cities including Cairo, Moscow, Baghdad, and elsewhere. This reliance on intermediaries meant that regional relationships could significantly shape the film experience even if a film's place of origin was thousands of miles away. Intermediaries could limit access to material, or they could expand access in ways that would not be authorized had the material traveled along a comparatively direct path. Having a variety of sources for films could make exhibition unpredictable, but it could also empower exhibitors to negotiate and nimbly shift allegiances when such shifts were appropriate.

This complicated system of intermediary exchange also meant that Iran was served by an inordinate percentage of flat-fee sales of films even after major cities, Tehran primarily, had established a robust network of cinemas. Outright sales, by design, give up formal oversight of licensing for lower risk and transport costs. And with that lack of formal oversight, and no expectation of return of films, comes more creative flexibility and opportunity with the material on the exhibition side. The flexibility of film functioned alongside that of publishing and vinyl pressing businesses in Tehran (a parallel highlighted in the second chapter's discussion of copyright). Reels of celluloid, film scores, graphic accompaniments, and audiovisual technology could easily be reworked, remade, or repurposed. Certain techniques, especially those related to the audio engineering of translated dialogue and imported music, flourished in Iran. They could be employed on an industrial scale and could hold up against external corporate capture for longer. These factors played out to varying degrees around the world. In spaces where they were concentrated, a conception of relay has useful work to do.

Given the book's attention to imported and recycled cinema in and around Iran, I hesitate to call it a straightforward book on Iranian cinema. A particular set of challenges arises when considering how a cinema might be of a place. Should one address the mainstream films, which may have been derived from foreign influences, or the realist examinations of social forces, or the modernist experiments? Or would it be useful to resist the call to distinguish a category of consequential cinema from the rest and attend instead to the undeniable tendency of these three categories to intersect in Iran? While this study is located in Iran, the first half of the book is concerned with imports and related infrastructures of distribution and exhibition. Even after the book shifts in its second half to films made in Iran, the context of circulation remains in the foreground. Samuel Khachikian, the director of *The Strike* and the standout figure discussed in the fourth chapter, helped many critics and fans to construct a sense of the possibilities of cinema in midcentury Iran. Yet his films have offered little to historians or critics interested specifically in work that made cinema unequivocally Iranian. His films engaged the vernacular of global genre filmmaking. They were preoccupied, to their detriment or to their glory depending on the critic, with an elsewhere--not necessarily a specific geopolitical elsewhere in the West but the cinematic elsewhere that was baked into his favorite genre, film noir, wherever and for whatever reasons the genre managed to thrive.

The question for me has not been to identify a genealogy of Iranian cinema or a prehistory of a well-known film movement, perhaps rooted in or leading up to a particular social phenomenon or to an artistic movement in Iranian film history. Such studies will continue to be important in this understudied field, but what this study takes as an imperative is identifying sites of encounter with cinema. In my choice of preposition in the title of the book, I take a guiding point from Blake Atwood: "I believe that the way forward is less Iranian media studies and more studies of media in Iran. For me, this semantic shift signals more attention to what media are, how they operate, and what they accomplish in Iran."[26] Presented to an audience of area-studies scholars, these remarks address the interdependencies of media and area studies. At the same time that media has gained attention in organizations devoted to the study of the Middle East, film and media history has increased its engagement with regional film practices that were not core to the formation of the discipline. In both cases, there has been a similar tendency to lean heavily on textual or representational analysis at the expense of the wealth of connections that stand to be made through the analysis of media systems or through archivally grounded media history.

To be *of* a particular location could simply mean to operate *in* that location for some time in a meaningful way. In order to assert this approach to locating cinema in a way that does not operate to the exclusion of other approaches, we might borrow Dudley Andrew's conception of an atlas of world cinema: a set of maps that are interrelated but not arranged in a linear or hierarchical form. Such a folio remains too thin if it excludes mechanisms of relay. Andrew offers a similar point when he makes a case for a historiography of French cinema that would triangulate imports and local productions rather than positioning them in competition. He goes so far as to add, "No study of French cinema, my own on the 1930s included, has attended to imports in this way."[27] It is not a straightforward methodological task, and research groups and journals such as *Transnational Cinemas* have devoted significant attention in recent years to discussions of appropriate regional variants and approaches. The political economy of Euro-American cinema studies is a question of imbalance but also one of emphasis. Some aspects of this imbalance are addressed by expanding knowledge of underrepresented film pioneers. Locating filmmakers excluded from Eurocentric interests marks an important intervention. But a more systemic challenge would consider new ways to speak for the medium in general terms. Since the labors and material conditions of relay are pervasive and enduring components of cinema, indeed the components that have positioned cinema as a global vernacular, the scholars of particularly inventive and active forms of relay have a significant claim to declare, "This is cinema."

Among recent studies of cinema in Iran, there is a range of new work that takes spatial or media archaeological approaches, or that suggests alternatives to national conceptions that might treat imports as noise. Claire Cooley foregrounds sound technology in her tracing of the infrastructures and networks of technical training that made it possible for film industries located in Cairo, Bombay, and Tehran to intermingle.[28] Negar Taymoorzadeh's work on the multiple adaptations of *Awaara* (Kapoor, 1951) in Iran and Turkey inflects studies of global melodrama in intra-regional terms.[29] Babak Tabarraee's work traces the long-form cult following around select locally produced and imported films in Iran in order to illustrate not just a trajectory of a film's significance to audiences but the ways that meanings overlap onto a specific object over a period of decades in which a film is continually remediated.[30] In each case, cinema's attachment points take priority over its roots, and its modernity is traced through a network of spatial relations that sometimes require counterintuitive uses of available material.[31]

My own efforts to track the labor of distributors, exhibitors, and journalists who worked to place cinema in Iran have led me to engage extensively with the archives of American film studios. Located in these archives are the largest collections that I have found of correspondence from exhibitors based in Tehran, original documents that can accompany interviews and memoirs produced in Iran about the midcentury film industry. The owners of several Tehran cinemas, including Diana, Rex, and Moulin Rouge have transactions, letters, and telegrams preserved in the archives of Selznick Releasing Organization (SRO), United Artists (UA), and Warner Bros. These collections may have been created in the interest of American film companies and preserved by American universities and organizations such as AMPAS, but, as collections of correspondence often do, they preserve the voices of the received correspondence, sometimes even more thoroughly than what was sent out.

These collections, housed in places where my own contingent location and travel opportunities have allowed me to arrange extended stays, provide more material than can be addressed in one book. But as those who work on film circulation through nodes including Bombay, Paris, and Durban will observe, this study is intended to be additive, not exhaustive. The reality of these networks, as Nolwenn Mingant makes clear, is one in which organizations grafted onto existing infrastructures.[32] When companies essentially had to rent space in others' intermediary channels of distribution, overlap, redundancy, and strange partnerships among competitors were typical. The archives of these overlapping circuits reward additive curiosity as they overwhelm ambitions of any one study to present an exhaustive history.

Taking industry archives as a primary source, this book thus travels alongside work on global Hollywood by scholars such as Ross Melnick, Daniel Gómez Steinhardt, and Nitin Govil, even as its vantage point in the Middle East means that it must remain attentive to what is obscured in available archival records.[33] The book replaces the question of which films or industries occupy dominant or marginal positions with an emphasis on how film objects move through intermediary systems. At the points where control over these objects breaks down, the study of circulation must attend to local networks with their own institutional configurations that align only partially, and sometimes not at all, with the producers of the secondhand prints they utilize. The archival work for the book does not, then, position Hollywood records as empirically authoritative. It looks for the conspicuous absences in the knowledge systems that produced foreign distribution records. To this end, it also attends to the archive of Hollywood abroad. Uncovering posters and exhibition records in Baghdad and Tehran that contradict American studios' affidavits of the films' prior destruction, as well as extant copies of these "destroyed" prints enhanced with dubbed mag-stripe soundtracks in the National Film Archive of Iran, reveals the limits of distributor knowledge and control. In this way, my project seeks not only to pursue a global perspective on Hollywood; it experiments with methods of globalized archival research practice. A relay system is not powered by its source, as time spent with documents will reveal.

The object life of cinema in Iran, when understood in terms of not just its origin and destination but also its nodal points, calls attention to miscellaneous devices and parafilmic material. These items can provide a history that sometimes runs contrary to what is made apparent by tracking only the major deals to import first-run lucrative titles directly from the distributor. Intermediaries are numerous in this space, and they are just as important to the life of the objects as any other stage. The comingling of cinemas in a location happens even in small-scale, everyday exchanges. Take Warner Bros., which in the early 1960s typically sent the Italian versions of its film publicity to Iran for everything from their B films to such enduring global successes as their James Dean melodramas and auteurist westerns like *Rio Bravo* (Hawks, 1959). When we look at the reassembly of these posters in Iran, even when we see the face of John Wayne or James Dean, we should consider how: when they were cut and pasted in magazines or repainted on marquee billboards (even when these billboards were re-created for fiction films, as discussed in chapter 5) they also bear the traces of the collection and design practices of the poster production houses in 1950s Rome. The choices made in the sourcing of posters can tell us something about how the status of a film changes over the course of its long life in theaters. Different intermediaries sometimes served different functions in the circulation of their films. They often demonstrated a film's achievement as a prestige picture that looked beyond immediate box office gains to more enduring patterns of reception. A change in print publicity can indicate a changed status for a film that had premiered earlier, as was the case with the posters for the evergreen Tehran run of *Rebel without a Cause* (Ray, 1955) at Cinema Rex.[34] Meanwhile, in 1961, the most successful music editor for films made in Iran, Rubik Mansuri, used Leonard Rosenman's music for *Rebel* to score the climactic fight sequence of the top-grossing local production, Khachikian's film noir *The Midnight Cry*. While *Rebel*'s status as a classic in Iran did not hinge on its poster or its recycled score, these exchanges of ephemera highlight the incremental labors by which its status was constructed. The film's chronology in Iran, dependent as it was on multiple channels of exchange and shifting points of relay, differs from better-known patterns in the chronology of classics. The patterns of evergreen films and mayfly films were reshaped by negotiations around, and reuse of, their material culture.

Material histories like these can get overshadowed by concerns about the transmission of Ray's or Dean's cultural memes through performance style or commercial fashion, which is admittedly no small phenomenon within the film culture in midcentury Iran. But tracking such forms of comingling of Hollywood imaginaries with the objects in the foreground allows us to maintain focus on how these media objects do what they do. Returning once more to the title sequence of *The Strike* and Mazaheri's connections to *The Man with the Golden Arm*, it would be illuminating to track the likely Italian source of the color illustration of Novak on the cover of the issue of *Setare-ye Cinema* that featured this film,[35] as would finding instances in publicity material that both borrow design elements from Bass's style and include samples of it in a discussion of the film. Those familiar with Saul Bass's title sequence for Preminger's film would likely have taken note of Barirani's 1957 design of *Film va Zendegi*. One would hopefully agree that an interest in this stylistic influence might be pursued by knowing more about how the print illustrations of the titles for *The Man with the Golden Arm* found their way into this issue's pages.[36] The publicity material was cut and inserted into the same issue of the magazine that experimented with this design format on its cover (the only issue cover that bears this resemblance). The artistic choices made by Khachikian and Mazaheri in forming this title sequence and by Barirani in his cover design, and the labor of Ashtiany in marketing these design elements, operate in an environment of recycled multimedia images. In a field with a wealth of miscellaneous archival sources, little of which has been subject to what Amelie Hastie has outlined as a method appropriate to miscellany, a lifetime of comparative compilation awaits.[37] The broader currents of

Hollywood's circulation contain swirls of miscellaneous objects including posters, recorded sound, odd reels, and repurposed footage.

The Chapters Each chapter takes a type of encounter as its point of focus: serial junk prints in the 1920s, postwar maintenance and re-engineering of film imports, the collage of found film scores in local productions, global film noir, and transnational commercial collaboration in the age of new waves. Each chapter foregrounds its disciplinary commitments to film studies, but these commitments are apprehended by way of investments in neighboring fields including translation studies, feminist STS, paperwork studies, infrastructure studies, and sound studies. While the encounters of each chapter run in chronological order, beginning with the exhibition of silent films in the 1920s and ending with the shifts of 1969, they present an interrupted chronology. The book is heavily weighted around (the Gregorian) midcentury and structured by types of archival material more than by progression or coverage. The bookend chapters in the chronology are also outliers that frame the book. The middle chapters verge progressively later in the twenty-year span between the return of postwar commercial cinema and the mid-1960s, but each offers some discussion of the span in its entirety. Missing from the book's chronology because of my focus on vernacular commercial flows are wartime institutions of cinema's circulation, particularly nonfiction, as well as a sustained examination of art cinemas in Iran. It is a privilege to be producing scholarship on cinemas of the Middle East at a time when enough simultaneous intellectual labor exists to relieve some of the pressure experienced by previous generations to reintroduce the span of an entire field with each new book.

The growth of commercial exhibition of silent films may be a chronological outlier in the book, but it is the circulation practices in this period that set up many of the questions that I follow up to the mid-1960s, when transparency of distribution and stable commercial formulae for local productions took hold. From the standpoint of the 1920s American film export business, the markets in the Middle East were largely seen as inaccessible or as failed opportunities. American firms failed to establish profitable infrastructures in the cities there, and these failures became all the more apparent to the industry as Hollywood assumed a dominant presence in many other film markets. The films that did show in many cities in the Middle East arrived much later and by paths far more convoluted than their producers would have wished.

Chapter 1 takes the convoluted relay of films seriously, as a positive attribute of the medium rather than as a lack. It offers a case history of the promotion and exhibition of serial adventure films in Tehran from the mid-1920s until the adoption of synchronized sound, a period when local film production was minimal and the geopolitical stakes of imported films were high. Using exhibition records from the regular advertisements printed in the newspaper *Ettela'at*, it is possible to infer a range of information about what types of films showed, about how complete and how old the exhibition prints were, and about the distributors who supplied them. The records show how Tehran theaters were supplied almost entirely by junk prints, mostly serials, amortized in other markets often a full decade before arriving in Tehran. Compared with other markets in Asia and Latin America, where the chronology of reception more closely followed the chronology of production, the lag in Tehran stands out. Because cinemas in Tehran and other cities in the Middle East were shaped by such a significant fact of distribution, a material history of serial film prints can reveal how the junk-print phenomenon helped to shape a distinct film culture and an awareness of films as historical objects.

The circulation of second-hand film prints continued as cinema exhibition grew after the war. Chapter 2 sheds light on the overlooked engineering labor and ongoing property disagreements that gave these prints their enduring material value. It follows the work of those who worried over forgotten copies of films, those who maintained technologies of sound and image, and those engaged in the practical management of copyright. To trace the afterlives of secondhand prints in formal and informal circulation, one needs to look at the postwar organization of distributors who owned major cinemas in Tehran and Abadan and the work of regional distributors who did business in Iran. When paired with exhibition records inside Iran, the studio correspondence with film dealers in the Middle East shows how the growth of the Iranian film industry, largely out of a network of exhibition venues that grew into dubbing operations and then production studios, depended in large part on Hollywood distributors' convenient obliviousness to the afterlives of prints that they did not want back. In lieu of a returned film, the circulatory network depended only on affidavits of the prints' destruction. Cost-sharing models carried undesirable risks. The very question of how to define a filmic cultural property led to legal and ethical disagreement. Though the affidavit of destruction did little to prevent informal circulation, it did provide a practical way to avoid financial risks and political disagreements. As a practical solution, it benefited parties at both ends of the relay chain. Focusing on a few high-profile moments of blockage, unprofitability, and physical reconfiguration of secondhand American studio prints, chapter 2 redefines these seeming barriers to circulation in Iran as moments of creative volatility within the industry and as foils to the ideological fantasy of pure circulation. At the same time, however, the slow labors of maintenance, repair, and repurposing of film temper the sense of media volatility as crisis or scandal. Worries endure. I look at image and sound reproduction technologies and infrastructures as examples of how work in media archaeology can and should inform a history of the work that moved famous films through cities in the Middle East. Technologies such as magnetic sound striping (applied to secondhand positive prints) thrived in this period in Iran precisely because these dubbing studios were largely unknown to producers of the original films until the early 1960s, and they were tolerated for much longer. The fact that this industrial-scale creative adaptation proved foundational for the local industry, even as unlicensed dubbed films crowded local screens, confounds any simple categorization of cooperation versus competitive control over the local market.

The second half of the book shifts from recycled foreign prints, however reconfigured they may have been, to commercial features produced in Tehran studios. This division marks a shift in perspective and not a suggestion of progress. It allows me to address imports and local productions with similar questions, not as "part 1" and "part 2." Directors and intellectual histories of authorship come to the foreground in the latter chapters, but only after being framed by earlier discussions of exchange networks, maintenance, formations of prestige, and challenges to notions of property and invention. Likewise, the chapters primarily about relay of imported films are also about creative labor found in the marketing of classicism in the press, exhibitor control, engineering prestige, and below-the-line work in film production.

A case in point is the collage scoring that underpinned Tehran studios' sound design, which is a practice that tells us both about recycled global media in Iran and about the films produced in Iran that rarely crossed national borders. In the popular films of the 1950s and 1960s, almost all of the final exhibition scores deployed found recordings. Sound editors for these films reconstructed and reassembled optical, vinyl, and magnetic sources. Their collections of recordings, built and maintained over decades, are mostly lost. They can be at least partly reconstructed by running digital audio recognition tools on the hundreds of films that are available to stream (the same tools being used to remove films from streaming sites on the basis of their unlicensed compilation scores).

Chapter 3 draws on the previous chapter's archival research on the paths of famous film properties into the Tehran film scene and links those findings with a working database of found Hollywood scores. It reconstructs the working music archives collected by studios and music editors and foregrounds the labor involved in the recycling of famous scores by Henry Mancini, Bernard Hermann, Max Steiner, and Miklós Rózsa in Iranian films. Iranian studios' scoring practices mark one of the most active practices of relay in the region. The creative uses of recycled sound in a growing industry counter simple readings of influence and imitation. In addition to uncovering the working methods of the collage score, the chapter identifies patterns specific to this period of experimentation with sound that announced its linkages with well-known films: the use of found sound as code switching, ironic citations of classic Hollywood scores, and the phenomenon of simultaneous Tehran premieres of Iranian and Hollywood films that use the same scores. These examples of resourceful sound editing draw attention to forms of intellectual labor that are typically elided in cinema history.

Relay, rather than remix, addresses the creative labor of these everyday works of collage. In addressing authorship and creative labor without seeking to rescue it as necessarily pathbreaking or countercultural, the discussions of recycled media in the book affirm recent work that has emphasized quotidian media piracy. Lawrence Liang's approach to piracy as access challenges both the cyber-libertarians who celebrate remix culture as entrepreneurial creativity as well as those who would want to cast the reuse of found sound as a form of charismatic resistance in the political economy of media.[38] There is wisdom in resisting the urge to put too much pressure on the oppositional effects or the remix-creativity of Iranian relay culture as the only conditions by which it might be historically relevant. An oppositional frame could neglect the entertainment dimension of the practice. These are practical solutions from a growing commercial enterprise, after all. Many of the films described in this chapter and the ones that follow it fit within a spectrum of melodramas and bawdy comedies derided by Iranian intellectuals as formulaic, crass, and technologically unsophisticated. These films were dubbed *filmfarsi* (written as a compound word to emphasize their corrupt hybridity) in the 1950s by the critic Houshang Kavousi in the weekly arts and culture magazine *Ferdowsi*.[39] A reliance on a notion of remix-creativity might try to disguise the quotidian nature of media work in this industry with a heroic canon of creatives who broke free from everyday media in order to make inventive remix work. Relayed film scores are not novel in exactly the way that remixers would want them to be. Part of their attraction lies in the ways they are not new. Their success, it appears, owes to the ways they immersed their audiences in a recognizable experience of cinema.

And yet it is hard to blame one for being drawn to the experimental energy of collage sound and recycled style. The emphatic ways the scores of these films are presented, like their title sequences and bold references to global genres, announce their relationship with cinema as a modern vernacular. Liang explicitly challenges what he calls the modernist dimension of intellectual property and creativity. It's a fair point, especially in a history restricted to inventors of a style or to founders of a film movement. The expansive definition of modernism in terms of a sensory-reflexive horizon of experience abates some of those restrictions, as does my approach to creative labor, which is inclusive of sound engineers' creation of collage tracks, dubbers' modes of performing through multiple degrees of alienation from the performance seen and heard in the sound studio, and film publishers' practices of compilation, cut, and paste. Genre, too, arrives in these films in a modular form that challenges a singular focus on even the prized labor of directors. While it would be an undue burden to imply that a modernist strain of creativity must be rescued in order for these films to be worthy of historical consideration, it also would be a shame to miss the glorious forms of creative practice on display. To set a firm boundary between these overlooked everyday labors and modernist experimental media forms would elide the playful gestures at work in both.

Of course, the critics and filmmakers writing in the film magazines in 1950s and '60s Iran were also wrestling with these questions. Film noir is a standout genre in this regard, both for the locally produced crime films that were capturing audience attention and for its discussion in the press. A cycle of prestige genre films emerges in the late 1950s Tehran, and so does an active film press. For this reason, chapter 4 is an effort to track traditions of engaging noir as much in Tehran film publishing as in the films themselves. The reception of film noir in Tehran film journals was enmeshed with the production of policier and thriller films in the studios. Together, they exhibit what I describe as an anxious exuberance (continuing the thread of worry set up earlier in the book) about modern film style. Classic Iranian crime films and celebrated film-noir imports contribute to a discussion of Samuel Khachikian as the most successful director of thrillers of this period. Nicknamed (to his chagrin) "the Hitchcock of Iran," Khachikian developed a reputation as a hitmaker and a stylist. His career faced challenges from critics such as Houshang Kavousi. In a critical landscape with more than its fair share of feuds, Kavousi, coiner of the pejorative term *filmfarsi* and director of his own policier, *Hefdah Ruz be E'dam* (*Seventeen Days to Execution*, 1956), referred to Khachikian's work, especially *The Midnight Cry* (based loosely on *Gilda*), as "counterfeit." The crime thriller enjoyed a heady run until, by the second half of the 1960s, it faced challenges from new popular films that rejected stylized thrillers in favor of a popular recipe combining comedy, action, and song. The crime film would continue in different iterations, but it managed to thrive as a prestige form before a widening of the gap between art and commercial cinema. Tehran noir's heyday, during a period that saw the rise of film publications and a growing intellectual culture around cinema, marks a florescence of modernist style drawn from the anxious enthusiasm for relayed genre films (which themselves feature anxiety as a pervasive mood). Film noir, from its earliest transatlantic imaginings to recent urban circuits between Bombay and Dubai, has always been about engaging with an elsewhere through cinematic style. It has also been as much about critics' labor as about a particular cycle of film production. This discussion of Tehran noir does not, then, suggest an echo of a phenomenon whose home is in another industry. It is noir itself at work. Here as elsewhere, the genre accompanies the globality of modern design with strong, but mixed, feelings.

The last major encounter of the book shifts into a more familiar orbit for the study of Iranian cinema, the era of new waves. It reconsiders the auspicious events of 1969 from the perspective of less examined forms of globalization. Whereas much of the pathbreaking research on this period has singled out the 1969–70 releases of *Gav* (*The Cow*, Mehrjui) and *Qeysar* (Kimiai) as a pivot point toward the Iranian cinema that is known worldwide, this chapter examines two of Masoud Kimiai's orphan projects in order to suggest an alternative historiography of Iranian cinema during a shift toward greater ambition for its films and increased institutional support for its new wave. *The Heroes* (Negulesco, 1969), a major Iran-Hollywood collaboration, and *Pesar-e Sharqi* (*Eastern Boy*, Kimiai, 1975), a sponsored film for adolescents, bracket this crucial period in a way that contrasts the constricting histories of a handful of groundbreaking art films. These forgotten works call for a method that attends to this period's ambivalent collaborations and its competing models of globalized cinema.

It is these works discussed in the last two chapters that hopefully offer perspective on a tradition of prestige in world cinema that borrows too wildly from disparate traditions to fit within the canons that have formed in film studies around national film movements. These films existed in circulation with the cinemas that we know and, I maintain, are best understood in the context of circulation. But this approach can be tricky. Identifying memes that run through these films, or singling out their occasional hints of well-known movements to come, if undertaken before developing methods adequate to their peculiar form of worldliness, might run the risk of atomizing the films from this period and hollowing out a tradition that is just starting to come into view. An archaeological approach offers one way to account for this misplaced cinema as a phenomenon, to account for all the tensions it generated in its own time as well as its invisibility in studies of world cinema today. Some of these films have recently been, or are in the process of being, subtitled for the first time. More will screen outside of Iran at festivals in the coming years, thanks to the patience and persistence of those willing to navigate the political and institutional obstacles of such tasks. If these new exhibitions generate a kind of revelation among festival-goers, as festivals always intend with these rediscovered programs, the hope is that an archaeological perspective will at least reorient the films for an alternative type of revelation--not as cut flowers extracted from an otherwise incoherent industry, not as films over cinema, but as works that call attention to the many relay points of cinema's charged itinerary in midcentury Iran.

CHAPTER I

An Afterlife for Junk Prints

It would make for a much simpler history had each newly released serial film or silent feature circulated provincially and globally with speed and uniformity. But the physical realities of film prints moving across trade borders and through intermediary institutions such as international exchanges and government censorship bureaus create messy periodizations. Quite frankly, the boundaries between early cinema and later film cultures are far more permeable than we have assumed. Their characteristics overlap in ways that warrant more focused attention. In a very general sense, any study of distribution attends to the intermediary life of film, but the speed and directness of film circulation vary enormously from region to region. In places that differ widely from general trends, the effect is not so much a local film culture lagging behind the production centers as a film culture out of sync. Rather than thinking about interruptions to circulation and damage to prints as incomplete steps toward more developed national film cultures, I want to consider how silent film's cultural translation can be shaped by the conditions of its physical translation.

Silent cinema in the Middle East and North Africa offers standout cases. The strategies of global distribution of films established in the 1910s suffered greatly diminished successes in many cities across the Middle East and North Africa. With some important exceptions, many of the predominant film export businesses considered markets in the Middle East as less accessible or as failed opportunities by the late

1910s. American firms in particular expressed disappointment at failing to establish profitable offices in the region. These failures were all the more conspicuous as American firms' decreasing dependence on intermediary distributors in London and elsewhere boosted efficiency and profitability in other parts of the world.

American trade press articles and letters in distributor archives illustrate a weakening of optimism as the basic situation failed to change through the 1910s and 1920s. In an article in *Motography* in 1912, the consul general in Beirut optimistically tried to tip off American companies to a potential market. He suggested that American firms route their films for the region through Cairo and Alexandria and claimed there was "no reason why a large business [could not] be immediately developed."[1] The relatively meager communication with Middle East and North African contacts in the Selig Polyscope collection of letters from the London office in the 1910s suggest some interest in potential markets in Cairo, Tunis, and Istanbul, but not necessarily a realization of that potential.[2] In the following several years, trade articles about the region reported similarly frustrating film import situations but attributed the continuing inaccessibility to larger cultural obstacles such as the Islamic ban on images or the difficulty of setting up gender-divided screening spaces. Locations with better film distribution, such as Cairo or settler communities throughout the region, were cited as the exceptions that proved the rule.[3] As one journalist emphasized, "Arabia, therefore, promises to be a difficult market, with the exception of the British administered Aden Protectorate, and the rather liberal Sultan of Mokalla."[4]

As the trade articles expressed hope for future business, they also frequently noted the age and poor condition of the prints. The films shown in Aden, for instance, were described as "an exceedingly common or archaic type" and "weekly exhibitions of pictures several years old."[5] An article regaling readers with descriptions of the high-fashion picture palaces in Egypt ends with a discussion of other, more rural and far from opulent, theatrical sites: "When the films have been the round of the various picture palaces . . . they are bought up cheap by enterprising Greeks [who] make quite a thriving business out of dilapidated old films" by exhibiting them in the villages.[6] The US consulate reported that theaters in Beirut, Damascus, and Tripoli were supplied by films that "would reach there only after having been used in a number of other towns and were often in bad condition and out of date."[7] These accounts of the troubled and interrupted circulation of worn and incomplete prints depict the diverse kinds of exhibition and reception of a considerable portion of the films screened throughout the region. These films were junk prints, forgotten by producers and amortized long before their arrival. Their life, a kind of afterlife, invites analysis as such.

As a term of admiration, not dismissal, *junk prints* organizes a rich set of associations. The term emerges in tandem with the growing circulation of goods in industrial modernity. It evokes a range of productive secondhand cultures dependent upon obsolescence, like the modern junk shop, but its associations with reuse date back much further. In the seventeenth century, *junk* described the reusable scrap line on sailing ships. This early definition might seem fitting for anyone who has worked with film fragments in an archive, in a projection booth, or on an optical printer. Someone with a reverent (and admittedly fetishistic) attitude toward junk film would likely notice how the practice of saving and mending frayed marine line does recall the modern labor of mending, saving, splicing, and threading old celluloid.

To refer to film as a kind of junk is nothing new. Importantly, the term described the circulation of secondhand prints in the silent era, and this usage noticeably features as the first modern example in the *Oxford English Dictionary*'s definition of *junk*. The OED entry cites Valentia Steer's 1913 study *The Romance of Cinema*, where the term is placed in quotes to note industry jargon: "The life of a film is very short. It is 'first run' today and 'junk' a few short weeks hence. What is now 4d. a foot, to be handled like a newborn babe, will, three months later on, be so much scrap, fit only for working up into varnish. Yet millions of feet of this worn-out rubbish are being reeled off daily at fourth[-] and fifth-rate picture theatres."[8] By *The Romance of Cinema*'s own coincidences of circulation, secondhand film has helped to define modern junk. Steer's revulsion for "worn-out rubbish" notwithstanding, this coincidence indicates the importance of *junk* as a historiographical imperative in film and media studies.

Like garbage and trash, junk is associated with waste, an annoying by-product, a slur upon the otherwise pristine efficiency associated with modern industrialism. Junk's visibility offends because it is nonsynchronous material.[9] It refers at once to matter out of date, out of place, and to matter that piles up over time.[10] A positive conception of junkspace can radically interrupt one-dimensional conceptions of media history, which, despite our best efforts, too often lean toward narratives of development and progress that overlook out-of-place historical material. These one-dimensional conceptions become even more dubious when tracing the histories of film's global circulation, as they tend to assume a kind of simple delay from one place to another. The notion of a simply delayed film culture (as opposed to an incongruous one) comes too close to the touristic fantasy that one (peripheral) place represents the past of another (central) place.[11] Junk, when foregrounded, confronts these assumptions, as junkspaces combine fragments of different historical periods in unplanned ways.

Junk augments the conceptions of *archaeology* that have influenced much of the post-1960s media historiography. Archaeology has proven an especially fruitful metaphor in film study, from classic work by C. W. Ceram to the authoritative recent history by Laurent Mannoni to experimental work by filmmakers such as Gustav Deutsch.[12] Archaeology and junk are intimately related, whether acknowledged or not.[13] A modern archaeology acknowledges the redundancy of a phrase like *archaeology of junk*. It aligns itself not with what the Futurists condemned as "the chronic necrophilia" of the archaeologists who fetishize antiquity but rather with the "perfume of garbage," to the modernist interest in the material culture of the everyday and its surprising revelations.[14] A modern everyday medium, periodically relegated to and rescued from junk heaps, with its own sour perfumes of decay, cinema proves an easier fit for this approach than most other media.[15]

To consider junk film's afterlife makes clear that the life of a film, while still painfully short to the preservationist, turns out to be nowhere near as short as Valentia Steer assumed. From a transnational perspective, Steer's "fifth-rate picture theaters" only begin the stories of the films' afterlives. The description of film as "worn-out rubbish" could be taken now as a testimony to the longevity and adaptability of these prints. It could draw attention to how the films' object-lives help to shape the translations that occur in new exhibition contexts. Case studies of the prints' age and the intermediary stages of their circulation in the region reveal inventive and often counterintuitive reuses of junk film. The labors of reuse created value by reordering film reels and transforming their themes.

FILM TRAFFIC AND REGIONAL INFLUENCE

In following silent cinema's steps toward sustainable commercial exhibition in Iran, the locations of regional relay points reveal as much as the places where the films were produced. Such relay points can often hide in plain sight. International commerce statistics provide some of the most accessible clues about the films shown on commercial screens in Tehran. There were around thirty cinemas operating in Iran in the late 1920s, with just under half of these located in the capital.[16] These cinemas subsisted on a steady stream of imports accounted for in one report by the US Department of Commerce. Statistics confirm that American and French productions far exceed those of any other country, and their share of the market remains fairly stable despite taking an obvious hit from the economic crisis. The low numbers overall and the decreased numbers in 1930 mark disappointment in what the commerce department hoped would be "a promising field for exploitation."[17] But the origins and number of these imported films do not tell the whole story.

Exhibitor advertisements from the 1920s and 1930s in the Persian-language daily *Ettela'at* provide more information about the films represented by the import figures. Launched in 1926, the paper is one of the best sources for evidence about the films from this period. Cinemas advertised in *Ettela'at* from the beginning. In the first few years of the paper's run, the only regular film advertisements came from the Grand Cinema operated by Ali Vakili in conjunction with the Grand Hotel on Lalezar Avenue (figure 5). Beginning around 1929, the film ads become more diverse, with cinemas Sepah, Zartoshtian (both also owned by Vakili), Pars, Tehran, and Baharestan among the frequent advertisers. These cinemas do not present a comprehensive view of film exhibition in Tehran, but the regularity of advertisements and continual experiments with tie-in stunts offer a glimpse into exhibition practices and policies at an array of major theaters in the city.

Ettela'at ads indicate that the basic numbers provided in the *Commerce Reports* article are interesting for what they conceal as much as for what they reveal. The films I have been able to identify were typically eight to ten years old, and they were mostly serials. The gap between the original release date and local screening date common throughout the region is substantial in this case. Notable also is the silent serials' prolonged popularity, which extended well into the early sound period. Some lag in exhibition chronology can be expected in any secondary market (including small towns in North America), but here the lag is particularly dramatic even compared with markets in China or major port cities in Latin America, where established exchange offices ensured rapid distribution. To say that the emergence of cinema was simply postponed in Tehran would neglect the most noteworthy aspects of this lag time: how elements of early cinema culture overlapped with 1920s modernism, how intermediary film exchanges exerted their own

FIGURE 5. Outside the Grand Hotel, Lalezar Avenue, Tehran. Private collection.

influence, and how mile markers of exhibition that were experienced elsewhere as continual sequence (the very premise of serialized stories) were often experienced in Tehran as simultaneity.

A cursory glance at the *Commerce Reports* article might suggest that American film dominates the market, followed relatively closely by France and distantly by Germany and Russia. But the circuitous trade routes and geographical intermediaries for these junk prints form as important a part of their story as their places of origin. Films and film culture routed through Istanbul or British-administered Baghdad seem to easily fit official culture in an Iran governed by a leader who would borrow many of his ideas about nationalist modernization from Atatürk and whose power was enabled by the British government. Intermediaries such as Moscow, on the other hand, created more complicated situations in the late 1920s.[18] The film exhibition scene in Iran during the constitutional revolution and the end of the Qajar dynasty was strongly tied to Russia. Many fledgling early exhibitors in Iran either had ties to Russia or were Russian immigrants themselves. As Reza Khan came to power (becoming Reza Shah in 1925), the dynamic shifted. The shah's government restricted Soviet cultural products, but American and French serials routed through Russia were imported more easily. That serials could circulate so freely becomes all the more significant when seen alongside the effort of cultural agencies in Moscow to flood the Caspian Sea region with Soviet productions as part of an effort, as Michael Smith puts it, to "civilize the Soviet East."[19]

However free they were from a certain kind of political influence, the junk prints that made it to Tehran by way of Russia were nevertheless physical reminders of a regional mania for serials. The early Soviet mania for adventure serials has been well documented. Historians of Russian and Soviet cinemas, such as Yuri Tsivian and Denise Youngblood, have shown how, by 1916, American films had become the main foreign import and the serial reigned.[20] Tsivian describes how pioneers of Soviet montage cinema, such as Lev Kuleshov, turned to American films—to the editing and staging of the Hollywood feature as well as to the anti-realist trick-based structure of the adventure serial—in the development of their own film practice.[21] While Kuleshov's serial-inspired films, such as his kitchen-sink adventure film *Luch Smerti* (*The Death Ray*, 1925), would have been less available in Tehran, the films that inspired him were part of the weekly program. Despite Reza Shah's resistance to Soviet cultural and political influence, some Tehran cinemas in the 1920s seem to have contracted a strain of "Americanitis" owing at least in part to the films' intermediary homes in Russia. Relay is never an uninterrupted linear process. Part of the story of the films' relay from Los Angeles to Tehran is the story of their triangulation by significant third parties like this one.

This particular distribution channel and its peripatetic cultural influence can also enrich an understanding of the early attempts to make films in Iran. The politics of serial circulation provide some of the context needed to position these early attempts, not only at the beginning of a trajectory of Iranian film production that ends with the popular movies of the 1950s, but also at the end of a tradition of exhibition and reception of early cinema's afterlife. The only surviving silent feature made in Iran, *Haji Aqa, Actor-e Cinema* (*Haji Aqa, the Cinema Actor*; Ohanian, 1933), stands as one particularly relevant example. Indeed, only a reading of *Haji Aqa* as belonging to a tradition of cultural reception of cinema could adequately account for how greedily the film appropriates early cinema. Reflexive from the start, the eight-reel comedy tells a conversion story about a religious man who learns to love the cinema after seeing a film that featured him as its unwitting star. The film basically follows the approach of early films like *Uncle Josh at the Moving*

Picture Show (Porter, 1902). It satirizes a naïve film spectator in order to simultaneously address the social anxieties surrounding the medium and create a comfortable position from which to understand these anxieties. Throughout his process of conversion, Haji Aqa (a naïve spectator but not entirely a rube insofar as he represents religious authority) encounters a range of characters from early cinema. These include a Méliès-like magician who makes people and animals disappear, a Luciano Albertini–like strongman whose strength is necessary to operate an absurdly large winch for removing teeth, and several slapstick characters who chase Haji Aqa around the streets of Tehran. More than a coherent narrative, the film functions as a collage of elements ranging from cinema of attractions–type interludes to 1910s-style stunt performances.

Haji Aqa is illustrative here because its all-inclusive, reflexive composition parallels the larger channel of circulation I have been tracing. Its assemblage of dancing, acrobatic stunts, and slapstick gags do recall the Hollywood genre films dominating the nearby cinemas, but equally important are the film's connections to similar filmmaking efforts to the north. A filmmaker of Armenian origin, Ohanian trained in Russia and, upon arrival in Tehran in 1930, he opened the school for acrobatics and film acting featured in *Haji Aqa*'s story. When Ohanian shows acrobats flying onto horizontal bars in reverse motion, Dziga Vertov's *Kino-Eye* (1924) footage of athletes seems not far in the background. When Ohanian presents as a rapid montage sequence the final screening in which Haji Aqa sees himself in a filmed performance, the influence is clear. The stunts and editing in the film seem to nod to American action films and to Soviet cinema at the same time.

There were certainly other distribution channels in addition to the one explored here, but the case of American and French films traveling through Russia and then to Iran over the span of a decade highlights the importance of regional circulation in questions of silent film's transnational influence.[22] Indeed, reconsidering film history in regional, rather than strictly national, terms can more directly address the political nuances and ironies of local cinemas characterized less by the stability of their industries than by their cultures of erratic but vigorous appropriation.

SERIALS OUT OF SYNC

In its heyday in the mid-1910s, the silent serial was a blockbuster genre developed by many of the same American and French firms that dominated the world film market. I have been arguing thus far that serial film "junk prints" played a key role in Tehran's silent moviegoing culture. Tracing the afterlife of a single serial, *The Tiger's Trail* (Astra/ Pathé, 1919), will provide a more detailed picture of the innovations of local exhibitors and the far-reaching flexibility of the serial form. But to grasp these innovations clearly means backing up a moment to understand current assessments of the serial film's form and its reception at home and abroad.

With their episodic format, serials remained amenable to the variety format of early cinema exhibition while also allowing for greater standardization. They followed a proven path (in literature) toward managing repeat business. Nicholas Dulac describes the effects of serial form as synchronizing the spectator with its regularity of content, just as its "to be continued" structure created a desire for more.[23] Hence, in the early and mid-1910s, when feature films were beginning to offer an alternative model of standardizing motion-picture entertainment, the serial's multi-reel format offered a compromise. Medium-length episodes suited the increasing trend toward longer films, but they allowed for standard repetitions from one multi-title program to the next. They could be promoted at great expense, like features, and still remain flexible for exhibitors' purposes. As a result, serials were far less self-contained as texts. Regularly released episodes benefited in the 1910s from intermedial promotions including public stunts, star discourse, write-in contests, and, most important, tie-in stories printed in newspapers to complement the film screenings. In many cases these tie-ins supported the aims of standardized management of film reception.

The serial's modern, sensational character continues to motivate a particularly active area of inquiry into its reception. Derived from sensational melodrama, silent serials rejected dramatic realism and instead exploited stunts, suspense, and action (usually in pursuit of a coveted object such as the parcel famously stolen by a human chain formed atop a moving train in *The Tiger's Trail*). As action spectacles, they stood at a charged division of lowbrow and middlebrow entertainment and form a prominent component of the cultural study of modernity in the 1910s.[24] And most important in the present context, these sensational melodramas had an extensive international reach. Adventure serials proved to be highly exportable commodities, fueling local manias for serials around the world, like the Russian "serialitis" noted earlier.

Investigations of the serial's transcultural circulation have led film historians to a sustained focus on the female star. In her discussion of the "technologies of stardom," Jennifer M. Bean points out the implicit transcultural dimension of the star discourse that made US serial stars like Pearl White such important modern archetypes.[25] Weihong Bao and Rosie Thomas have analyzed these translations of Pearl White's stardom, showing how her star persona and the character types she embodied proved highly adaptable to local character types such as the *virangana* warrior woman in India and the *nüxia* female knight-errant in China.[26] While not exactly my focus here, I've chosen to look at *The Tiger's Trail*, a Ruth Roland vehicle, in part because it adds another local variant to this recent scholarship. Roland, like White, worked in the United States for the Pathé company. She had, by 1919, succeeded White as the company's principal serial star. Her success on Tehran screens points to the growing relevance of transnational studies of the serial star. The broader cultural implications of this success deserve more attention than the scope of this chapter will allow.

The exhibition records of *The Tiger's Trail* mark it as a significant, but not atypical, film event in Tehran. In terms of the number of episodes screened, the diligence of the advertisements, and the tie-in material, *The Tiger's Trail* was among the more complete serials promoted in *Ettela'at*. The newspaper provides a wealth of material about which individual episodes screened and where. It had a long run at the Grand Cinema and then screened shortly after at Vakili's Cinema Zartoshtian for women on the north side of the city.[27] *Ettela'at*'s premiere announcement for *The Tiger's Trail* signals the importance of its acrobatic star, its cost, and its international success.

Grand Cinema, Lalezar
Friday, Saturday, and Sunday Evening.
The 1st through the 3rd of the month of Dey [December 23–25, 1927].
Famous and unparalleled serial—*The Tiger's Face* [*The Tiger's Trail*]
In six episodes
One of the most celebrated masterpieces by American artists.
With astonishing acrobatic action—by Ruth Roland, the famous actor.
This serial cost millions and has a cast of thousands. Seeing this story of a bravehearted young girl, who is fighting for what is rightfully hers, you will sympathize with her sensational courage.
This serial has been shown all over Europe and America numerous times. Each day it attracts more and more viewers.[28]

As one of the more extensively promoted serials, *The Tiger's Trail* might seem better suited than most serials in Tehran to the strategies of synchronizing audiences, printed texts, and images with the organized release of each episode. But the tie-in material in this case actually undercuts this assumption. While studies of other reception contexts highlight the serial's connection to planned efficiency and emerging mass marketing, this case highlights its less examined affinity for improvised, creative presentation in local markets. The *Ettela'at* ads offer evidence of the attempt to replicate foreign serial promotion, but the physical changes to the available footage, the damaged or otherwise missing reels, subjected the mechanisms of serial exhibition to continuous redesign. The modular format and tie-in promotion may have been designed to manage a certain type of relationship between film and spectator, but in the films' afterlife these modules and their tie-in stories proved much more pliable.

The Tiger's Trail had undergone multiple transformations even before reaching Tehran. It was made in the United States and distributed by Pathé, but it came to Iran by way of the French Pathé release. The French Pathé version, *Le tigre sacré*, had twelve episodes, unlike the American version's fifteen, and it appeared on French screens seven months after the completion of the American release. Seven years after the Paris premiere, the film began its Tehran run at the Grand Cinema as *The Holy Tiger*, a translation of the French title, and occasionally as *The Tiger's Face*, a title derived from one of the episodes. The episodes were promoted with tie-in stories as well as advertisements that also came from France (although the advertisements describe the serial as an "American" masterpiece). The novelist Guy de Téramond had published feuilleton tie-in stories in *L'Avenir* concurrent with Pathé's release of each episode. These were compiled shortly after as a *ciné-roman* (figure 6).[29] *Ettela'at* published one thousand– to two thousand–word translations of all twelve of de Téramond's chapters over a three-week period beginning December 20, 1927.[30]

Exhibitors in Iran partly replicated the promotion strategies that accompanied serial episodes when they were first released nearly a decade prior, but a combination of intentional and unavoidable changes to the programs radically altered the outcomes. *Ettela'at* published feuilletons that were often not in sync with the corresponding film episodes, and patrons of the movie theaters further down the chain of distribution would see the films long after the newspaper printed the tie-in story. *The Tiger's Trail* was no exception. Since only about half of the series made it from the original distribution centers to screens in Tehran, the exhibitors had to modify the timing of the releases. The gaps in the film program offer some indication of the modifications necessary for such a spotty program. Feuilleton episodes five, six, seven, and eleven appear to fill in

FIGURE 6. First three episodes of *Le tigre sacré* (Guy de Téramond, 1920).

for missing footage. They are accompanied only by general ads promoting the Grand Cinema, while other story episodes carry announcements that the corresponding film episode will be screened at the cinema that evening. Like many of the serials that played at the Grand Cinema, the episodes were then given a second run at Vakili's Cinema Zartoshtian. Here, they fell further out of sync with the printed stories.

These serialized story versions of the films, as a result of their loose fit with the film programs, often exceeded the function of clarifying plot points for filmgoers.[31] While exhibitors did utilize printed plot summaries in many cases, live narration was still the most effective way to ensure that audiences engaged with the films' stories. Even with the translations of de Téramond's chapters, *The Tiger's Face* screenings were preceded by "an oral introduction for the gentlemen who had missed some of the episodes."[32] This makes sense given that the viewer base could be unpredictable. The Grand Cinema was attached to a hotel, after all. It was a business dependent on the circulation and variation of people in its spaces. The translations of de Téramond's work could thus not really substitute for on-site narration. Low literacy rates aside, his story episodes often spanned wide and erratic gaps in the film programming. Live narrators could always improvise. The printed stories' regularity and completeness set them apart from the irregularly sequenced films. The printed stories had a definite value, but it was not primarily as a substitute for live narration.

During the intervening decade between production and exhibition, reels, scenes, and titles inevitably went missing and were re-edited. The shipments must have been a programmer's nightmare, with odd reels, unreliable labeling, and translation issues. In many instances, the films were shaped more by the intermediary distributors' scissors than by the original production company. In *Esquisse d'une psychologie du cinéma*, André Malraux offers a rare account of these kinds of transformations: "In Persia, I once saw a film that does not exist. It was called *The Life of Charlie*. Persian cinemas show their films in the open air, while black cats look on from the walls surrounding the audience. The Armenian exhibitors had artfully compiled Chaplin's shorts into a single film. The resulting feature film was surprising: the myth of Chaplin appeared in its pure state."[33] In explaining how Chaplin transcends the physical manipulations of his films internationally, Malraux indicates how extensive these manipulations could be. The film he describes is closer to a compilation film than to a program of shorts. It is likely that exhibitors were compelled to give incomplete imported serial episodes a similar treatment.

Ettela'at advertisements give little indication of modifications to individual episodes of *The Tiger's Trail*, but if the missing and re-edited footage within reels was comparable to the percentage of missing episodes, then the divergences between the *ciné-roman* (itself a double translation) and the films were considerable. Mistakes in the programming schedule offer some clues about the state of the films upon arrival in Tehran. At the outset of the Grand Cinema screening of *The Tiger's Face*, the advertisements announce repeatedly that the cinema would show six episodes.[34] By mid-January 1928, eight episodes of the series had screened. The eighth episode corresponded to the twelfth and final feuilleton episode. These mistakes in counting the episodes were repeated in different ads. The exhibitor may have tracked down another two episodes elsewhere, or he may have eventually discovered them within the shipment. Whether these specific mistakes in the program resulted from assessments of the prints or the printing of the advertisements, shipments containing half of the original footage would have made these kinds of revisions difficult to avoid.

All these factors worked in concert to disrupt the timing that had made the serial such an efficient organizer of mass audiences across other national borders. As Paul Moore has shown in a detailed study of exhibition history in Toronto in the 1910s, the serial format helped to consolidate multiple episodes, promotional materials, and screening locations and thus to synchronize a mass audience across North America.[35] Since it enabled many episodes to play "at once" in multiple locations, accompanied by tie-ins in the daily papers, the serial form fashioned an integrated network of multiple texts. One essential feature of this network was a tiered hierarchy based on first- and second-run theater locations. Moore's systematic analyses of these effects on imported films in Toronto cast the serial's diversity in Tehran into sharp relief. Whereas brief planned delays reinforced synchronization and mass organization in Toronto, extended unplanned delays, missing reels, and unpredictable tie-ins undermined or even reversed these effects, even as Tehran exhibitors partially imitated strategies of synchronized promotion.

One aim of this planned organization of the serial was to engage a wider public with a sensational genre often considered more narrowly as lowbrow entertainment. And just as serials did not foster mass culture in the Middle East the way they began to in North America, the association of serial melodrama with lowbrow culture did not exactly fit their reception in Tehran either. The prestige of the films and their tie-in stories could vary widely. For a newspaper made up of only a few pages per issue, it is remarkable that the translations of tie-in stories for each serial episode sometimes spread over multiple pages (figure 7). *Ettela'at* likely devoted so much space to the film stories because serialized stories (often translated work by foreign authors) already formed an important component of the Iranian periodical press. The translated serial story's special-feature status in some papers, combined with the arrhythmic pairing of *ciné-roman* and serial, mark these stories as special features, as amusements in themselves for a reading public that primarily represented the educated class far from the lowbrow.

Because the serials in Tehran were undeniably out of date, exhibitors faced a challenge in marketing these films as legitimate works. The blurbs in the ads would, of course, not want to give any sense of the film programs as being obsolete, so it might seem counterintuitive to make note of a film's age and intermediary life. But rather than attempting to conceal the reality of their films' age, exhibitors often embraced it as an asset for promotion. The last line of the *Tiger's Trail* advertisement cited above, about "attracting new viewers daily," is one example among many. Other advertisements, such as those for *The Secrets of an Invisible Woman* (probably episodes from Pathé's *La femme inconnue*), are billed as having more cultural merit because they played in the United States for many years (a tradition that can be found in film advertisements all the way into the 1970s).[36] The promotional line for the American serial *The Invisible Protector* boasts, "The film has screened around

FIGURE 7. Advertisement for *The Tiger's Trail* (1919, billed as *Chehre-ye Babr / The Tiger's Face*) with one installment of a translation of *Le tigre sacré* (Guy de Téramond, 1920), *Ettela'at*, October 20, 1927.

the world."[37] These ads express a cosmopolitan sentiment that turns the films' road-worn status on its head through a rhetoric of world travel. Exhibitors used their long trade life, the same trade life that rendered these scratched, warped, and heavily spliced prints little more than the waste products of yesterday's business, to elevate their films' status to something like "classics" of the international screen. The trickier it was to promote junk prints as of-the-moment fashions, the easier it was to creatively promote them as modern "classics."

These "classics" endured, even as they lost legitimacy to dramatic realist forms and feature films in other parts of the world. Some of the accounts of early Iranian film history, which frequently return to pioneering work by Farrokh Ghaffary and Jamal Omid, argue that the serial form lost prestige after the introduction of *The Thief of Bagdad* and *The Count of Monte Cristo* in the late 1920s.[38] This is already an extension of the serial's longevity, but the screening notices indicate that one could stretch this periodization even further. By the early 1930s the advertisements do reflect an increased concentration of feature films, but they also show how serials continued to maintain a strong presence by adapting to the increase in feature exhibition. One discernible trend involved "featurizing" the serials by projecting two or three episodes at a single screening. The serials do not appear to be any more complete in the early 1930s than they were in the mid-1920s (still not much more than half the number of original episodes), so this adaptation would have served the exhibitors' practical need to assemble a program out of odd reels while also serving a demand for longer-format evening entertainment. *The 2000 Year-Old Woman*, *The Brass Bullet* ("with the famous Juanita [Hansen]," 1918), *The Fast Express* (retitled *Death Train*, 1924), Louis Feuillade's *Barrabas* (in only six of the original twelve episodes, 1919), and *The Iron Man* ("the international serial with Luciano Albertini," 1924) each screened two or three episodes at a time.[39] On occasion, perhaps because of the familiarity of this screening format, the exhibitors mistakenly (or creatively) billed feature films as screening in two-episode segments. The early 1930s notices for Jean Epstein's *Mauprat* (1926) and Harry Piel's *The False Verdict* (1924) make this mistake, even as they provide details concerning the actors in the features.[40]

The act structure in features and the episode structure in serials appear to be, to some extent, interchangeable in the film descriptions. Like *The Tiger's Trail*, with its imported tie-in story and well-traveled reputation, these examples indicate how widely serials' cultural legitimacy could vary depending on the exhibition context. Positing sharp distinctions in prestige between the serial and the full feature format might in this case belie the ways in which cultural capital could be imaginatively constructed through shrewd programming and promotion. The standing of an evening's entertainment depended less on any standard respectable film form than on the labors of artful exhibitors working with varied film shipments and managing how these objects would be encountered.

IRONIES OF APPROPRIATION

I want to follow up these observations with a final non-serial example of a reconfigured "classic." The Tehran exhibition of D. W. Griffith's *The Fall of Babylon* shows just how counterintuitive and politically significant the afterlives of these silent-film prints could be. Long before its wide global circulation, the film had already endured one of the most famous re-editions in the silent era. In an effort to salvage something more marketable out of his epic *Intolerance* (1916), Griffith extracted its Babylonian story for release as a stand-alone feature in 1919. In this form, the film did prove marketable in Tehran, enough to reappear with some frequency in the early years of *Ettela'at*. Notices for the screenings as celebrations of Iranian history were listed on the front page of the paper as well as in the advertisements section. They indicate that the reels of *The Fall of Babylon* were dusted off regularly for screenings promoted as special events.

The film proved well suited to local and official appropriation, where its import status and the draw of its stars worked in concert with its local appeal. The acting talent of Constance Talmadge competed for space in the advertisements with the historical interest of the setting.[41] In some cases the exhibitors adapted Griffith's own famous gestures toward historical authenticity for this end. Their advertisements paraphrased the film's intertitles that footnote the historical sources for the film's images. A 1926 screening notice for the Grand Cinema invites viewers "who have read the history of Iran . . . to get acquainted with the forefathers of your country personally" by seeing "the great historical city of Babylon, its buildings, gardens, and towers, with your own eyes."[42] A 1930 screening notice at the Cinema Sepah explains, "For this glorious film the filmmakers built an accurate replica of Belshazzar's famous fortress walls."[43] The advertisements borrow wholesale the rhetoric of moving-picture re-creations as guaranteeing historical accuracy, a rhetoric that Griffith had honed in *The Birth of a Nation* (1915). As accurate replicas the architectural details enabled the film to function as a kind of local, place-specific tourism while remaining recognizable as a featured import in which "one scene alone cost millions to make."[44]

The greatest irony of this afterlife of *Intolerance* lies in its mistranslatability. The film regularly screened as part of celebrations such as the Iranian New Year. Its claims to historical accuracy, transparency, and universal appeal were freely borrowed, but the film's message was not.

New Year's Festivities
—Grand Cinema—
On Wednesday and Thursday, the first two evenings of spring
Film—*Cyrus the Great*—Conquering Babylon
The Grand Cinema, the preeminent film exhibition hall, has organized an event to honor our customers and celebrate our Iranian history on this special occasion of the New Year. We will show the famous film—*Cyrus the Great*—about the conqueror, whose name is the pride of Iran and Iranians. No one who is interested in this story should delay seeing the film.[45]

It is tempting to speculate how many times this print may have been re-edited prior to this screening. But scissors are only one tool among many. Radically recut or not, this film clearly conveys a new message. A story about a fall has become a story about a conquest. The narrative of *Intolerance* and *The Fall of Babylon*, in which the Persian army represents the bellicose intolerance of the era, is aggressively misread in *Cyrus the Great*. The advertisements for the screenings of this film present a lesson in a history of an exalted civilization rather than the film's original warnings of catastrophe. Sidestepping Griffith's aims of realizing film's potential as a universal language, promoters of the film in Iran constructed an alternate epic narrative. The film was subsumed within a nationalist discourse founded on the construction of a pre-Islamic golden age.[46] In other words, these special-event screenings enabled local misreadings of a film famous for its ambition to eliminate local misreadings.

In *The Fall of Babylon* and in each of the examples outlined here, these inventive promotions challenge simplistic conceptions of periphery and center. An interpretation would be lacking if it framed the liberally translated tie-in stories one-dimensionally as fostering progressive variations on film fandom without recognizing how they also functioned as special features imported by a savvy promoter for a small, mandarin reading public. In searching a cinema culture for adaptations to dislocated films, it is just as important to identify some of the entanglements of cinema's modern vernacular.[47] Imported, translated silent-era films could integrate with a regime in which sovereignty relied more on the centralized spectacle of modernization than on its sustainability. The advertisements and tie-in publicity, developed during an earlier period in these films' history and creatively misused to promote the films as modern classics, could overlap with the visions of social order promoted by nationalist intellectuals and by the state.

Whether in service of progressive improvisation or demagogic appropriation, these uses of junk serials and other "masterpieces" betray secondhand film as a conspicuous living artifact. Even if the 1920s readership of *Ettela'at*'s tie-in publicity was limited, the "world travel" rhetoric was commercially motivated, and the modernism of certain films was appropriated as a spectacle of authority, there is also the possibility that the filmgoing public in Tehran, because of the various adaptations to the serials' age, wear, and missing reels, could experience these films as objects with histories in a way that resonates with other re-viewing cultures. The increase in scholarly work on the institutions that redefined films as historical objects after their commercial viability had waned speaks, albeit in an oblique way, to the types of film cultures I have been tracing here.[48] It is certainly important not to overstate affinities in placing these local appropriations in some relation to the well-known secondhand ciné clubs in, say, London or Paris that famously fostered an early historical awareness of cinema in the silent era. Important differences will always need to be acknowledged between the deliberately out-of-date programs at 1920s European film clubs and the necessarily out-of-date programs pieced together in the commercial cinemas of 1920s Tehran. But the motivations and methods used to understand and evaluate each of these practices might reveal something compelling about the other. Just as film historians such as Malte Hagener have worked to show how avant-garde secondhand screening practices, which he associates with "the birth of film history," were more eclectic, mainstream, and improvisational than the participants' writings would lead one to assume, research into the eclectic, mainstream screenings at cinemas in Tehran can begin to show how these events generated another sense of film's historical value through their creative adaptation to supposedly obsolete footage.[49]

I make these kinds of assertions here, and throughout this book, with the intention of inviting more discussion about the historical reflection at play in emergent, secondhand exhibition contexts. The question of the connection between a film culture's historical awareness and the awareness of celluloid as material is not a geographically limited question, nor does its relevance end in the silent era. As I discuss in chapter 5, the practice of collecting fragments of celluloid from Hollywood films became a widespread practice among preadolescent boys more than a generation later in Iran and was mythologized in films and published stories. Personal stories of these film-notebook collections and the inventive attempts to project still film frames (in need of oral histories) are well known among the children of those who grew up shortly after World War II in cities across Iran.[50] These broken pieces of junk prints lovingly gleaned from projection booth floors stand as reminders of the extended life of celluloid and its importance in the history of the material awareness of film. They draw attention to the morphologies of the print in the silent era and beyond.

CHAPTER 2

Circulation Worries

The systems that relayed cinema through the Middle East into Iran did more than simply transmit feature films as capsules of creative labor from abroad. They reorganized the sites and conditions of cinema's creative labor. Without this reorganization, traceable through archives of distributors, lawyers, accountants, and technicians, cinema could not have become the vital and sustainable component of everyday urban experience that one encounters in midcentury Iran. Even in the cinemas around the world in which Hollywood productions occupied the majority of screen time, the direct institutional presence of Hollywood should not be immediately assumed.

Products and technologies circulated through local infrastructures that were barely visible to the industries that created those objects. For this reason, as I demonstrated in chapter 1, such objects were neither static in their form nor self-evident in their meanings. They were continually reshaped physically in the process of translation, they needed to be reconstituted, and their contexts needed to be constructed. I maintain my focus in this chapter on physical films and film technologies circulated in Iran, but I position them here in relation to cultures of maintenance, debates about the geography of rights to intellectual property, and the business of distribution. The infrastructures supplying prints and the technologies used to reproduce them and retool their dubbed soundtracks deserve attention in their own right, and such attention requires a cultural history located at the intersection of archives related to engineering, law, and trade.

Moving into the postwar decades requires a few shifts in emphasis. As circulation of secondhand prints accelerated and grew in the 1950s, their afterlives needed to be managed and engineered. A series of tasks emerge in the effort to foreground this logistical and technical work. How exactly were film prints, posters, and sound recordings routed along shipping lines? Which versions were routed? What were the structures of the business transactions and the definitions of intellectual property? What kinds of machines and components were engineered to present the material at every stage of their circulation? What kinds of creative maintenance reworked these objects in transit? Finally, how do we integrate these different constructions of industry leverage, success, or prestige, and how does media archaeology figure within them?

In conceptualizing this particular constellation of questions at various stages of research, I have returned to the phrase *circulation worries*. *Worry* was material before it was emotional. The archaic meanings of the term describe process of wear and tear, either rapid and violent or protracted and subtle. To worry an object is to disintegrate it, as a pet worries a chew toy or furniture (like the desk at which this book was written). The term is also used to describe persistence through difficult work or challenging travel. Both of these material definitions highlight the driving factors of my materially focused cultural history of cinema in Iran: the fragility and the endurance of films in circulation. Films are worried in an instant by sprocket teeth, but they also worry along through formal and informal distribution networks around the globe.

The common affective meanings of worry, as anxiety about unpredictable challenges, point to legal and technological concerns central to this chapter. The legal and financial obstacles to transparent film circulation seem to multiply in the postwar Middle East. They caused distributors and exhibitors alike to fret over the best way to handle complicated issues of copyright. Only after agreements about the licensing of film properties had been reached—if not philosophical agreements, at least practical ones—could the technical work with the material begin. Because these films had traveled far, they required an outsize network of technicians and engineers to worry over them as they were handled, reassembled, re-edited, and duplicated.

The cultural history of media in modern Iran is distinguished by an intense love of cinema, a *cinemadusti* linked at each phase in its long history to forms of uncertain access. Given these persistent circulation worries, we might consider the moodier inflections of this love as a form of what Sarah Keller terms "anxious cinephilia" wrought by cinema's circuitous travels.[1] Later chapters will revisit this mood in places where it might be expected, but I introduce it here through a kind of stage door: a collection of documents and devices that kept the systems running behind the scenes.[2] While I would not characterize worry as the single defining tone in an archive that includes business correspondence, trade and fan press, legal debates, and engineering achievements, there is something in the sense of worry as an expression of care, as a feeling associated with maintaining rather than dominating or disrupting, that unites these archival traces of love and frustration in an archaeology of a fragile medium in midcentury Iran.

SUSTENANCE: ENGINEERING AND MAINTENANCE

The first decades of industrializing cinema in Iran depended on a kind of engineering labor usually overshadowed by the premium placed on breakout inventions. To work against such habits of omission, it is helpful to turn away from norms centered on engineering achievements as disruptive innovations and focus instead on the ongoing labors of maintenance and repair that make a media industry adaptable. In their call for a revision to engineering pedagogy, Andrew Russell and Lee Vinsel emphasize that "creativity, invention, imagination, and artfulness—are . . . distributed more broadly in the technology landscape than our dominant discourses of innovation . . . are keen to acknowledge."[3] Given that 70 percent of current engineering graduates go into fields maintaining infrastructures, they argue that it is inaccurate and sometimes unethical to obfuscate that creative labor with rhetoric of entrepreneurial innovation.[4] While they are careful to point out that their intervention could have adherents across the political spectrum, it is compatible with a critique of neoliberalism in engineering and in the field of science and technology studies. A key question of the Maintainers Research Network is ultimately one of value.[5] It is an approach influenced by feminist discourses on science and technology's relationship to the ethics of care.[6] From a geopolitical perspective, if one emphasizes individual innovation and corporate R&D over conceptions of care, maintenance, and repair, one risks aligning creativity in the field with metropolitan capital accumulation rather than interrogating those alignments. In other words, the question of ethics in tech pedagogy frames a challenge for media historiography.

To write a history of cinema that includes the labors of care and maintenance means dwelling in the material of the trade and decoupling creative thinking from narratives of the progress of an industry. Such an approach is imperative when studies are located in the media environments of the Middle East, as it helps to avoid the frustrating search for parallels between the methods for understanding its cinema industries and the established methodologies used to study others. So Steven Jackson's question "how might we begin to reverse this dominant view, and reimagine or better recognize the forms of innovation, difference, and creativity embedded in repair?" offers a useful way to redirect concerns toward the pressing needs of this study.[7] Prints that played on Tehran screens were sustained by professionals who knew how to work with the available material, how to source, maintain, repair, and send it in a useable format through projectors and speakers. This was the case in the exhibition spaces of the 1920s and '30s, but it was more dramatically the case with the industrialization of cinema after the war. This period witnessed a significant growth of exhibition infrastructure, particularly in Tehran, and a formalization of dubbing practices that expanded the audience for imported films. The multiple or hybrid formats and processes of bringing films to screens make for unreliable markers of progress. An adaptive and sustainable moving picture business in parts of the Middle East needed to accommodate larger audiences to be sure, but it also needed to play with asynchrony. Creative engineering of motion pictures meant creating systems of production and exhibition flexible enough to cycle back to earlier technologies in patterns that fall out of sync with the decisive steps forward in the technological progress of moving pictures. Histories of this creative labor should consider forms of achievement and prestige not only in those moments when the industry clearly forged ahead but in the sustained work with asynchrony.

Let's take as an example a public-facing curatorial project in Iran from 2016. The curators at the Museum of Cinema in Tehran take a notably engineering-heavy approach to cinema history. The way they frame the creative labor of film engineers offers some guidance in thinking about the history of creativity and craft in relation to maintenance and repair. Throughout the museum, the devices associated with the typically less glamorous labor of an industry interlaced with more familiar stories of celebrity performers, auteurs, and international awards. Even before entering the museum, devices of below-the-line labor greet visitors as museum objects. The display on the front terrace of this repurposed

اسباب سینماتوگراف

مجموعه ابزار و وسایل بکار گرفته شده در حرفه های گوناگون دوره های گذشته سینمای‌ایران اینک فرسوده و
بلااستفاده شده اند . لیکن برای پژوهشگران تاریخ سینمای کشــــورمان هر یک نشـــان از سیر تحول و تکامل
تکنولوژی و گویای مبداء اخذ آنها از کشورهای صنعتی و بضـاعت فنی تولید و نمایش سینمای ما در هر دوره
بوده و یادآور خاطره و خاطرات تکنیسین هائی هستند که با آن ها کار کردند و جان گذاشتند تا سینمای ایران
پا بگیرد و گام های آغازین را بردارد.

FIGURES 8A, 8B. Object card and equipment exhibit, Museum of Cinema, Tehran.

palace includes machines used to edit films, reproduce them, and record sound onto their magnetic stripes. The object-card text explains,

> This collection of equipment was used for a variety of professional tasks during past generations of Iranian cinema. While these worn-out devices are no longer in working order, each of them provides researchers in the history of our country's cinema with clues about the evolution of film technology. For each period in cinema's history, they simultaneously bear traces of acquisition from industrialized countries and demonstrate the technical capacity of film production and exhibition within Iran. They also encourage us to remember the experiences of the technicians who operated them. These technicians sacrificed their lives for Iranian cinema as it emerged and took its first steps (figures 8a, 8b).[8]

This prologue to the museum's exhibits is remarkable in its poetics of obsolescence and unseen labor. Likewise, its allusion to the devices' points of origin abroad is paired with the significance of their use in Iran; acquisition and local capacity are components of the same history. Other examples of such devices feature at major milestones in museum's chronology. These are devices that circulated but were also maintained over years by the labor of technicians whose memory the museum evokes before it tells visitors anything about awards at Cannes and Venice.

Inside the museum, several engineers are showcased in this manner, with at least one prominent figure standing out. Engineer Mohsen Badi's professional life in cinema is particularly suited to an ethics of repair, since it actually began in a repair shop in Tehran in the early 1940s.[9] Before that, Badi studied in Paris and London and opened a radio shop in Paris, which he ran for several years until the escalating events of the Second World War forced him to return to the Middle East. He eventually settled in Tehran around 1940, across the street from the National Bank, establishing a shop like the one he had in Paris. In the evenings, after the shop closed, he developed sound recording and film duplication systems that would be used in the film industry in the decades to come. As the industry grew, he assumed multiple roles as a sound engineer, lab and studio owner, cinematographer, director, and producer. Badi's semiautomatic, darkroom-free, 35 mm continuous contact printer features prominently in a section of the museum's timeline primarily devoted to midcentury engineers (figure 9). A small controversy around this device is as important to the story as the device's enduring utility. It is framed as an example of a particular kind of creative achievement. The card describes how it was developed in 1949, retooled over the next twelve years, and copied by several other studios in Iran. In 1971, the story goes, it caught the attention of Bell and Howell engineers who were installing film equipment in local laboratories. They recognized their company's J printer in Badi's machine and suspected a reverse-engineered violation of what they perceived to be their intellectual property. Upon further investigation, the card explains, they discovered that Badi had never seen the J printer and had developed the suspicious components one year prior to the company's patents.

This lesson about Badi's device hinges on an alternative notion of prestige and success. An intellectual property challenge, won by an Iranian engineer, forces a company in a superior position in the political economy of media to confront its own assumption that all creativity trailed its own innovations. Working without the R&D budget of a major corporation, Badi had out-engineered the engineers at Bell and

FIGURE 9. Exhibit of Mohsen Badi's device, Museum of Cinema, Tehran.

Howell. Badi's elegant machine, built in his storefront workshop in response to a specific set of local problems, had leapfrogged the massive company's research and development for fast and relatively portable reproduction technology, and it had remained invisible to the global suppliers of this technology for over twenty years. Badi's machine was not the copy, the card indicates; it was in fact the prototype copied by other studios in Iran. The exhibit creates a narrative of creativity specific to a small industry working in relation to global infrastructures of circulation. Its model of creativity emphasizes uncommon stress points in its conception of what cinema is, why it is significant, and how it achieves that significance. These points of stress offer an object lesson for film studies.

The exhibition of items from Badi's career supports a historiography rooted in questions of maintenance and repair. The little work that exists on his contributions tends to highlight this dimension by linking it to tropes of engineering skill and perseverance that offer a contrast to the heroic inventor tropes used in publicity material for cinema inventors in Paris and New Jersey in the 1890s.[10] Badi's multiple roles in the industry also reflect the ways that technical and creative labor intersected in Iran. Badi tailored machines and laboratory processes to the specific prints made available by importers, to the need to dub those films with available materials, and to local use of magnetic as well as optical sound—requirements that will each be elaborated in the following sections. While the commercial cinema would continue for decades to derive most of its revenue from imported prints, Badi's work made the industry less dependent on imported technology.

Such a construction of creative prestige returns to the concerns about the use of a term such as *bricolage* to describe the experimentation within the industry at this time. To call someone like Badi a bricoleur in the sense widely used within cultural studies, in opposition to the category of the engineer, might indeed highlight a certain counterhegemonic aspect of his underdog story. But it may also benefit from a caveat. The term fits awkwardly from the outset in everyday speech. In Iran, as in many parts of the world, *engineer* (*mohandes*) is a title of respectful address as common as *doctor*, so a categorical separation of these two terms should be careful not to obscure the social position and cultural capital of "Mohandes Badi" as he produced experimental film equipment afterhours in his shop on Ferdowsi Avenue, with its sign that read, "Radio Maker Mohsen Badi, with Diplomas from Paris and London" (figure 10).[11] And yet, if engineering maintenance thinking applies primarily to labor that does not alter the context of the system being maintained, then there is value in holding on to a certain inflection of *bricolage*. The terms used to describe this labor should identify countercurrents within otherwise top-down histories of media technology and technical labor while steering clear of a neoliberal salute to workshop innovations as a precursor to global entrepreneurial citizenship. Junk prints in Iran were maintained, and they were reanimated. In addressing these concerns, film historiography stands to benefit from attention to recent work in engineering ethics, communication, infrastructure studies, and science and technology studies that has placed a critique of cultures of workplace innovation at the center of questions of the contemporary global circulation of technology.[12] Badi's contact printer and his magnetic sound recording equipment were devices of creative relay. They were technologies that aided the growth of a commercial cinema but that also were

FIGURE 10. Storefront of Mohsen Badi's radio shop. From *Mohandes Badi: San'atgar-e Cinema / Engineer Badi: Craftsman of the Cinema* (Aziz Sa'ati, 2008).

developed as experiments in a maintenance and repair shop. They demonstrate that relay is not exclusively a question of trade. It also involves the work of building and caring for machines.

COPYRIGHT: THE PUBLIC GOOD AND CREATIVITY

Badi's exchange with Bell and Howell highlights an overlooked type of creative technical labor, but it does so only alongside the knotty issue of intellectual property. His printer, like the sound recording technologies to which I will return later, was itself an instrument of copying. Here devices of duplication, which were also used to modify copies along the way, form part of a museum's timeline of the creative labor of cinema in Iran. This timeline mirrors what was happening on the other side of the chain of distribution, where challenges of licensing and duplication, and the piratical rhetoric generated around these challenges, are essential circulation worries of the postwar media networks. Douglas Brunger, whom David O. Selznick tasked with pursuing copyright violations throughout the global export network, complained in multiple letters that the Middle East was "the toughest territory in the world."[13] Such a statement echoed earlier challenges with a greater sense of urgency as the volume of circulation increased. Brunger advocated for increasing royalties and regional licensing fees in the economic model, which brought complications. These expressions of frustration remained consistent throughout the 1950s and early 1960s, until studios established offices in Tehran and the system of accounting for prints shifted to a more direct measure of ticket sales in which multiple businesses shared profit and risk. I present concrete examples of risk management and modification later in the chapter, but given the uncertainties surrounding the definitions of property and its licensed usage, I will first address the debates about copyright policies and practices around modification ahead of the specific films that were modified and circulated. Among these disagreements about property, even when they may seem trivial or contingent, can be found a recurring ethical concern about how to sustain access to everyday media.

The archives of Hollywood's foreign distribution departments in this period document decades of managers' calls for tighter restrictions on international copyright. Interoffice memos regularly featured complaints about the ease of circumventing distributor oversight. What these complaints might fail to reveal if taken at face value is that cross-border copyright is an issue of legal disagreement, not simply a problem of legal enforcement. These disagreements stem from ethical concerns about the political economy of media and diverging cultural understandings of the function of intellectual property. Global media distributors, and their allies in policy, could hardly be expected to describe these differences as anything other than obstacles to profit from material exported at their discretion. Their rhetoric of injustice and scandal around the uncertain licensing and copyright situation in the Middle East expresses a common fantasy of the region as a chaotic media environment, which is always constructed in relation to a fantasy of neatly policed borders of copyright in production centers.

Such a construction overlooks the historical realities of copyright, described by Peter Decherney as "not a watertight monopoly that protects against all forms of copying and reuse. It is designed to leak at the sides, and it has strategically placed holes throughout."[14] A subculture's misuse of property can be monetized if given a chance to form a pattern. Off-label uses of a technology in a large population can function as outsourced R&D. It is only by making way for such leakages, Martin Fredriksson and James Arvanitakis point out, that corporations that control intellectual property can identify and work to enclose the creative reuse of intellectual material once it proves profitable.[15] Corporate enclosure of innovation depends practically on leakage and ideologically on the rhetoric of global piracy. Both the enclosures and the rhetoric have only intensified with the digital circulation of media. Their analog media configurations at midcentury reinforce the contemporary work by Kavita Philip and Lawrence Liang, scholars of global copyright who have traced discussions of digital piracy in their racialized and civilizational terms.[16] If the aim is to incorporate some of these questions of postcolonial legal scholarship into media historiography, maintenance thinking might offer a way through midcentury cinema history in Iran that remains attuned to the concerns of these scholars.

While exporters in the silent era certainly discussed piracy in the region, the licensing of film prints for commercial exhibition makes piracy a point of focus after the coming of sound and especially after the war. Piracy was discussed extensively in United Artists' "Black Book" on Persia (UA grouped Iraq, Iran, and Afghanistan as "Persian territory"). This company resource was essentially a scouting report on all aspects of film export in the territory, including data on corporations and competitors, insurance, selling instructions, and contact information for local attorneys, banks, and exhibitors. It compiles documents on these subjects written between 1935 and 1949. The booklet includes an excerpt of a report from the Bureau of Foreign and Domestic Commerce that describes "film pirating" as "undoubtedly the subject of greatest interest and concern to American film interests as regards Persia": "This situation arises from the fact that there are no laws whatsoever which may be invoked for the protection of film rights. . . . Should needed legislation be passed the question would not be settled entirely inasmuch as it would be comparatively simple to change the name of a picture or forge a document which would make proper identification difficult. Such subterfuges are already used by unauthorized exhibitors to avoid detection by rival rightful exhibitors, and as a consequence certain importers create considerable difficulty by importing films from other territories."[17] The report, in this early stage of organization of licensing in the region, describes the kinds of circulation worries that reoccur in exporter correspondence throughout the 1950s and early 1960s.

The major work of legislating international copyright in Iran came to a head in the early 1970s and made explicit the stakes of long-standing disagreements. A growing local economy, aided by shifts in the global economy and rising oil prices, renewed diplomatic pressure on Iran to address concerns of copyright holders in Britain and the United States. In the opinion of British ambassador D. J. Makinson, "The history of action to obtain copyright protection for British authors and publishers is the history of a 'cat's cradle' with the Shah, vested Iranian interests, the publishers, and HMG pulling in different directions; when one party gives ground, the others tug, but not together."[18] Makinson expressed this opinion privately in response to two major overhauls of Iranian copyright law passed by the Majlis (Parliament) in 1970 and 1974. The first law granted protections only to works published in Iran for a comparatively slim term of thirty years beyond the death of the author. It included cinema and television alongside published writing and musical compositions, but it notably did not include audio records. In an effort to enhance the uses of material for the public good, it exempted educational materials from these restrictions and established the Ministry of Culture and Art as the recipient of the postmortem copyright term in the absence of a clear heir.

This law spoke to some concerns voiced as far back as the 1935 bureau report, but it did not please British and American diplomats and the industries for whom they advocated. The music industry, in particular, lobbied for increased protection and pointed out instances of Iran serving as a hub for pressing and circulating reproductions of commercial vinyl throughout the Middle East. The International Federation of the Phonographic Industry described the law as "a considerable step forward, as previously there was no kind of copyright protection whatsoever," and noted attempts by American and British agents to get their industry to lobby Iran in 1961 and 1965.[19] They cite favorably the public tension created around this issue at the Geneva conference convened by UNESCO and WIPO (World Intellectual Property Organization), where a special display of these duplicated records highlighted Iran's involvement. "[Iran's representative in Geneva] Dr. Hedayati and his delegation were very upset by the inclusion of many records pressed in Iran in an exhibition on pirate records and by references to Iran as a major source of pirate records in the Geneva press at the time of the conference."[20] This event, as well as other meetings in the intervening years, led to the revisions of 1974, which prohibited facsimile reproductions of books (but not translations or other reformatting) and audio recordings. The 1974 law maintained, however, its educational exemptions as well as its primary focus on work first published in Iran, which led the embassy to suggest that concerned publishers consider setting up dummy publishing houses to release work in Iran before the US and UK publication dates.[21] In any case, there still was a considerable degree of freedom, particularly with regard to audio material.[22]

The ambassadors' and industry representatives' strong preference was for Iran to sign on to the Universal Copyright Convention, which went into force in 1955 and established formal copyright notices, basic terms of copyright after the death of the author, and the rule of equal treatment of a country's authors and those of other signatory nations. But such restrictions have created asymmetrical effects around the world, which have threatened to undermine copyright's aims of promoting creativity and a healthy public of readers, viewers, and listeners. An article in the *Tehran Journal* titled "The End of Pirating?" expresses concern for the new law's impact on readership, let alone full participation in the convention's protocol, stating that "additional costs should not place books beyond the reach of the average citizen or the student."[23] The prominent journalist Houshang Vaziri outlined these challenges in a 1974 editorial in *Ayandegan* in which he stresses the financial and cultural costs of joining the convention despite "strong . . . moral foundations of such reasoning." He writes from the perspective of an intellectual concerned with maintenance of the public sphere, telling his readers, "No, we are only losers if we join the International Copyright convention [*sic*]."[24] In this context, it is worth emphasizing the degree to which both of these legislative achievements in the early 1970s carried an implicit critique of the asymmetry of international copyright. The laws passed in Iran maintained provisions that framed intellectual property as a public good. The fact that they were passed while resisting pressures from foreign diplomats highlights these stakes.

To their credit the British embassy did acknowledge the ways in which the global distribution of wealth affected the ostensibly neutral agreement. The Paris revision of the agreement in 1971 was meant to address these imbalances for "qualified underdeveloped countries," but as the copyright hawks themselves acknowledged, "even then all is not plain sailing. The majority of the underdeveloped countries whose adherence [to the Paris revision] was quoted to the Shah as a reproach—Pakistan, India and so on—were not free agents when they signed, and are in favor of only limited protection for authors from 'rich' nations."[25] Each of these various points of interest in the "cat's cradle" were ultimately motivated by similar worries about impoverishing the public domain, however incompatible their solutions may have been. Their agreements and impasses highlight the stakes of certain legal restrictions on circulation of media, which were just as much of a reality in the decades leading up to these reforms as they were in the public discussions of the early 1970s.

These legal structures, and the industry norms that form around them, give shape to patterns of creation. Decherney argues that "piracy battles denote the most innovative periods in media history," and Lawrence Lessig has advocated for copyright reform by making the historical argument that nearly all media forms begin as instruments of piracy.[26] This chapter and the next identify forms of creative labor only possible in sustained periods of contested cultural property.[27] The shift from compilation soundtracks to film composers discussed in the next chapter corresponds with the legal discussion of copyright of recorded sound in this one. In the period before and after the adoption of copyright restrictions, we see a creative landscape made possible by a legal framework, business organization, and capital accumulation as much as by innovations of individual sound designers. The conditions of possibility of the creative work of these individuals are formed in relation to existing infrastructure. The soundtracks of films exhibited in Iran (local productions as well as dubbed imports) might be seen as a historical instance of the category of transformative piracy that Lessig has held up as a justification for protection of the public use of property. Their literal remixes illustrate historically and geographically diverse instances of the creative forms Lessig celebrates in *Remix*.[28]

But such confidence in public domain advocates' definitions of creativity also raises a few concerns. These central chapters of the book do maintain, in some form, a narrative of duplication, modification, and informal distribution as creative work. To completely exclude practices of cross-border reuse in Iran from a history of modernist collage or remix culture would narrow the understanding of both the inventiveness of those practices and the global geographies of remix culture. Such acknowledgments should, however, be considered with the less romantic dimensions of reuse in full view. Embedded in the Iranian critique of the pressure to commit to international copyright agreements are concerns about everyday access. These quotidian concerns set up cultures of reuse to fall short—of ethical legitimacy and of historical significance—if understood only in terms of transformative creativity or resistance. As Liang argues in a critique of the global viability of Lessig's approach, "the public domain deploys classic terms of representation, which borrow from either political or cultural theory; these include categories of citizenship, resistance, and creativity. Piracy often does not fit within any of these categories."[29] Red flags in Lessig's formulation include his rhetoric of freedom and anarchy (critiqued by Ramon Lobato) as well as something he calls "Asian piracy," for which Kavita Philip's critique bears relevance.[30] This is the term he uses to categorize forms of piracy that cannot be redeemed since they are not "transformative." The bad practice of bootleggers in the global south casts into relief the good practice of Bay Area coders and electronic musicians. Such an unreflective model casts Asian piracy, Philip points out, within a "discourse of the not yet," a kind of adolescent phase of parts of the world "awakening to the joys of shoplifting but still unprepared for full-time shop-keeping."[31] Echoes of this discourse of "not yet" can be found throughout the archive of relayed cinema in Iran. It is articulated by Hollywood distributors, but also by those who took on the task of building the film industry and film press in Iran. A history of creative labor in the region should certainly highlight its innovations, possibilities, and achievements, but it also must take a reflective approach to the discourse of the not yet. Narratives of creative achievement in the film industry against a background of copying and informal circulation must be careful not to import geographically coded binaries of good and bad piracy into historiography.

Maintenance thinking offers one possibility for a reflective approach. It remains rooted in everyday media and questions of access while also addressing creative labor in the film industry. A historical approach informed by public domain legal scholars' goal of singling out innovation is not antithetical to quotidian notions of access, but neither is it identical with them. The question of access mentioned by intellectuals like Vaziri does not stop within the typical liberal-market boundaries. Educational exemptions are a clear part of ethical and legal debates in Iran, but so are questions about private publishing outfits and their ability to stay in the business of producing affordable translations and facsimiles. Notions of creativity that neglect the everyday horizon of experience around usage (the vernacular in vernacular modernism), might misidentify how transformative uses of media work across geopolitical imbalances.

Everyday maintenance thinking creates a space for different notions of transformative circulation. It includes the cut-and-paste reuse of sound and the rich performance cultures of dubbing artists in Iran alongside the problem-solving of engineers and the need for exhibitors to make material accessible at a price that can foster a robust film culture. Transformative use should not narrowly describe an escape velocity out of bad piracy to a form of (also narrowly defined) modernist creativity. It describes a media landscape in which the creativity of one practice must be conceived in constellation with often excluded practices. Reflective historiography might then suspend romantic inclinations in order to show how cultures of copying and circulation actually work in everyday space. The archive of correspondence around the Middle East film trade reveals that even when the rhetoric of piracy is discussed by interested parties as a kind of crisis or pressing question, this rhetoric is often a superficial distraction from the everyday work punctuated by technological achievements like contact printers and magnetic soundstrip systems, global distributors establishing what forms of circulation are permissible or unavoidable, and exhibitors driving the hard bargains that create access in this "toughest territory in the world."

LICENSE: JUNK PRINTS AND AFFIDAVITS OF DESTRUCTION

Even as those who worked in the foreign distribution offices in Los Angeles and New York dutifully pursued export to as many territories as possible, the profits for the Middle East remained minimal through the early 1960s. For Selznick, Warner Bros., and United Artists, the three studios for which there is the most extensive archive of foreign circulation in the Middle East, annual revenue reports indicate many markets in the Middle East had barely noticeable revenues. The 1947 accounting report of global grosses of Selznick for the previous year put Egypt at 0.14 percent, Syria and Lebanon at 0.03 percent, Iraq at 0.02 percent, and Iran at 0.01 percent.[32] Revenues from Iran totaled less than rounding errors in markets around the world. These four territories in the Middle East were usually listed on the spreadsheets, but their revenue sections were left blank more often than they were noted. In the ledgers kept by United Artists in the early 1950s, the figure for the entire Middle East hovers around 4 percent of all foreign distribution revenues.[33] The majority of that number was generated from principal markets in Beirut and Cairo. The cities further along the chain of distribution, despite having significant film cultures and large populations of moviegoers, were even less likely to be captured by these calculations. Baghdad, for example, was already partly a secondary market for what had played in Cairo or Beirut, or in oil company cinemas in the Persian Gulf. Of the 230 film imports officially counted by the US embassy in Baghdad in 1954, 80 percent were outright sales of junk prints, which were hard to track and typically offloaded in blocks.[34] Baghdad's revenues were a fraction of those of larger markets in the Middle East, and Tehran's was a fraction of Baghdad's—at least from the perspective of foreign distributors. Moving into a period of accelerated trade with "Persian territories" in the 1950s, direct communications from distribution offices in Hollywood and New York still infrequently extended east of Baghdad.

And yet the filmgoing population of Iran was many times that of Iraq. Reports from the time give uneven information, but the general numbers are revealing. The Annual Motion Picture Report obtained by United Artists in 1951 accounts for forty motion picture theaters in Iran with thirty of those in the capital, making for a total Tehran seating capacity of fifteen thousand.[35] It calculates, based on weight totals from customs offices, the equivalent of 650 feature films imported in that year with "four out of five films shown [being] United States productions.[36] The *Asian Film Directory* of 1952 identified eighty cinemas in Iran, half of them in Tehran, with a seating capacity of sixty-five thousand.[37] By the early 1960s, Selznick's agents were reporting back information about more than seventy cinemas in Tehran.[38] This was enough space for a significant cinema culture; it was just less legible to distributors from abroad. To some extent this was by design, and the system was structured around this inaccessibility. Hollywood distributors in this period mostly treated the Middle East, especially Iran, as a territory where the economic risks of actively managing distribution outweighed the potential for profit. They valued the advantages of each stage of distribution being unable to see or capture the transactions of the next. This relay system was a way of getting around obstructions and impediments to a top-down distribution method, and it was maintained through the early 1960s.

Such minimal financial motivation for more than a decade after the war suggests that, before thinking of the everyday work of the releasing offices as capitalist ambition for rapid expansion, it might be beneficial to think of it as maintenance work on their end as well. The economics of *disposal* drive maintenance thinking as much as the economics of reuse. The term *junk prints* in fact describes both of these interlinked economies. Shipping costs, relative to licensing fees, were high enough that even new prints were not returned. And the majority of the prints in circulation in the Middle East at midcentury were still secondhand after the war, even as trade volume increased. Part of the value of sending these prints abroad was the reduction of storage costs, and fire risks in the case of nitrate, at home.[39] Returned prints would reintroduce the very storage and disposal costs, and the maintenance liabilities, that the foreign releasing offices were tasked with writing off. For this reason, requests for return of prints were rare at midcentury, even in places with robust shipping networks. From a studio accounting perspective, the export business in relatively tiny markets amounted to a modestly profitable practice of externalizing liability of film prints that turned from valuable commodities to running taxi meters once their maintenance costs had exceeded their economic viability at home.

A system of disposing of prints and verifying such disposal was, in fact, the precondition of these prints' viable circulation. In cities such as Cairo and Beirut, where there was some transparency of communication, studios sometimes authorized exhibitors to keep films on site beyond the expiration of their (typically two-year) license. The hope was that proximity would draw interest for new license agreements. As one of Selznick's agents described the possession of expired prints at the Roxy in Beirut, "we have been holding the prints in storage primarily for use as a form of bait to a future distributor in a desire to eliminate the cost which this storage would involve.[40] If the prints failed to attract local distributors, they were eventually requested to be shipped to a neighboring country where there was a successful deal for a rerelease. Exhibitors, hesitant to allow this administrative and maintenance cost to be externalized onto them, were known to refuse this burden. They offered to destroy prints instead of shipping them off.[41] Facing such challenges along with a financial motivation to reduce the number of old prints in storage, ordering the film prints' destruction became the predominant method by which studios tried to control the informal economy around secondhand prints in the region. The affidavit of destruction, produced by an official witness, made continued trade in outright-sale prints possible. At this time the term *tabari shodan* (to be axed, literally) came into ordinary usage in Iran to describe the fate of prints for which an affidavit of destruction was requested. The term, and the ways a film could avoid the ax promised by its affidavit, is part of a rich oral history shared by film collectors and archivists.[42]

Focusing on the adaptability of the affidavit of destruction suggests a chronology of the film trade that does not adhere to a developmental timeline. In some markets, it made sense to require box office records. This was not uncommon in Egypt, the Levant, and sometimes in Baghdad. But more often, agreements depended on outright sales and affidavits of destruction. And whenever a point of instability or a challenge to communication interfered with an attempt at profit sharing, a return to outright sales was a possibility.[43] A purely linear history that describes profit-sharing models as the inevitable maturation of relay forms might obscure the ways that these different trade strategies operated simultaneously and cyclically rather than in sequence. It might also conceal the ongoing negotiations around risk and the burdens of maintenance, of which both exporters and exhibitors were well aware, that animate the archive of memos in distributor correspondence. The negotiations that made exhibition of imported prints possible in the Middle East continually adapted as risk burdens shifted alongside fluctuations of the availability of secondhand stock, changes in distribution intermediaries, and rerouted channels of communication.

For Iran, which remained further out on the spectrum of risk, the most visible dealer to emerge from the archives of correspondence in these years was an exhibitor and importer in Iraq.[44] Naim Aizer owned the King Ghazi Cinema in Baghdad, which served as a first-run exhibition site as well as a distribution hub for films and general merchandise. He had worked for the Anglo Iranian Oil Company and had connections with many other import-export institutions, including the British General Supply in Baghdad, Arthur Rank's releasing company for British films, and the import-export business of his brothers Joseph and Edward in New York. It was Edward Aizer who linked Naim in Baghdad with American distributors working for United Artists, Universal, and Selznick Releasing. A meeting described in a 1947 letter from SRO's New York office to the Paris correspondent describes some of the conditions of this relationship. Edward, "who evidently own[ed] the Princess Hosiery Shops, Inc.," detailed Naim's language skills and connections in Iraq and Iran and offered to "assist his brother by making dollar payments in New York on account of film purchases from [Selznick Releasing]."[45] This forged an enduring trade relationship with American studios. Edward absorbed currency risks. His dollar guarantees for Naim's purchases ensured that the Baghdad side of the accounting was none of the studios' concern.

Letterhead sometimes tells a story of the layers of mediation in communication networks. One would likely not be surprised to find a great deal of oil company letterhead in Hollywood distribution archives for Iraq and Iran in the 1950s. Less expected, but no less of an essential conduit for access to these markets, was the letterhead of a small chain of hosiery shops based near Times Square. United Artists was even notified when the Aizers changed the name of the shops from Princess to Lady Oris (figure 11). Many details of these transactions were invisible in the United States, and so was, to a large extent, the life of the physical print.

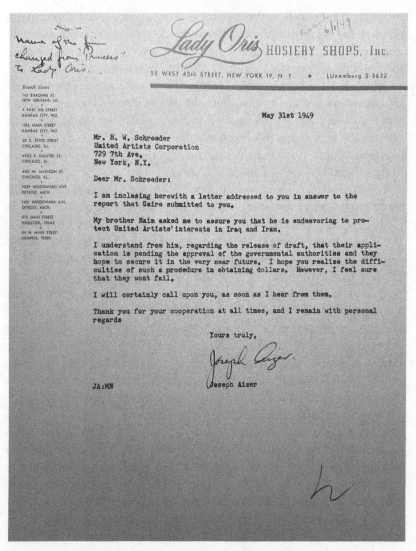

FIGURE 11. United Artists correspondence regarding Iraq and Iran on Lady Oris (formerly Princess) Hosiery Shops letterhead. Wisconsin Center for Film and Theater Research.

By the time prints reached this primary distributor/exhibitor in Baghdad, they had already undergone multiple degrees of separation from the organizations that would be able to reliably capture these screenings as part of the actuarial picture of a film's commercial life. And yet Aizer was one of the main distributors of films into Iran. He visited his contacts there several times a year to sell his used prints. Some of them, according to the records of the studio distribution offices, were listed as officially destroyed after receipt of affidavits of print destruction sent by Aizer and his associates, and yet they survived the ax.

The copyright owners appeared to have been mostly fine with this situation. The system would occasionally run into trouble when, say, a studio made a push to distribute its back catalog in the region. A reissued license for a territory increased the visibility of the informal market. The fact that many of these prints had not actually been destroyed then became a source of complaint by owners of regional rights. Releasing offices were obliged to show a good faith effort to account for informal circulation. What is revealing about the archival record in even these cases is the degree to which the energy seems directed not at getting to the bottom of piracy but at minimizing it or negotiating around it. Maintenance thinking often won out over hard-line defense of ownership. Take Selznick's 1952 campaign to redistribute the company's catalog around the world. The office began with high aspirations, which took close to a year to solidify into an agreement. They first tried to sell at unrealistic prices to each territory individually. The tone of this early correspondence bore a cavalier orientalism: "We have 12 pictures free for Irak [sic] and Iran and I have sent a note to the Intersales Commercial Corporation giving them the titles and suggesting an average royalty of $2000 per film. May Allah smile upon us!"[46] Several months later, with no takers, they wound up licensing the films to a distributor in Cairo named George Mansour. These were new prints, to be struck in Fort Lee, New Jersey. Mansour wanted to be responsible only for Egypt, but SRO pressured him to take on the rights and risk for the Middle East. Mansour then spent the coming years complaining to SRO about unauthorized versions of these prints on screens, particularly in Iraq and Iran. Selznick's team made inquiries and were easily satisfied when they discovered documents of destruction.

Information to the contrary would not have been hard to find. These same films, such as *Duel in the Sun*, listed as officially destroyed, were not clandestine screenings; they were playing at commercial cinemas in Tehran, with reviews and ads in the newspapers. A few years after this dispute, a poster for *Duel* made the color back cover of *Setare-ye Cinema*, in which the film was described as a "work produced by the famous David O Selznick."[47] A few years after that, Hollywood agents in Iran were still quietly responding to rumors that this print remained in circulation.[48] Hitchcock's films were doing well in Iran, and so Mansour was particularly upset about unlicensed copies of *Spellbound*. He insisted that the film was still showing in Iraq and Iran despite Aizer's assurance in a telegram that the print no longer existed. "Spellbound destroyed 1945 stop according instructions United Artists stop affidavit American Embassy our possession stop King Ghazi."[49] Selznick's further investigation involved interviews with Iranian exhibitors, who told him that the rumor was started by a confusion over an Iranian film with a similar title, *Broken Spell*.[50]

Both explanations, it turns out, misrepresented the facts. Aizer knew the film was not destroyed in 1945 because he himself had prepared a detailed box office report of the film's run in Baghdad.[51] He kept record of every seat sold, and a researcher in the UA archives can still learn whether and how much someone paid for a box seat to see *Spellbound* on a Tuesday evening in 1949. The *Broken Spell* mentioned by Aizer's and Mansour's contacts in Iran may have been referring to *Afsungar* (*The Enchantress*, Koushan, 1952), which appears to borrow from *Spellbound*'s plot and style, or to the preproduction of a film with a closer title (*Spellbound* was usually billed as *Telesm-Shodeh* in Iran) to the *Broken Spell* named in the letter, Siamak Yasami's *Telesm-e Shekasteh* (*Broken Talisman*, 1958). The latter film would have only slightly overlapped with the years of Mansour's continual complaints about the infringement and could not have caused the original complaint. While Aizer's deflection and the subsequent productions in Iran may not have been completely apparent to SRO at the time, the correspondence reflects a predilection on the part of Selznick management to push this unlikely story of a misunderstanding as reality. These investigations were taken far enough, at least, to resist Mansour's request for an extension of his license as compensation for its infringement: "At the present moment I do not think there is reason to grant George Mansour an extension of his rights. When reissues are brought for Middle East countries like the [*sic*] Lebanon, Syria, Iraq, and Iran it is with the knowledge of existing laws and bad practices and the risks inherent in such purchase under such conditions."[52]

The archival record here, when paired with the exhibition record in Iran, indicates a kind of strange cooperation. In showing unlicensed prints of *Spellbound*, Selznick and the exhibitors were, in a way, working together. The same producer who was publicly describing these exhibitors using piratical rhetoric was, in interoffice memos, siding with these same exhibitors *against* the regional distributor to justify passing off risk to Mansour. Ironies like these mark some of the differences between fluid circulation and relay.[53]

Mansour's challenge to unlicensed exhibition in Iran shone a harsh, but temporary, light on a mutually beneficial (to everyone except Mansour) system. As long as calls to investigate remained minor and infrequent, this odd collaboration could continue to enable the relay of films. It is copyright's tactical rather than systematic enforcement that allows it to function in a porous and adaptable manner. But the risks of this system were also vulnerable to exploitation by agencies able to shine a light more powerful than Mansour's. An official illumination of an informal screening of a film could be used to enact censorship in accordance with geopolitical maneuvers. The US Department of State was not above using its own bully pulpit to reveal small-scale copyright violations to its political advantage. In one case, the embassy successfully nudged the Iranian government to ban the Soviet-produced *Padeniye Berlina* (*Fall of Berlin*, Chiaureli, 1949) from Tehran theaters. It failed, however, to also silence the Hollywood production that replaced it, *North Star* (Milestone, 1943). Milestone had been blacklisted in 1949, and the embassy deemed his war film too sympathetic to Soviet interests to be tolerated in this political moment: "The Embassy is interested in preventing a repetition of the showing of this film."[54] It seems that the US Cold War policies, which were strongly felt in the nonfiction production initiatives in Iran, were at work in the commercial cinema as well. Only, control in this arena could not be as direct as with sponsored nonfiction. To enact their censorship beyond their legal control and diplomatic influence, the embassy evoked precisely the porous affidavit of destruction system.

> Feature films are normally licensed by exhibitors in Iran for a period of three years. As NORTH STAR is quite an old film, in all probability the lease has expired. It is a common practice for exhibitors in Iran to run films when legally they do not have the right to do so. . . . The Embassy would like to suggest, however, that the Department approach the U.S. distributor to request that prints of this film be withdrawn from circulation. . . . The distributors could assist the Embassy's information program by making every effort to see that such films are not shown in critical areas such as this.[55]

The embassy had no genuine intention of reforming copyright violations at this time. The letter makes clear that it was only films deemed sympathetic to Soviet interests that should have been subject to copyright scrutiny. Here Goldwyn and United Artists are being enlisted, by US government officials, to selectively enforce their copyright. The embassy appealed to their patriotism in an effort to get these US distributors to assist in making commercial film offerings in Iran favorable

to the American "information program." While some informal agreements, such as the one that brushed aside Mansour's complaint, helped
to keep old prints moving through the Middle East with minimal risk
to American studios, others called upon these same studios to obstruct
that movement in the interest of Cold War containment. The relay system encouraged odd collaborations, indeed.

OBSOLESCENCE: DUBBING TECHNOLOGIES
AND LEVERAGE

The Iranian case in the 1950s was not categorically different than
others around the world, but there were many degrees of separation.
At many points someone along the chain of distribution either chose
to ignore or had to accept a lack of information about the full afterlife
of a film print. With each point of invisibility, the effects become more
pronounced. They are more pronounced, still, because Persian is separate from the languages not only of production centers but also of the
regional distributors. This combination of factors in the media environment enabled creative reuse on an industrial scale. As the negotiations
between studios and exhibitors such as Aizer and Mansour illustrate,
the intermediaries in this system are numerous. They are just as important to the life of the objects as any other stage. There occurred, at each
stage, a negotiation around risk and an assessment of a film as an object
that can generate value but also generate costs, if its maintenance and
disposal are not properly managed. While studios favored a system of
outright sales, affidavits of destruction, and staying out of intraregional
licensing disputes as a way to reduce liabilities (in their storage vaults
and on their accounting books), they also handed over a large degree of
control over the objects that they considered their intellectual property.
Film distributors, exhibitors, and engineers could take advantage of
these freedoms by unlocking value from prints that the releasing offices
considered depleted.

The key to the value of these circulating prints in Iran lay in their
sound stripes. Dialogue from films was often summarized and tran-
scribed into Persian, with the text distributed in print form or projected
in superimposition or along the margins of the screen. Exhibitors also
spliced in intertitles, a practice carried over from the silent era into the
1950s and '60s. Executives at Fox and Selznick marveled over Iran's use
of "insert titles instead of subtitles adding as much as forty-five minutes
to the film's running time."[56] None of these systems were able to engage

FIGURE 12. Dubbing artists at Azhir Film. Private collection.

large audiences the way a dubbed print could. Dubbing did not require literacy as a precondition for understanding, and, operating at a remove from the companies that delivered the prints, it enabled significant cultural translation of situations and characters. Moreover, once Persian dubbing operations in studios in Italy, Egypt, and Turkey proved successful and such work began to be consolidated in Iran, technical and performance laborers could move between studios and develop the practice by building on the innovations of other colleagues at work in the same city. The period of exhibitor control over commercial prints was long over in the United States and Europe, where it had moved from a dominant practice in early cinema to a practice rarely seen outside of experimental and nontheatrical screening contexts. In midcentury Iran, the relative freedom to modify prints meant that exhibitors could develop postwar audio technologies and link the publicity around global Hollywood stars with configurations of celebrity around local actors and radio voices (figure 12). I focus on technological and infrastructural aspects of dubbing here, as studying performance history of dubbers and their translation process would require another book.

One of the most striking technological innovations around dubbing, one that was able to leverage the relay system to the advantage of the film industry in Iran, was the systematic use of synchronous magnetic sound applied to the film print. Optical sound came standard on projectors and was the most efficient process for standardization of printing and exhibition, but the prints of foreign films in Iran had already been freed from such standardizations. Magnetic systems were capable of producing higher quality sound. Studios in the United States did market them as special hi-fi alternatives to optical sound, but their cost as an add-on technology kept them from gaining much traction outside of small-gauge and some widescreen applications.[57] In Iran, it was precisely this modular quality that made magnetic sound thrive alongside optical systems. A mag-coat track may be a costly extra step for prints made from scratch, but in an environment populated with secondhand prints, it could simply be added to an existing positive print without requiring expensive and image-degrading duplication. Remember that the prints they were working with were usually graded B and C when they left American warehouses on their way to only their first stop in the Middle East, which was not usually Iran. Creating internegatives from scratched and spliced exhibition prints had limited practical benefit. Sound engineers in Iran developed their craft by working within these parameters. They recorded the optical track as raw material for the dub, then applied a new magnetic emulsion onto which the rebuilt soundtrack was then rerecorded. Using this method did not require negatives or separate music and effects tracks, and some parts of the original soundtrack could be left alone entirely. This was particularly the case for films with prominent scores and intermittent dialogue, as can be heard in the Persian dub of *Psycho*. The score and effects are left untouched until the moment right before dialogue, which is briefly punched in. These brief inserts are sometimes marked by evidence of their cut-and-paste methods, such as repetitions in the score and momentary increases in distortion. The long stretches of the film without dialogue, carried by slowly unfolding action and Bernard Herrmann's score, were able to remain intact. The audio distorts briefly for each line and then returns to clarity. The designers of these soundtracks patched together original and new with some attempt to maintain the sound's construction of space and perspective.

Iranian sound engineers began experimenting in the late 1940s with a liquid magnetic emulsion and then standardized their practices with laminated mag tape. Early experimentation with the emulsion process, conducted by Jalal Maghazei for a dub of *Song of Scheherazade* (Reisch, 1947), reused magnetic tape stock obtained from Germany: "When submerged in a solvent, the emulsion on the tape dissolved and yielded a thick brown liquid. Maghazei used a device of his own making to cover the optical sound track of the print with this liquid. He recorded the soundtrack, which included separately recorded dialogue and sound effects mixed with the film's music, on this stripe."[58] The print of *Scheherazade* was reported to have problems. While its sound quality was better than that of previous attempts, the emulsion was unstable and began to fragment and peel off as it ran through projectors.[59] The long-term advantages of this method, however, were clear. Constructing the dubbed exhibition print in-house reduced the cost and delay of shipping out to a lab in Italy, and it allowed a level of creative control over the repurposing of film prints. With this ability to control the process came the innovation required to grow these experiments into a sustainable practice. Maghazei soon brought his devices and expertise to Golden Age (*Asr-e Talayi*) studio and continued to develop the craft of dubbing processes for imported and local productions.

The Minnesota Mining and Manufacturing Company (3M) had developed a desirable system for affixing magnetic tape to celluloid in the early 1950s, and media organizations in Iran were eager to import this equipment. Radio Jahan imported magnetic sound production equipment and was in communication with early dubbing engineers.[60] The import records of vital laminating machines used in the application of magnetic sound are rarely archived, but I have located one record of acquisition from 3M in the archives of the USIA nonfiction film initiative in Iran.[61] This laminating machine, which cost the significant sum of $2,700 for a ten-year lease, was adaptable for work in multiple gauges. It could adhere mag stripes at 100 mils (2.7 mm) for high-quality 35 mm films down to 30 mils for 8 mm or double-track 16 mm.[62] Its sonic advantages were detailed in an issue of 3M's *Sound Talk* bulletin by the (impossibly named) magnetic audio engineer R. F. Dubbe. He compares the new laminating process to the uneven surface and lower sound quality of rival processes, those attempted by Maghazei, of applying liquid magnetic emulsion to the film. In the mid-1950s, Dubbe lists only seven labs in North America capable of laminating mag track onto film.[63] That Tehran was equipped with more than one lab for this work underscores its importance there. It also indicates another example of asynchronous circulation of technologies in which one market jumps ahead in the use of a particular process when it proves adaptable to specific conditions.[64]

Multiple currents of media circulation were brought together by engineers in Iran into a regular industrial process. Positive exhibition prints mark one current. They were manufactured and struck in the United States and sent to Iran through the circuitous channels of commercial film licensing and distribution. An audio laminating device on long-term lease from 3M was incorporated through another initiative, the USIA program in Iran. This device was intended for use in the production of 16 mm educational films, but its adaptability benefitted the creative maintenance of other media objects. The laminator's ability to add high-quality sound to an existing print meant that it was suited to an industry reliant on dubbing into a language that set it apart from distribution hubs in the region. The cinemas needed Persian dubs, but importers did not have regular access to the dubbing kits and optical tracks used in more capital-intensive dubbing operations elsewhere in the world. Nor did they necessarily want such access, since the supplementary material would raise the cost of exhibition beyond the reach of many moviegoers, to the detriment of the thriving cinema culture in Tehran. Instead, a technology exported for nontheatrical production merged with a used-print distribution network and an infrastructure of sound studios, with their engineers and dub performers, to create an applied-sound format that became a mainstay of commercial exhibition in Tehran. Dubbe likely was not aware of his device's dubbing duties in Iran, but its significance should not be doubted.

Examples of dubbed films from this period are abundant in digital circulation. They provide a wealth of information about techniques, translation strategies, and performance styles. To address media archaeological questions about this process, specifically pertaining to the ways the film industry integrated standards of film trade with the technology of magnetic dub tracks, one needs to examine the surviving prints from this period. They provide their own indications about where they have been and when. The archivists at the Filmkhaneh (National Film Archive of Iran) allowed me to inspect a collection of mag-dubbed Hollywood films in their collection for edge information and to listen to them on a Steenbeck with an add-on magnetic sound head. Three prominent examples from this collection from the late 1950s, *Al Capone* (Wilson, 1959), *The Long, Hot Summer* (Ritt, 1958), and *North by Northwest* (Hitchcock, 1959), give a sense of the intermediaries and the range of processes involved. The magnetic stripes indicate that all three were actual exhibition prints used in 1960s Iran, not copies made later. The prints of both *Capone* and *Summer* bear edge markings of Kodak negative stock and Agfa positive stock (figures 13a, 13b). This indicates that the positive exhibition prints were created in Europe for those markets. The magnetic track for *Capone* was applied in Iran, but the stereo magnetic track on the Cinemascope print of *Summer* appears to be original to the imported print. In the second case, sound engineers were able

FIGURES 13A, 13B. *Al Capone* (Richard Wilson, 1959) and *The Long, Hot Summer* (Martin Ritt, 1958). Magnetic soundtracks over prints on Agfa stock. National Film Archive of Iran.

to extract, remix, and rerecord the critically acclaimed soundtrack for that film using only the technology embedded in the print itself. Film-khaneh's print of *North by Northwest* bears markings that suggest a different route (figure 14). The original optical track, rendered unusable by its magnetic stripe, is still partly visible underneath. The new track, tape laminated at the 100 mil standard, still has excellent sound quality today even as the images on the celluloid have faded to magenta. The edge codes on the print reveal that the film stock was manufactured in 1959, the year of the film's initial release. A black dot between the first and second letter in "SAFETY," printed along the edge, indicates that the film stock was manufactured in Rochester and not in Europe. So this print was an original, English-language print, made in the United States for domestic markets, that made its way to Iran after its first run. It was prepared for exhibition without being duplicated in Europe or

FIGURE 14. *North by Northwest*
(Alfred Hitchcock, 1959). Magnetic
soundtrack over a print on Rochester-
manufactured positive stock. National
Film Archive of Iran.

Iran while reviews and translations of criticism were published in newspapers and journals. In each of these examples, an original print was
routed through different intermediaries and became part of a reusable
collection of material. The soundtrack tells the story of the technologies applied to the print in this market, or, in the less common case of
a preexisting print with magnetic sound, a reuse of existing technology
within a dubbing infrastructure that was well equipped to turn that
uncommonly formatted print into a valuable new object.

The dub system was so carefully constructed by the time these prints
were repurposed that it had finally drawn the attention of foreign studio heads. The exchange that followed illustrates exactly why the system of copyright is designed to leak at the sides. With the success of
such technological and business innovations, an attempt at corporate
enclosure was not far behind. In the early 1960s, Hollywood companies' interest in the region shifted. Brunger at SRO took interest in the

number of bodies in seats in Persian-speaking cinemas and wrote to Selznick with the news that "this is a territory which has possibilities of much greater scope than in the past and perhaps it might be considered as having priority over Syria, Lebanon and Jordan, or Greece."[65] He attributed this to his own detective work around "something fishy" in current dealings with Iran, which revealed that "all films were now being shown in a 'dubbed version'—I put this in quotes because they . . . do not seemingly call for music and effects tracks but merely dub the dialogue and perhaps put in their own music and effects—and this has, of course, enabled them to show films to a vastly wider audience than was hitherto possible."[66] Brunger's sources told him that a quality color print like *Duel in the Sun*, once dubbed, could gross $20,000 in Tehran. These were prints that were being offered at under $2,000 at the time. Selznick and Brunger then learned of the quality of Iran's sound engineering achievements through the Iran sales representative George Chasanas, a relative of Louis B. Mayer who had run MGM's operations in Cairo since 1948 and had contacts throughout the Middle East.[67] Interested in this process as a form of innovation on cost and access, Selznick strategized an enclosure of the creative labor of these maintenance thinkers. He suggested establishing Tehran as a dubbing center for the entire Middle East: "I am fascinated by your information about the dubbing development in Iran. . . . I would also think that dubbed versions for Iran would enormously increase our values for all the Arab countries. . . . With all the labor costs in Iran getting about as much for a month's work what a German would get in an hour, I should think the dubbing costs extremely small, and could multiply our grossing potential many times over."[68] This was Selznick's response to studio representatives tasked with assessing violations of licensing in Tehran. They had expressed surprise at the dubbing studios' ubiquity and talent in working with available prints and magnetic sound systems, and rather than try to stop it, Selznick suggested growing the operation. The archive of correspondence around this initiative provides a historical example of the everyday process of leakage and enclosures of intellectual property in modernity. Selznick's plan, activated through communications networks of memos and telegrams, illustrates what Fredriksson and Arvanitakis describe as a "corporation['s] attempt to enclose and commodify innovations created by the very same outlaws it rails against."[69] It took nearly a year of debates with his employees and a consultation with UCLA Arabic professor Charles Wendell for Selznick to finally concede that Persian is a completely different language from, not a dialect of, Arabic before his plans to enclose Iranian dubbing processes were finally scrapped.[70] Unrealistic as it was, it is remarkable that Persian dub processes had become a persistent thread of conversation in the home office memos of Selznick's company for almost a year, only after being invisible for years of formative activity.

The increase in direct communication and trade with exhibitors in Iran in early 1960 provides one way to delimit the periodization for this chapter. In just a few years, distribution networks shifted significantly. Naim Aizer permanently relocated to New York in 1962 to be closer to the export side of his business as he continued to serve as an agent for films shipped to Iraq and Iran. MGM established stronger connections in Iran in the 1960s. Warner Bros. began communicating directly with the Cinema Rex, Lalezar, in Tehran, selling company prints and publicity material stored in Rome and Cairo.[71] More cinemas in Iran displayed neon Hollywood studio logos in their windows as agents from these studios spent more time there. Television broadcasts of these films also became a regular concern, which begat a new urgency in company communications to locate affidavits of destruction whenever the record was uncertain. These transitions opened up new possibilities as they closed off others. They were considered markers of progress by many at each end of the chain of distribution, but in terms of the innovation made possible by delays, miscommunications, and circuitous networks of circulation, this greater transparency also increased opportunities for enclosure.

New designs on the territory were not without their own continued obstructions, and examples of these sometimes took on dimensions that seem comic in retrospect. It is difficult, for example, to write of Warner Bros.' successful entry into the market when reading letterhead full of so many miscommunications. For example, the Cinema Rex company letterhead was imprinted with "Sherket Sahami Cinema Rex" in Persian and Roman script. The fact that Warner Bros. sometimes addressed its letters to "Mr. Sherket Sahami" (Mr. Joint Stock Company) illustrates the persistent opacity in their dealings with cinemas in Tehran.[72] Small failures in communication like these are legion in the archives of communication between film companies. A history that considers film company business letters and memos as media, not just as sources of information pertaining to the medium of cinema, will find valuable material in this texture of miscommunication even during periods of greater transparency.[73] Untidy paperwork is sometimes necessary to get the job done, and when it is necessary, its little malfunctions shape what exactly can be done and how.

Chasanas's time in Iran marked a period of greater transparency but was also an example of a difficult deal that left exhibitors in Iran at an advantage. Chasanas listed the challenges to selling reissued prints in a market where extant copies continued to reappear. He relayed to the home office a series of stalled negotiations with a long list of exhibitors in Iran, including the owners of Cinema Niagara and Cinema Plaza in Tehran. His recommendation was to take the slim offer from Moustafa Akhavan, who owned the Moulin Rouge cinema complex and "showed very little interest in the whole deal."[74] Brunger, who made no effort to hide his eagerness to fire Chasanas on suspicion of "collusion" with Iranian exhibitors, tried and failed to push Selznick away from any such deal. Selznick's answer indicated that, while ambitious dubbing projects intrigued him, he still preferred to offload risk rather than actively police profits from one-time sales. "Possibly we must accept [this] bad beating [from the] present Iranian deal and charge [the financial loss] to experience and growing knowledge values[—]especially but not limited to Hitchcock's far transcending previous computations."[75] What was for Brunger a moral issue was for Selznick a "charge to experience." It was a financial write-off on the way to greater transparency. Such charges, however, reduced as they might be in the coming decade, provided resources that had sustained film production in Iran through its industrializing years.

It is difficult to overstate the importance of this creative leveraging of obsolescence for the formation of the industry in Iran. Dubbing practices were not an impediment to the Iranian film industry at midcentury, as was feared in places like Egypt with its dub quotas; rather, they were an essential part of the formation of the industry.[76] Magnetic sound fits with secondhand prints both technologically and financially. Producers selling to these uncertain media environments were willing to give up control and visibility in order to pass the liabilities of objects they understood to be nearing obsolescence onto regional distributors. The fact that they could not really see that these films were being dubbed on this scale meant that they could not extract the box office capital from these value-added versions by profit sharing or by charging triple the rate for dubbing rights in an outright sale. Local exhibitors were thus able to drive hard bargains and keep capital at home. Since the dubbing studios were often integrated with exhibition spaces, this meant that much of the investment was directed there, and dubbing thrived in the 1960s. Moreover, dubbing formed an economic hedge for local production risks. If a local production lost money, a studio could return its attention to low-overhead dubbing projects that would steer them back into the black for the short term.[77] Technicians could move freely from one type of project to another, as could voice actors. Many of the foundational film production studios grew out of dubbing studios, and most of the studios took on at least some of the work of dubbing imported prints.

The networked labors of Badi, Vaziri, Aizer, Akhavan, and the Selznick team, maintenance thinkers all, guide a history of cinema in Iran through spheres whose interconnections are not always self-evident: the cultural reception of cinema at its point of exhibition, the business of traffic in films and audiovisual technologies, and the techniques of using and remaking films. Describing the negotiations among distributors within the same frame as the creative labor of those who work in the craft professions of making films might raise questions. The straightforward, financial reasoning displayed in the communication between Chasanas and Akhavan might not immediately present itself as of a piece with the labor of dubbing engineers and artists, let alone above-the-line creative talent working in film in midcentury Iran. This work would fall outside of Lessig's neoliberal definitions of creativity, but as anti-imperial scholars of copyright argue, there is an ethics to the pursuit of what lies outside of those definitions. Shifting historiographical focus to maintenance thinking, to its traces in the artifacts of cinema history, means shifting emphasis away from the film as a singular production or a pristine object whose changes are only understood as forms of degradation. The emphasis, instead, can turn to the film as the site of continual processes, leakages that created value where it did not previously exist. The innovations intellectual property is supposed to protect in modernity are present not only on the master negative at the Technicolor plant in Los Angeles. The applied magnetic stripes bear traces of creative labor that came later in the life of the objects, as do the archival records of engineering processes and distribution infrastructures that maintained and reanimated prints deemed obsolete junk.

An expanded historiography of creative media practice takes rather literally some of the models that have been widely used to interpret instances of cross-border film cultures. The terms *haggling* and *cultural translation* have proven useful as metaphors that account for the reception of these imports against the grain by local audiences in the Middle East.[78] Here, I have been exploring the material dimensions of these terms in order to examine how they can affect methodology. Actual haggling often provides a strong foundation for cultural haggling, and this is especially the case in an industry with a discrete infrastructure for turning secondhand prints into valuable commodities. A common emotional tone in the memos of Hollywood distributors dealing with Iranian exhibitors was lament. They were rarely in a position to challenge the hard bargains driven by owners of Cinema Niagara and Cinema Moulin Rouge in Iran. Before critics and audiences in Iran began their own work of haggling with the icons of 1950s Hollywood, their experience had been shaped by months, and sometimes years, of literal haggling over which films could be shown, in which formats, and to which degree of financial accessibility.

Likewise, in order to understand the kinds of cultural translations at play, translation-studies scholars would remind cinema historians that we must take seriously the actual translations that had a role in shaping the experience of cinema for most of the world.[79] This awareness positions histories of dubbing as central to the understanding of global cinema, and it foregrounds the kinds of aesthetic and ethical questions Mark Nornes has posed in playful and personal terms as "reconsidering my gut-level hatred of dubbing" in favor of an "attempt to come to love what I call the ventriloquist's art."[80] This chapter takes the histories of such gut reactions (as old as dubbing itself) to heart. But instead of focusing on the dubbed dialogue itself, I position media archaeology, specifically the machinery of film translation, as a complement to work in translation studies. That is, if one can agree that the study of cultural translation of cinema in (not only) Iran should include practices of translating dialogue, then a history of those practices should also include technologies and processes designed specifically for the purpose of translation of secondhand positive prints. This material aspect of the dub process resonates with Nornes's epithet, if one takes an insight from sound studies, that all film sound can be considered a form of ventriloquism.[81] The path by which one might learn to love the dub, as a central feature of global cinema, does wind through the careful consideration of translators' choices. It also runs, I argue here, through an archaeology of the sound stripe—one that loves the ferrous sludge painted over an optical track as much as it loves the opposing voices covered and carried by this sludge.

Consider, as a final image, another exhibit at the Museum of Cinema in Tehran. Toward the end of the path through the museum, a path that began with a wall of obsolete technology, visitors encounter two rooms devoted to the technology and performance of dubbing. The rooms display sound engineers operating midcentury audio technology. The prestige histories told by cinema museums converge with the history of this creative reengineering of secondhand positive prints. Yes, there were traditions of Iranian critics who railed against dubbing as a kind of violence to the original print. And these arguments did follow along lines that are familiar in other scenes of encounter with dubbed film. They turned on notions of class, accessibility, and market saturation just as they did elsewhere. But what also stands out in Iran is how Persian dubs carried with them alternative discourses to this one.[82] They were also markers of prestige, even before blockbuster multitrack feats of dubbing in the mid-1960s such as *The Sound of Music*, also known as *Tears and Smiles* (*Ashk-ha va Labkhand-ha*), in which each of the film's songs was rewritten and rerecorded. Dubbers shared the culture of film celebrity, and the engineers that made their work possible have a prominent position in histories, even public-facing histories and those created by fans themselves. To this day an avid cinephile culture exists around dubbed films. And dubbing figures prominently in histories (even official ones) of prestige cinema in Iran. Moreover, these instances of admiration were not, as in the case of dubs in many other places, only evident at moments when the dub was more or less invisible—when it did not call attention to itself. There are respected dubbing artists and dub translators around the world for whom the measure of quality of their work often lies in the ability to deflect attention away from the mediation that the museum places on a pedestal. The Museum of Cinema and a half century of cinephile culture (however worried it may have been) in Iran remind us of counterintuitive formations of prestige, and that these formations should be integrated lest the invisibilities of midcentury circulation reinscribe themselves as a stagnant disciplinary divide that prevents cross-archival work on this period.

CHAPTER 3

Collage Sound
as Industrial Practice

A few assumptions have guided this study so far. Writing a cultural history of relayed cinema means being attentive to unseen forms of labor that refashioned films, to expectations about hierarchies of creative control, and to the shifting relationships between what can be captured by an industry and what remains uncontainable in the afterlife of media objects. These points remain in the foreground even as the book shifts its focus to feature films that were produced in studios in Iran. A cinema that industrialized after the Second World War but did not consistently record sound on location or compose its own scores until the late 1960s and beyond cannot help but offer an education in the possibilities of the uncontainable elements of global cinema. With this in mind, it seems appropriate to begin a discussion of production with the industry's primary found material—its archive of film music—and the creative labor that repurposed it.

In the films made before the emergence of regular composed scores, almost all of the nondiegetic music, and some of the diegetic music, was assembled from a working archive of imported commercial recordings collected by each studio or its sound editors. These music archives supplied the only scoring material for hundreds of films. For most of the 1950s, film studios in Iran released between ten and twenty features per year. The number fluctuated but steadily increased to around thirty releases per year by the early 1960s.[1] The first composed film score, for *Shores of Anticipation* (*Sahel-e Entezar*, Yasami, 1963), premiered a decade after the industry achieved sustainable commercial production. Film scores did not really become a familiar occurrence until the late 1960s with the rise of respected composers such as Esfandiar Monfaredzadeh. Given the enduring demand, the task of selecting the music for each scene grew into a specialized profession with its own creative constraints.

With little reason to follow industrial norms of the source music, sound editors in postwar Iran could make very different kinds of choices from those of their compilation-score peers elsewhere. We hear the theremin in romantic comedies or cowboy music in urban thrillers. And this flexibility is evident at differing scales. It occurs across the large archive of films, but one also encounters it within the work of one studio, and even within an individual film. A single film would regularly include music from multiple genres and countries, and from multiple films. Abrupt shifts would occur, even within a single scene. I take this aesthetic practice seriously as a form of collage that, due to its configurations of authorship and labor performed by below-the-line professionals, has been hiding in plain sight.

Other industries used temporary reference tracks to help with cutting while the films' scores were being composed, and the labor of music editors in Iran shares some attributes with that work. They both assembled found material in a way that influenced the film's pacing and point of view. In Iran, however, these were final scores. They would ultimately face a public as Iranian film scores, and they did so with cues that had their own public life on the radio, on sidewalks in front of gramophone shops, or in neighboring cinemas with imported new releases. Unlike temp tracks they were made to endure, and they made public reuse of enduring scores. Their citations were not from just any old films. They regularly came from films and records that had done, or were doing, particularly well in Iran. Their familiarity intersected with the circulation histories of films and with the LPs that were being duplicated and pressed in Iran for regional distribution.

A study of collage sound in Iran can thus analyze the patterns of a craft without dropping the thread of media's afterlife. A thorough archival definition of a film encompasses potentially every copy of that film, every physical location in which it was exhibited, and the provenance that linked each of those objects to each of those places.[2] The same is true for its detached score. The records of, say, a Miklos Rózsa score for a Selznick film present one aspect in the Selznick and Rózsa archives in Austin and Syracuse. The afterlife of that score in archives around the world, moving from vinyl to the sound stripes of films made in Iran, discussed in critical reviews, amortized by distributors, and accounted for in exhibition records, reveal another aspect and other functions of that same material. By using audio recognition software for the available films from this period and comparing their samples with circulation records, I have been able to target the ways that sound collections formed, the timing of the release of films that make use of these collections, and the citational structures of the scores. Since film music is particularly well suited to the study of collection, timing, and referential qualities of film objects in circulation, compilation scoring presents a valuable chapter in a study of the relay of cinema in the region. An industry with few copyright restrictions took advantage of the flexible resource of found sound. As an additional component, one incorporated along with dubbed voices in the final stages of postproduction or remixed for a second release, this resource proved particularly nimble and adaptable. It lent itself to a sustained form of collage in a generation of industrial practice.[3] This dimension of the films of a small industry complicates the familiar tension between national narratives of invention and worries about influence from abroad.[4]

FOUNDING AND THE FOUND

Take *Afsungar* (*The Enchantress*, 1953) by the foundational director Esmail Koushan. The film was an ambitious commercial production in an emergent industry. It helped to cement careers of performers who were on their way to setting standards for stardom in Iranian cinema: the songstress Delkash and the actor Nasser Malek Motie'i. The plot combines a drama of seduction and murder with a framing device of a protagonist with amnesia. Nasser (Malek Motie'i), an engineer, is the favorite employee of an industrialist and marries his café-singer daughter, Forough (Delkash). Forough's stepmother, Shokat (Zhaleh Olov), attempts to seduce Nasser and poisons her husband. These actions set into motion a series of further deceptions, deaths, and wrongful imprisonment that cause Nasser's amnesia. This film is one of the earliest films by the pioneering filmmakers at Pars Film that is currently accessible for close listening.

Given the context of the film's production, it would not be wrong to approach *The Enchantress* either as part of a foundational national film history or as a transnational remake. Koushan's name and Pars Film stand out in origin stories of Iranian cinema. Working at a Turkish film studio in the 1940s, Koushan created early dubbed films in Persian. He returned to Iran in 1946 to establish Mitra Film Company and Pars Film and then produced the first postwar commercial feature in Iran, *Tufan-e Zendegi* (*The Storm of Life*, 1948). Pars grew quickly and, upon rebuilding after a fire in 1952, became a formidable film studio—the largest in Iran. Koushan was also one of the pioneers of magnetic sound and took part in the gluing (the literal collage) of mag tracks to unduplicated imported exhibition prints. Like many studio founders, he remained involved in dubbing activities even as his film productions increased. His work in dubbing, production, and infrastructure expansion place him rightfully in a history of firsts.

On the other hand, Siamak Yasami, who worked on *The Enchantress* and was slated to receive credit until a creative disagreement prompted Koushan to remove his name from the film, has said that he adapted some of the script from an Italian film with the Persian title *Khashm* (*Anger*). This was most likely *Furia* (1947), although much of the film diverges from the plot of Allesandrini's film and its 1880 source novella, *La Lupa.*[5] *The Enchantress*'s clinical take on the common melodramatic trope of lost memory bears strong resemblances to *Spellbound*. Hitchcock's film was still fresh in the minds of moviegoers and journalists in Iran, and Koushan's film is, after all, a story with a kind of spellcasting in its title, about a main character who has lost his memory as a result of trauma, and a drama that hinges on his re-exposure to that trauma so that his memory may return and the wrongs of the film may be righted. The film rewards both approaches, the national industrial narrative and the analysis of cross-cultural stylistic influence. I pursue a complementary path, one that does not center on the borrowing of plot elements from *Furia* or *Spellbound*. Nor does it seek to either reaffirm or challenge *The Enchantress* in relation to genealogies that have addressed Koushan as the father of the film industry in Iran. The media artifacts embedded within the film, on its sound stripe, reveal its role in networks of circulation that questions of adaptation, remakes, and cinematic paternity often do not address.

The music in *The Enchantress* is an index of its ambitions. It was noticed in the film press, and it set a form that would continue and develop for years in Iranian cinema.[6] Close attention to the sound of this film reveals music from a variety of sources. The diegetic music is Iranian. It includes nine songs performed by Delkash in cafés and private reception rooms. The nondiegetic music relays found recordings. The three dozen musical fragments used in the film come from only a handful of recordings. Two classical recordings, Berlioz's *Symphonie*

Fantastique (conducted by Pierre Monteux) and Kodály's *Dances of Galanta* (conducted by Victor de Sabata), provide escalating tension leading up to a murder and a wrongful imprisonment. A recording of Brahms's third symphony, released along with the film noir *Undercurrent* (Minnelli, 1946), recurs throughout the film.

The most frequently sampled film scores, the cues that do much of the work in the film or accompany its spectacle, come from none other than *Spellbound* and *Duel in the Sun*. Knowing something of Selznick's plans for their reissue in the Middle East, George Mansour's complaints in Cairo about the ineffectiveness of his regional license, and the promotional efforts surrounding these films in magazines in Iran, it should seem serendipitous but not particularly surprising to find actual recorded fragments from these films put to work in this early industrial talkie. The haggling over distribution offers one glimpse into the afterlife of these films in Iran. The archive of their scores tells another part of the story, one interlaced with the efforts to preserve the copyright for, circulate, and promote the film.

Fragments of music from *Spellbound* and *Duel* do significant work in the film. They announce the arrival of specific characters. They code space as public or private, indoor or outdoor. They highlight narrative progression, accentuate action scenes, and command attention during reversals in the melodrama. *Spellbound* is used extensively to accompany Nasser's scenes in the mental hospital, which marks the most direct connection with the score's original associations with traumatic memory loss. *Duel* often serves as a leitmotif for the main male characters in the film, particularly in outdoor scenes. All of these samples are patched together with evidently little concern for concealing the discontinuities created by abrupt cuts from one cue to another. Even when a single musical theme is used throughout a scene, it is not uncommon for that theme to be cut three or four times to clear dialogue, to signify a dramatic shift, or to call attention to an eyeline match. In each of the key pivot scenes in the melodrama, the seduction and the poisoning, there are no fewer than five musical fragments spliced end on end. Each abrupt cut marks a small situational climax within the scene. In the seduction scene the music cuts to articulate each situation: when Forough sees Shokat's intentions with Nasser, when she storms out of the house, during her eyeline match and swish pan to reveal the father coming home early, when she reenters the home, and when he reenters the home. In the poisoning scene the music cuts to emphasize each incremental movement: as Shokat mixes the poison into the glass, when her husband takes the first sip, and so on. Audiences listened, through the cuts, clicks, and punched-in dialogue, to elaborate patchwork soundtracks created by the craft labor of the film's sound editors, Kairov Boric and Eskandar Minai.

An analysis of the practices of collage scoring complements ongoing work on directors and performers central to the formation of the industry. Layered within this early production by the "father of Iranian cinema" are other media-historical currents. The film does conclude with a popular Iranian song, "Biqarar/Restless," performed by Delkash in a domestic interior to finally break the spell of amnesia (an illness marked by the score from *Spellbound*) and reunite the couple. It is important that Delkash draws the film to a close with a popular Iranian song, and it is also important that Nasser is delivered to Forough in a scene that includes underscoring from *Spellbound* and *Duel*. In this film, as in the compilation scores in hundreds of films made in the following decades, audiences listened to familiar cues from the imported films that still commanded the bulk of screen time in Iran. This film offers multiple stories of authorship, industrial norms, cross-media tie-ins, and audience expectations. It is an index of media circulation, and as such it operates within and beyond a heroic story of cinema pioneers. Like those of the films that would follow it for more than a decade, the score of *The Enchantress* calls attention to its polyglossic layers.

This is not to say that the status of the director did not face its own challenges of respectability before the late 1960s. Commercial postwar cinema in Iran has been vexed, almost from the start, by questions about the validity of its authorship. Hamid Naficy has described commercial films from this period as authorless and followed by the development of the authored new wave films in the late 1960s. He addresses a long-standing discourse about these films as recycling elements rather than presenting "a consistent worldview or coherent film style."[7] Filmmakers derived these elements locally from "a deep sociocultural encyclopedia" of tales of particular character types, most notably the neighborhood tough guy, coded negatively as a thug (*jahel* or *lat*) or positively as a chivalrous protector (*luti* or *javanmard*).[8] Elements were also borrowed from abroad in the form of Hollywood car chases, fight sequences, or genre typage.[9] It is not that such films did not have directors, creative hierarchies, trade unions, and the like. Rather, these structures played only a marginal role in the crystallization of a conception of authorship around festival ambitions, archiving, intellectual film critics, and the translation of auteurist texts into Persian. So even major directors of the commercial cinema of the 1950s, including Koushan and Samuel Khachikian (discussed at length in the next chapter), while certainly recognized in histories of the film industry in Iran, have had difficulty fitting into broader critical canonizations. Their films have faced challenges both by critics in Iran and by an apparatus of cinema and media studies that often engages with histories of world cinema according to the definitions of authorship keyed to the emergence of national art cinemas.

The scoring of this body of work in Iran compounds these concerns, as it uses material composed elsewhere as found fragments in a composition. With important exceptions this tradition of scholarship and criticism, imbalanced but not incorrect in itself, has persisted even as great strides have been made in decentering media infrastructures and unpacking the complexity of the labor process in industries or nontheatrical film communities. What has been a challenge to the respectability of the films' directors is compounded for those who labored to produce their compilation scores. The intellectual labor involved in creating and circulating these scores is full of omissions and points of invisibility. *Duel* and *Spellbound* both had famous scores. They were associated with famous composers and were part of David O. Selznick's efforts to redistribute his back catalog in 1952. But these soundtracks also conceal forms of labor in Hollywood. Both scores, in the early phases of their assembly, were shaped by the crucial but largely unacknowledged craft labor of Audray Granville. Her temp tracks formed reference points for the films' composers. Nathan Platte traces the labor of Granville in the construction of *Spellbound*'s sound. Working with documents in the Selznick archive, he shows that Granville's work uniquely positioned her in regular communication with the producer, director, and composer. The archive of correspondence among them reveals that Selznick and Hitchcock had an early case of temp love. They preferred Granville's choices over Miklós Rózsa's in multiple instances, and those choices affect character sympathies in the final score.[10] If we expand our perspective on the scores to include their origins, afterlife, and travels, the names of composers, and the names of the films' copyright owners, do not provide a sufficient picture of their authorship. The music that we hear as a motif for Nasser's amnesia in *The Enchantress* was born as a collage score and was reworked into another collage score several years later. Granville and Minai (who would go on to score dozens of Iranian films), are linked in the way their labor of sound collage contributed to the long creative life of this score. They are also linked in the ways their authorship was obscured by the industry and within cinema studies. Layered within this early success by a prominent name in the industry are other forms of authorship. The film speaks in different voices. Its collage score invites a closer look at narratives of the rise of a national cinema as it raises questions about negotiations of licensing, divergent legal copyright structures, import and engineering of recording technology, and the diversity of craft labor that such logistics of circulation made possible.

ARCHIVING, ASSEMBLY, AND RECOGNITION

Compared to the patterns of compilation scoring and temp track construction in industries that had their own composers, the sound work in these films challenges assumed hierarchies of authorship. One might imagine that much of this work would elude credit, but in my database of opening title credits from films of this period, around three hundred films currently, there are few such instances. Industry colleagues, critics, and fans often acknowledged this craft labor as intertwined with other conceptions of authorship. In the first decade of postwar film production, sound roles were combined, and sound engineers sometimes also edited the films. The composition and recording of the diegetic songs performed in films were entirely separate roles from the scoring.

Differentiation of the scoring labor occurs in the early 1960s. After this point, sound recording, mixing, and synching were distinctly credited and typically performed by someone other than the person who arranged the score. Compilation scoring was credited from the 1960s on as *muzik-e matn* (literally, music of the text) or *tanzim-e muzik* (arrangement of music). Several names reoccur, and these help to periodize and trace the formation of the industry and company allegiances. The field is a small one, and many names occur with regularity in the film credits, including Vartan Chaparian, Hassan Mosayyebi, Eskandar Minai, Fereydoun Badi'ian, Jalal Maghazei, Varuzh, and Dariush. The film credits indicate that the most prominently credited names in film scoring in Iran were often more mobile than their colleagues, with Rubik Mansuri, Vartan Chaparian, and Varuzh creating soundtracks for multiple studios within a given year. We can follow names like Eskandar Minai, who worked as an assistant on *The Enchantress* at Pars Film and went on to take a key role in sound editing for Atlas and Iran Film studios. Other sound editors formed stable working environments. For example, Dariush teamed up with Gorgin Grigorian to produce steady output for Golden Age Studio in the 1960s (figures 15a, 15b). In several

FIGURES 15A, 15B. Caricatures of Dariush and Grigorian from the titles of *Aqa-ye Haft Rang* / *Mr. Chameleon* (Amin Amini, 1963).

instances, the directors themselves stepped in to select the music for their film scores. This occasional tendency of well-known directors to accept credit for this work further unsettles the boundaries between technical and artistic labor and points to the ways in which scoring could be used to indicate a kind of authorial brand.

If one were to pursue the history of collage sound around the work of an individual, Rubik Mansuri stands out in the field (figure 16). He built public and critical recognition for the work of compilation scoring over a career that extended from the experimental period through popular and new wave films of the 1970s and into the films of the 1980s. Mansuri started work in a dubbing studio owned by Stephen H. Nyman,

FIGURE 16. Rubik Mansuri. Private
collection.

an American rug merchant who became involved with film when he
assisted in the shooting of Arthur Upham Pope's nonfiction film work
in Iran. Nyman published narratives of his work on "the New Iran" in
a series of articles for *Movie Makers*, where he describes the process
of importing equipment and Kodachrome film stock through Beirut,
Baghdad, and western Iran.[11] As Nyman's film footprint expanded, he
became a representative for 20th Century Fox, shooting B-roll and other
newsreel footage for Fox in Iran, and he founded a dubbing and documentary studio with Esfandiar Bozorgmehr and Abolghasem Rezai.[12]
Mansuri's first dubbing job was as an apprentice to Hassan Mosayyebi
on *Sheytan-e Farari* (*The Runaway Devil*), which he remembers completing in 1955 as a separate recording. They synched it each night with
the film print in theaters. After three years working at Nyman's Studio Brenton (later renamed Dubbing Cinema Iran), Mansuri achieved
early success with the score for the Azhir Film production of *Tufan dar
Shahr-e Ma* (*Storm in Our City*, Khachikian, 1958).[13] In the years that
followed, Mansuri was in high demand, working on more than thirty
films per year at the height of his career. His style and music selections
were imitated by other sound editors, and the musical choices he made
in his collage scores influenced composers. In my database of credited
music editors, Mansuri's name appears in the sound credits of more
than one-third of the available films made in Iran before 1970.

In interviews, Mansuri described two essential elements of the craft of the collage score—archiving and assembly—which established it as a well-compensated profession within the industry.[14] He began to build his collection of vinyl records and magnetic tape from his earliest projects. By the time he was consistently scoring films, he had an extensive archive, which he updated regularly by placing orders with film importers. He made biannual trips to Europe to buy classical records unavailable in Iran and to procure the latest commercial releases of film scores, jazz, and mambo. The collection needed not only to provide reliable material to match any mood or tempo, but to keep current with new recordings. During times of easy circulation, Mansuri's archive swelled and was up to date. During times of scarcity, it fell out of sync.[15] Working with these cycles of circulation was part of the maintenance labor required of Mansuri and his peers in order to deliver sound to Iranian films. It required an attention to logistics as well as the cultural knowledge of a record collector.

On the process of assembling scores from his working archive, Mansuri notes the challenges in cutting up music not intended for a scene. Sometimes shifts in dialogue or action would require several musical cuts within a single scene. He describes his own transition from a collage approach to an inconspicuous method based on musical similarity, which sometimes included his own flute and piano melodies dubbed over a found score. He attributes the choices that can be found in the films the early period of film scoring to his youthful irreverence:

> Many years ago, I used to cut freely from Chopin to Beethoven and Beethoven to Tchaikovsky. I was young and made my selections based on whatever I happened to like. Some years later, I saw this as a mistake. My method was . . . I can describe it with an example from traditional Iranian music. In the *Homayun* mode, for example: a *Homayun* can be edited with any other *Homayun*, but one cannot edit a *Homayun* with a *Chahargah* or a *Chahargah* with a *Chaharmezrab*. I was editing together symphonies based on points where they seemed to fit together. I would cut two symphonies together on a matching drum beat or on a flourish of a particular instrument. This montage created a new music whereby audio tape was shaped from the work of several musicians.[16]

In describing his strategies of compilation, Mansuri effectively theorizes sound montage. It is characterized by the changing standards from a period of experimentation before the 1960s to a shift toward professionalization in that decade and then another shift adapting to norms set in the 1970s and beyond. As the musical tastes of Iranian film audiences shifted, perhaps as a result of the introduction of Iranian composers creating music for the screen after 1969 (but not for all films), his archive adapted to include more Iranian, Turkish, Indian, and Greek music. Jazz, or western symphonic music, he says, seemed incongruous for 1970s audiences except in certain cases.[17]

Like almost any broad narrative describing a shift in approach, however, it is important to consider the many exceptions to this tendency. Mansuri continued to use eclectic found material in his later work. One striking example is the soundtrack for the multiple-language coproduction titled *Homa-ye Sa'adat* in Persian and *Subah O Sham* (Chanakya, 1972) in the Hindi version. *Subah O Sham* had a composed score that could have been used in the almost identically cut *Homa-ye Sa'adat*. Instead, Mansuri was hired to construct a different score for this version that played in Iran. Mansuri's score includes recognizable jazz fragments from Henry Mancini and other composers. The date of this release indicates that the practice of collage sound endured, and the specific situation of this coproduction (its readily available composed score) suggests that a collage score could be preferred even when unnecessary.[18] These eclectic compilations did not just solve budget and technical constraints. They also established stylistic norms.

The craft of the compilation score was pulled in two directions. It should reward attention to its author's skill in collecting and editing, but professional skill in compilation should avoid drawing too much attention to itself. Mansuri's discussion of his career suggests that industry norms gradually favored subdued choices. The experimental phase, despite Mansuri's sheepishness about its films' perceived lack of taste, entertained a wider range of possibility. Music editors' choices could be made to be noticed. In either case, Mansuri stresses that what he produced on his reels of magnetic tape was a new form of music. As with many established traditions of collage, the vitality of the sound practice was often counterintuitive. It was eclectic but also immediately recognizable. The sound recordings sampled before the mid-1960s demonstrate interchangeability and flexibility, but they were not detached from their sources. Far from anonymous default stock sound, these compositions announced their sources. They played with forms of recognizability. They featured hooks or standout gimmicks from found sources. If the goal had been to reinforce the world of the diegesis and its characters, or a singular aesthetic vision, it might have encouraged the use of less conspicuous scores, or at least, in a fifteen-second scene, a less conspicuous part of a famous score. Sound editors took the opposite tack, often enough to suggest a particular attraction to this type of material. They regularly chose recognizable motifs, the ones most likely to stick in their audience's heads. They invited awareness of the musical cues, and these invitations persisted and built upon one another.

The midcentury score was rarely tasked with supporting seamless narrative or consistent style. The films themselves bore little allegiance to these principles. The modular structure of the films, whether constructed from citations of imported genre cinema or from Iranian folk typage, was reinforced by the modular collage of film music. An earworm such as the opening title theme of the television show *Peter Gunn*, sampled in *Sodagaran-e Marg* (*Merchants of Death*, Malek Motie'i, 1962), does not *support* the car chase and action scene so much as accentuate the scene with its own familiarity. The borrowed style of the chase, a modular spectacle, authorizes a fragment of a score that played widely and was unlikely to be forgotten once heard. The film's creators were not afraid of the well-known musical fragment upstaging the film with its recognizability and incongruity. And even in cases where there was a generic convergence, music editors were not afraid of choosing the scores that would stand out and have their own gravity. When Mansuri used Leonard Rosenman's score for *Rebel without a Cause* in *Faryad-e Nime-shab* (*The Midnight Cry*, Khachikian, 1961), he did so in the spirit of its function in *Rebel*. He used the original knife fight cue for *The Midnight Cry*'s final fight sequence. But given the enduring popularity of *Rebel* in Tehran in the early 1960s, the knife fight cue was a conspicuous choice no matter how well it fit the scene.

These patterns of recognizability apply just as readily to the home-grown modular elements in the films. When folk types appear in a film, we often hear the same familiar hooks and sonic gimmicks used with other character types. A melody from *High Noon* (Zinnemann, 1952), with its clomping rhythm of horse hooves, accompanies a tough guy delivering a monologue about chivalry into the mirror in *Avval Heykal* (*The Strong Man*, Yasami, 1960). In *Jahel-ha va Gigolo-ha* (*Tough Guys and Dandies*, Madani, sound by Dariush Azizi, 1964), the tough guys make an important entrance to the whistling "Colonel Bogey March" from *The Bridge on the River Kwai* (Lean, 1957), and they are accompanied by the theme for *Bonanza* while they all take off in their cars. The associations seem to follow a pattern closer to the animated film, where musical citations are typically more pronounced and often serve as humorous leitmotifs for characters who are also a kind of citation. The modular structure of the films complemented the noisy patchwork of recognizable samples. In other words, it was precisely those borrowed types from folk stories and from Hollywood, types that prompted early debates about the authorlessness of Iranian popular cinema, that authorized sound editors to make attention-grabbing choices.

In this professional environment sound editors could approach household-name status, and above-the-line names could be attached to the musical selections of a particularly bold score. Mansuri became a celebrated name among film fans, a status not (yet) achieved by Granville, and directors including Khosrow Parvizi and Samuel Khachikian took on music editing work even after they had achieved fame as directors. When Parvizi (credited as Kh. P.) selected music for his cowboy movies, and when Khachikian (credited as "Samuel" or mentioned in the press as "Samvel," as his friends called him) created the score and sound effects for some of his thrillers, they apparently did not do so to restrain or homogenize the selections. They chose standout compositions and aggressive musical montage. They interspersed famous soundtracks and classical recordings with mambo and jazz. The role of the films' directors in making these choices seems to counteract the concern expressed by Mansuri later in his career about the subdued aesthetic consistency of a given track. The directors' hands-on approach to compilation scoring could function as an opportunity for aesthetic risk taking. Bold choices might have created some unwanted noise, but they also could aid in the branding of a film around a name. Mansuri himself appears to have gone along with this notion of the director authorizing a particular type of selection, if his bold scores for Khachikian are any indication. His score for *The Midnight Cry*, in addition to its musical fragments taken from blues standards *Rebel without a Cause* and *Desire under the Elms*, samples *Alfred Hitchcock Presents: Music to Be Murdered By* (Alexander, 1958). It would be difficult to find a selection more on the nose for a film about murder by a director known as the Hitchcock of Iran. Both director-credited collage scores and director-branded themes reorder the distinctions between above- and below-the-line labor. Listening for the signature cues in stylized films can reveal author functions within the modular form of the films.

TEMP LOVE, OUT OF SYNC

Consider the asynchrony of the trends in compilation scoring in Iran and the United States. What creative and marketing opportunities did this asynchrony afford? The studios in midcentury Iran used American scores composed when the pendulum had swung away from compilation scoring norms of 1930s Hollywood. Then, by the late 1960s both industries had swung past each other in the opposite directions. Just as Hollywood was rediscovering the compilation score and directors were rekindling their temp love, the film industry in Iran began to favor original scores from its own composers, and its remaining compilations turned away from their rowdier past. The cyclical trends for or against compilation were, for these two industries, about as far apart as they could be.

This was the period in which Max Steiner, Hollywood's celebrated golden-age composer, famously spoke out against the compilation score.[19] It was a period in which he helped to consolidate control of the score around the composer, and film studios packaged and sold this music apart from the films as part of a campaign of tie-in branding. These efforts created the conditions of recognizability that inadvertently gave the scores their currency in compilations abroad. It is important to see these scores made in Iran as a creative interaction not just with found melodies but with the commercial life of this branded property. The patterns of sampling at midcentury were wildly out of sync with the commercial trends that produced the source material, which made it possible to resynchronize new forms of recognizability and commercial viability.

Taking as examples a few of the most globally recognizable film composers and compositions regularly sampled in Iranian films, the history of these citations intertwines with the history of tie-in marketing and promotion of film albums. The commercially released albums of Miklós Rózsa, Henry Mancini, Elmer Bernstein, and Steiner consolidated various forms of sound labor around the branded composer. This helped the recordings to travel efficiently on the currents of the market and to create crossover marketing synchronization. But outside these core markets they circulated in an asynchronous manner through exchanges around the world. Here *Spellbound* bears another mark of distinction to add to the discussion above. It was not only Rózsa's first tie-in album; it was an early experiment in this very practice, which would become a norm fifteen years later. With this four-record album, film music tested the possibilities of circulating separately from the film. As Kyle Barnett has described, the release of the score marks a web of commercial entanglements with Selznick's Vanguard Films, radio networks, and ARA records, which released and distributed the LP.[20] Despite its robust promotional efforts, bolstered by Rózsa's Academy Award and liner notes by Hitchcock, the album stumbled commercially (figure 17). But

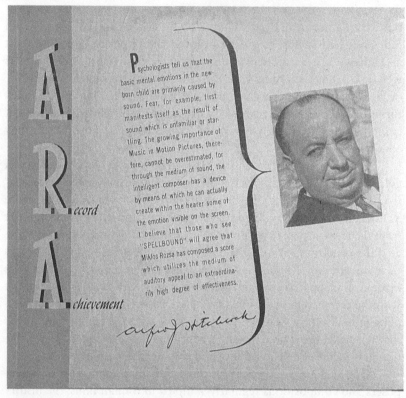

FIGURE 17. Foldout sleeve of the *Spellbound* album (ARA Records, 1945).

its marketing missteps did not prevent it from traveling far. It became a leitmotif in *The Enchantress* in 1953 and featured prominently in other notable Iranian films such as the urban social melodrama of crime and redemption *Chaharrah-e Havades* (*Crossroads of Events*, Khachikian, 1955). As tie-in film albums became more common in Hollywood, new recordings found their way alongside early examples of this practice in the working archives of music editors in Iran.

Once Rózsa's compositions offered an early model of the possibilities of popular tie-in music, Henry Mancini's and Elmer Bernstein's careers grew intertwined with this practice. By 1952 MGM was a major manufacturer of records, and by 1958 United Artists, Paramount, Warner Bros., 20th Century Fox, and Columbia all had purchased or started their own record companies. The possibilities for cross-promotions and the vogue for big themes expanded as a result.[21] Rózsa's noir modernism had traveled far on vinyl, but Mancini made his career with an album-friendly integration of jazz and mambo. *Touch of Evil* was his first film album and *Peter Gunn* his first real blockbuster.[22] Both of the main themes from these compositions feature prominently in Iran over the years. The *Touch of Evil* title sequence was used seven years after the film's release in the title sequence for *Sarsam* (*Delirium*, Khachikian, 1965), and *Peter Gunn* was used a few years earlier in *Merchants of Death*. Bernstein's music underscores a number of Iranian films. His most useful tracks appear to have come from *Desire under the Elms*, which can be heard in a courtroom drama (*Dast-e Taqdir* [*Hand of Fate*], Ovadiah [Gorji Obadia], 1959), a melodrama of divorce (*Bim va Omid* [*Fear and Hope*], Ovadiah, 1960), and a noir thriller (*The Midnight Cry*) all within a few years of the album's release.[23] The music editors' repetitions of these famous musical cues in film after film form part of the history of the Hollywood majors' move into the record business. The scores' cross-promotional possibilities and big themes carried over into cinema in Iran, but during this process of relay they intersected with forms of publicity not intended for the albums or their films.

Music editors in Iran apparently had a fondness for overtures, which they found a way to fit into a variety of situations. Whether from recordings of classical compositions or from American film scores, overtures were overrepresented on the soundtracks of films made in Iran. Twenty years before the sustained entry of Hollywood into the record business, Max Steiner's score for *Gone with the Wind* held a special status as a prestige score as well as for the particular recognizability of its overture. "Tara's Theme" functioned as a sonic nametag, which identified the film and marked its status as a prestige picture as it traveled long distances.[24] Selznick certainly pursued opportunities to continually export prints to the Middle East and South Asia. The export of Technicolor prints of the film along British trade routes was one way he moved his capital out of Britain during a wartime currency freeze.[25] But as with many of these ventures, the company remained largely unaware of the ways in which the film was relayed.[26] The film still stands among the best-known Persian dubs of classical Hollywood. Babak Tabarraee traces the multiple dubbed versions of the film, produced in 1963, 1968, and in the 1980s, describing the fan culture around this film in Iran as it was continually reshaped by famous Iranian dubbing performers and technicians who opened the film to a wider audience and Iranianized its characters and situations.[27] Tabarraee notes the emphasis on enduring classicism in the *Ettela'at* advertisements, pointing out the newspaper's repeated tagline for the release of the 1963 dub: "Generations come and go. Thousands of films are screened, but only *Gone with the Wind* remains eternal."[28] The melody's robust afterlife meant that it was recognizable in diverse and unplanned ways.

In the decades between *Gone with the Wind*'s 1939 release and its first Persian-language dubs in the 1960s, its soundtrack turns up in several films made in Iran. When we do hear it, keeping with the pattern, we hear the most conspicuous part of "Tara's Theme." The earliest example I have found of this relocated sonic nametag is in George Ovadiah's *Bipanah* (*Abandoned*, 1954). The cue announces a character's entrance and then clears the dialogue with an abrupt shift to a subdued melody in a different style. The film was fifteen years old at this point, but the album, released in 1952 to correspond with Selznick's push to redistribute his back catalog around the world, was new. The use of the melody would have spoken to at least some of the cinephiles and record store patrons in the audience. Each subsequent citation of the cue rendered it recognizable beyond those who knew the original film or had heard the soundtrack on a gramophone or broadcast. If the fame of the cue served nostalgic pleasures in these later instances, it may not have been for an original film classic. "Tara's Theme" plays itself again and again as it accompanies important narrative transitions in Iranian films.

Whatever associations the film audiences may have had with *Gone with the Wind*, when they heard a few seconds of its recognizable theme in an Iranian film, it usually meant that it was time to cry. In *Amu Nowruz* (*Uncle New Year*, Yasami, 1961) the theme wells up at a key sentimental moment, when the magical title character appears in a flame and gives the weary protagonist the affirmation she needs to move on with her life. In *Shabneshini dar Jahannam* (*Party in Hell*, Sarvari and Khachikian, 1957, sound by Jamshid Boyuki), an abrupt mid-scene musical shift to "Tara's Theme" works within the scene rather than as an opening or concluding flourish. The plot follows Haji Jabbar, a character set up as a kind of Iranian Scrooge who is transported out of the living world during an early-cinema-inspired fever dream. He crosses the *Pol-e Serat* (the bridge into the underworld) and encounters demonic variety acts in a Méliès-like setting and voyage. "Tara's Theme" marks the turn in which Haji Jabbar realizes the error of avarice. He enters a room that resembles a decadent parlor occupied by the souls of a wealthy couple. He scrambles to gather loose cash from the floor as the man behind him begins to laugh. The music fades from the playful *Barber of Seville* to "Tara's Theme," and Haji Jabbar begins to cry (figure 18). The score was coded as a marker of cinematic sentiment, and it remained in the

FIGURE 18. Haji Jabbar is brought to tears as the score switches to "Tara's Theme." *Shabneshini dar Jahannam / Party in Hell* (Mushegh Sarvari and Samuel Khachikian, 1957).

sound archives to be used for this purpose. It even returns in redubs. In the available version of the first Persian-language talkie (made in Bombay), *The Lor Girl* (*Dokhtar-e Lor*, Irani, 1934), "Tara's Theme" accompanies the sentimental dialogue.[29] When sound editors updated the score for a 1969 rerelease, after *Gone with the Wind* had received significant press in Iran, they added the theme to the central love scene in the film. When the melodrama pivots on an outpouring of sentiment, as occurs in each of these films, Steiner's overture signals this shift in a way that could have been apprehended by a viewer paying rapt attention, someone distracted from the film while retrieving a snack, and someone listening to the film outside. The uncontainable fragments of this sonic nametag well up as if to announce "This is cinema" at the moments designed to move an audience to tears. The new functions of the old score fold the scenes into a long history of an "eternal" film's global reception.

The global classicism of evergreen Hollywood scores accounts for one common pattern of reuse, but other recycled scores appeared at the speed of global fashion. Remember that while some of these scores came from film prints themselves, better sound quality could be transferred to mag tape from commercial LPs. Vinyl was both stable and fast. Music editors' collections were archived over years to be sure, but vinyl could circulate in ways that distributor-controlled film prints could not. This portable format met with a nimble soundtrack technique in which all dialogue, music, and effects were recorded and assembled last, with the rapidity of a temporary preview track. This resourceful production method not only saved time and money, it gave the industry opportunities to create novel forms of tie-in simultaneity. One way to trace this simultaneity is to compare newspaper exhibition records for Hollywood films in Iran with the release dates of the Iranian films that recycle their scores. It turns out that some Iranian filmmakers were able to integrate music quickly enough to score their own films with musical themes from imports that were still playing in first-run cinemas.

The score for *Fereshtei dar Khane-ye Man* (*An Angel in My House*, Aghamaliyan, 1963), edited by Dariush Azizi at Golden Age studio, opens with the piano theme from Billy Wilder's *The Apartment* to accompany its nighttime shots of busy Tehran streets. The LP, *Theme from The Apartment*, was one of several cross-promotional efforts that succeeded on the music charts in the early 1960s. With this film, United Artists piloted rack sales of albums in cinema lobbies. The company expanded the program when the promotion proved profitable.[30] *The Apartment* hit US theaters in 1960, but it premiered in Iran in October 1963 at the Moulin Rouge cinema.[31] *An Angel in My House* was released this same year. The soundtrack played in Iran simultaneously for Aghamaliyan's urban melodrama and Wilder's cynical sex comedy about the postwar managerial class. The choice gives *Angel*'s opening a contemporary feel. Wilder's ironic uses of the song's sentimentality are not conveyed in the new context, but something about its source still stands out. It would not have been unreasonable to expect it to be recognized given the commercial success of the album, the film itself, and the narrative significance of that particular song within the film. The *Rickshaw Boy* LP features visibly in the diegesis of *The Apartment* as a running cynical gag. Wilder's film also had prestige associations in Tehran. The Moulin Rouge was a high-end cinema, and Jack Lemon was on his way to becoming a major star in Iran (figure 19).

The same accelerated sampling happens with the score for the James Bond film *From Russia with Love* (Young, 1963). The film was released in Iran two years later with the descriptive title *A Trap for James Bond*. John Barry's score for the film follows the other big-theme composers with its pop melodies tuned to marketing opportunities. It was Barry's first in a series of Bond scores, which helped the franchise become famous for its branded music. The theme tied record sales and radio

FIGURE 19. October 1963 advertisement for *The Apartment* (Billy Wilder, 1960). Courtesy of Ehsan Khoshbakht.

play to the film in most markets, but in Iran audiences may have heard it first in a locally produced thriller. *Delirium* (sound by Mohammad Mohammadi) was released in Iran the same year as *A Trap for James Bond*, and it makes use of two cues from Barry's score.[32] The musical cues in *Delirium*, as in *Angel*, do not call back to time-tested classic scores. They play simultaneously with anticipated new releases at first-run theaters. The business ties between Hollywood film companies and record subsidiaries by 1958, and the stylistic changes in theme music that followed, encouraged multimedia commercial viability. Simultaneous screenings of films that were produced seven thousand miles apart but that make use of the same scores illustrate how such commercial strategies could be repurposed.

In some cases, collage sound in films made in Iran may have traveled faster to cinemas than the original films for which the scores were composed. Take Hollywood's orientalist battle spectacle *Taras Bulba*

(Thompson, 1962). The film did fine in the United States, but Franz Waxman's score received radio play, multiple commercial releases, and awards nominations.[33] I do not have an Iranian exhibition record for *Taras Bulba*, but I have found an instance of its soundtrack in the Iranian film *Zamin-e Talkh (Bitter Earth*, Parvizi, 1963), which was released less than three months after a limited American release of *Taras Bulba*. The Iranian premiere of the score, in a compilation credited to Parvizi himself, must have *preceded* the local distribution of the film by at least a year. It even preceded some key US markets, as the film followed a standard staggered release pattern. As a result, when moviegoers in some US cities heard Waxman's score for the film on opening night, they were hearing a score that Parvizi had already presented to Tehran audiences weeks earlier in his own take on the western genre. The score for a Yul Brenner action film set in the Eurasian Steppe had been reattached to a cowboy movie made in Iran before the Hollywood film had completed its first run in its own domestic market. The Waxman-Parvizi vector, outpacing the United Artists domestic release schedule, offers an acute example of what can be discovered when one replaces linear arguments about temporal delay with inquiries into circulation's layered chronologies.

Iran's temp love was all about the odd timing. Commercially available recordings of film music, products of one industry's rejection of compilation scoring, transformed into a working archive for another industry's exploration of the possibilities of compilation. The products of the cross-promotional strategies of Hollywood and its record subsidiaries around 1960 could be retooled for other kinds of crossings on the sound stripes of films and in the public venues that screened them. These processes help us to challenge assumptions that circulation follows a linear chronology from origin to destination with a kind of dilution marking each step. It shows that Iranian sound editors, who (like the composers they sampled) were keen to craft music with publicity in mind, took advantage of these records' acclaim while reshuffling their linear timelines. They could return to a 1930s soundtrack over decades, create resourceful affinities with contemporary films, and even leapfrog Hollywood films' domestic release schedules. Tracking patterns of recognizable sound draws attention to these essential networks of exchange without implying that asynchrony is a one-way street.

Rather than closing off the world of the individual film, the citations, repetitions, and tie-ins of relayed scores opened the films to the kind of participatory media culture that Anahid Kassabian describes in her celebration of the compilation score. For Kassabian, composed scores offer assimilating identifications, which extract audiences from their own histories and identity positions. Compilation scores, by contrast, offer affiliating identifications, which "depend on histories formed outside the film scene and . . . allow for a fair bit of mobility within it. If offers of assimilating identifications try to narrow the psychic field, then offers of affiliating identifications open it wide."[34] The collage scores of the cinema industry of midcentury Iran offer a particularly elaborate form of affiliative identifications. Their peculiar irony is that they were constructed out of samples, unbeknownst to Steiner, of golden-age assimilating scores. The film music formed part of the larger urban experience of sound cinema. These scores jumped across media and across the boundaries between private and public space. They announced links to popular films and television programs, and beyond their play in theater spaces and broadcasts, they also permeated the streetscape.[35] Many cinemas in Iran were airdome operations that attracted paying audience members as well as listeners on the sidewalks, walls, and open lots outside the cinema. For indoor cinemas, too, it was common practice to transmit the scores through loudspeakers onto the street. Record stores played film scores along with pop music on the streets of fashionable neighborhoods. The experience of listening to film sound outside the movie theater has been documented in memoirs of film fans and filmmakers alike, and it has been mythologized in multiple films and texts. Careful attention to this sound has been portrayed as a kind of vernacular film school by one of Iran's most celebrated filmmakers of the 1970s and beyond, Masoud Kimiai (discussed in detail in chapter 5). Some cinemas continually reward an analysis tuned to the medium's pathways of affiliation. The asynchronous collage scores in these films helped to announce affiliations with global cinema, but it was cinema as a participatory process and not as a static product or a distant ideal.

RELAYING THE POPULAR SONG

Familiar overtures and underscoring mark one facet of the compilation score in Iran, but what happened when the films relayed pop songs and singers from abroad? Cinema in Iran was a site of transaction around globally recognizable popular songs just as it was around prestige scores and big themes. While these modular films supported a range of musical forms, the pop song had a different compilation pattern than the composed score. Such songs moved beyond a fabric of familiarity to a specific referentiality, and for this reason they required more diegetic framing than samples from familiar scores. As performances of foreign pop, they occupied a different status, too, from the rich traditions of Iranian music found in montage sequences and café performances, which is one of the reasons I link this (often diegetic) found material to an analysis of the nondiegetic collage score.

Rock, mambo, and jazz songs were often introduced through (elaborate) reflexive gestures, or they were authorized by a particular stock character. Familiar instrumental scores did the work of affiliative identifications in these films. They were recognizable, and they were cut to set mood, provide leitmotifs, and mark reversals in the narrative. Pop singers amplified the familiarity of the source material and created additional layers within this texture of citation. The modularity of pop fit the modularity of the films, but it required intensified switching to authorize its place in the films. Just as the silent-era advertisements for films in Iran showcased their value, and long history, as objects of global media circulation, popular songs, particularly when played in English, were accompanied by acts announcing a commercial recording's status as media product. In other words, the more conspicuous the recording being relayed, the more one is likely to find elaborate structures of reflexivity around it. These films did not emulate rock films or musicals in their entirety; they inserted their songs into spectacular scenes marked by techniques of code switching.[36]

Johnny Guitar (Ray, 1954) traveled to cinemas around the world, including Iran, but Peggy Lee and Victor Young's "Johnny Guitar" proved especially suited to circulation. The song was covered extensively, in English and in translation, in the late 1950s and early 1960s. At the same time that it was being performed in Sweden by the Spotniks and in Lebanon in Arabic by Fairuz, the song found its way into an Iranian melodrama of a separated couple told from the point of view of their daughter. *Bim va Omid* (*Fear and Hope*, Ovadiah, 1960) turned out to be one of Ovadiah's notable works before he began making films in Israel. It features the debut film performance of a nine-year-old Googoosh, who would become one of Iran's superstar singers and film performers. Her performance of "Johnny Guitar" concludes a ten-minute hallucinatory variety act. The infirm father laments that he cannot afford a television, and his daughter tries to cheer him up by saying that *she* is in fact a better television than one bought at the store. As she announces a series of song and dance numbers from around the world, Googoosh's face is framed by an opening in a wall that resembles

FIGURE 20. Announcing the performance of "Johnny Guitar"
through a room divider as if through a television screen. *Bim va
Omid / Fear and Hope* (George Ovadiah, 1960).

a television tube. The father perceives the performance through the haze
of illness, which provides a loose justification for the fantastic elements
of a scene with several elaborate costume changes. Googoosh returns to
the television frame to announce the final performance in a combination of English and formal Persian. "Ladies and gentlemen, good morning. *Aknun beh ahang-e engelisi-e* 'Johnny Guitar' *tavajjoh farmaid* [At
this time, please direct your attention to the song "Johnny Guitar" in
English]" (figure 20). She performs on banjo in a flamenco costume as
her father's condition slowly worsens. A medium shot of her from the
father's point of view dissolves with a liquid effect to a shot of her in
the dress she was wearing at the start of the scene as the music switches
to underscoring. For this (and other scenes throughout the film) sound
mixer Eskandar Minai used the familiar cue from Elmer Bernstein's
Desire under the Elms. To achieve this movement from somber melodrama to diegetic variety show and back, the film stacks one reflexive
transition atop another.

A costumed performance of "Johnny Guitar" could hardly be
expected to fit seamlessly into this tearful family drama with moody
underscoring and no other songs. The scene as a whole is essentially a
stage act featuring seven costume changes (two of them in drag). Instead
of mitigating the amount of time given to the performance, the film
showcases the precocious talents of its child star with a dense series of

alternations in code. The scene alternates between external and internal diegesis with its fever-dream framing, between formal and vernacular Persian, and between Persian and English. It switches from one musical genre to another and includes codes from cinematic, stage, and tele-visual performance. Before Googoosh can perform her version of the popular song, her character has to refer to herself as a television. Her diglossic switch from vernacular to formal Persian marks the switch to television, and the switch to English marks the finale of this tour-de-force performance.[37] The entire scene is bracketed by the fever dream, a common enough frame for a musical performance, with the shift out of the father's hallucination signaled by a transition wipe but also by the underscoring from *Desire under the Elms*. The crossing into television and the switch from a Hollywood cross-promotional song to Hollywood underscoring reflexively position the modular virtuoso comic stage performance of a child star within the incongruous story of child's pathos-filled quest to find her father's heart medicine.

The chameleon performance of a child star offers one standout example, but the films more commonly leaned on stock characters to mediate jazz, mambo, blues, and rock. One of the most common char-acter types to stitch in a famous pop song was the dance-hall dandy, or gigolo. Like the tough guy, the dance-hall dandy was a ubiquitous caricature based on an actual subcultural formation. Dandies were con-sistent mediators of music in the films in which they appeared. Whereas café singers and tough guys usually performed Iranian film songs, dandies relayed imported pop. Code switching was built into early twentieth-century caricatures of the Iranian dandy, and it accelerated in midcentury popular culture when the caricature became a popular way of poking fun at city youth intoxicated by media from abroad.[38] Dandies used English and French phrases, they were preoccupied with fashion, and they were steeped in popular music. It was an indicator of membership into midcentury dandy subculture, as important as a joyfully mismatched wardrobe, that one would have spent enough time outside a downtown record store to "know by heart and be able to hum at least six foreign songs such as 'Johnny Guitar.'"[39] When these characters appear in films, they assert this musical knowledge in a way that authorizes pop music in the film but also allows for a kind of comic reflection on its reception. They were rarely the heroes of the films and functioned, instead, as agents of media reflexivity.

In addition to "Johnny Guitar," dance-hall dandies in these films appar-ently loved Bill Haley and His Comets, an attraction that illustrates their role as mediators of waves of popular forms of rock, jazz, and mambo. Haley's music is a particularly active object of midcentury intermedial circulation. It marked changing radio and gramophone cultures, and it was integrated into a cycle of Hollywood dance films. It found its way into advertising media, world expos, and even experimental films of the late 1950s. *Don't Knock the Rock* (Sears, 1956) premiered in Tehran as *Piruzi-ye Rock 'n' Roll* (*Rock 'n' Roll Victory*) in May 1957 and was accompanied by extensive advertising and discussion in the press about rock as a global phenomenon:[40] "And now young Iranians hang out from morning to night in front of record shops on Naderi Street. . . . They will do anything they can to get their hands on a Bill Haley record, they collect pictures of Elvis Presley from foreign magazines, and at evening parties they imitate the moves they have seen in rock-and-roll movies—showing off their 'art' to their rivals."[41] As can be expected, these discussions spanned from the celebratory to the reactionary (tensions that animated the plots of the Bill Haley films themselves, although without the subtext of westoxication), and quips about the Tehran dandy subculture, wherever one stood in the debates about Haley and Elvis, were usually ready to hand. The character type allowed media makers to stage a push and pull of admiration and satire.

Complete songs by Bill Haley and His Comets from his recent films can be heard diegetically in at least three Iranian feature films from the period. Each one cites the rock-and-roll movie, but in modular dance scenes rather than full remakes. Such scenes appear apropos of nothing and rely on the dandy figures within them to manage their incongruities. Given that *Party in Hell* premiered in the fall of the same year as the Bill Haley film, it should make perfect sense that this film made use of Bill Haley's music with enthusiasm. The film offered a kind of model for modularity with its variety act format. The film greeted pop trends, as well as attractions from cinema history, with a warm embrace. Raj Kapoor appears in what is perhaps a gesture to the dream-song sequence in *Awaara* (Kapoor, 1951), which is partly set in Hell. The Haley scene (let alone the rest of the film) includes a host of codes incongruous with any rock-and-roll film. The film gestures to Georges Méliès in its style, its costuming, and (based on surviving photographs of the set) its mode of production. The Haley scene in particular makes use of living cards that call back to early trick films. The dissipated dandies in the scene revive when one of them holds up a large record that he has brought with him from the land of the living, which he identifies in a slow and deliberately pronounced English. "Rock and roll?" The rest

FIGURE 21. Displaying a Bill Haley record to a group of dandies and living illustrations before the "Rip It Up" dance sequence. *Shabneshini dar Jahannam / Party in Hell* (Mushegh Sarvari and Samuel Khachikian, 1957).

repeat, "Rock?" He replies, "and roll." We see a closer view of the disk before it is placed on its own oversized gramophone (figure 21). The gigolos and gigolettes dance together to Haley's "Rip It Up" from *Don't Knock the Rock*, and the middle-aged Haji Jabbar joins in. This pattern repeats in *Storm in Our City*, in which a group of dandies drive up to the hills outside of Tehran for fresh spring air. One of them ironically recites a nature poem about spring flowers before they turn on Haley's "Mambo Rock" from their car stereo. A middle-aged village couple, traveling with two donkeys, sees them and joins in. Their donkeys kick to the rhythm of the saxophone solo. Finally, *Akharin Gozargah* (*The Last Passage*, scored by the director, Parvizi, 1962), a kind of western, seems an even less congruous place for an extended Bill Haley dance sequence. It is a rural film about property rights and inheritance, with a subplot of smuggling and corruption. A brief detour in a dance hall, aided by the presence of a large console radio and gramophone player, introduces the dance sequence to "Rudy's Rock" from *Rock around the Clock*.[42] When the manager of the dance hall switches the records on the gramophone, he turns to the camera and says, in English, "Excuse me, dance?" The swing dancing extras, costumed like the dancers from *Rock around the Clock*, populate the musical interlude before the start of the film's third act. In each case, these dance-hall dandies' switches of code, and their facility with oversized gramophones, become useful devices in the global relay of pop. It took a world's worth of participatory media cultures to keep Bill Haley and his band in orbit, a world that included the dance-hall dandies of midcentury Iranian cinema.

Dance-hall dandies rarely performed without foils in these films. Rubes (such as the country couple), traditional patriarchs (such as Haji Jabbar), or tough guys offer another position of affiliation within each musical scene. One of the most elaborate examples, in which the subculture is central, is Iran's 1964 recasting of *West Side Story* (Robbins, 1961), *Tough Guys and Dandies*. The dandies in the film, outfitted in their official uniform of loud-patterned shirts and mismatched ties, call themselves the Jets. Their rivals, the toughs in black fedoras and matching jackets, are led by a man named Esmail Aqa Westside. Just like in the other gigolo examples, the Jets perform music within the diegesis. During the film's dance hall sequence, the actors mime playing jazz instruments to a recording of Bert Kaempfert's "Cerveza." As with their association with rube characters in other films, they are interrupted by their foils in a comic back and forth. The dandies' performance allows a popular song to play in the film in its entirety while the toughs offer both a target of humor and a vantage point from which to mock the dandies' musical excesses.

The film does not reproduce full songs from the musical, but it incorporates some of its choreography and is permeated with cues from the album, another LP that topped the charts in the years between the two films. Together, the dandies and the toughs mediate the relay of the popular recording. The early scene of the Jets' snapping in unison is restaged with *West Side Story*'s music overdubbed as the only sound. This opening theme repeats throughout *Tough Guys* and returns with important variations in the rumble scene. Instead of exclusively using the music from *West Side*'s rumble, *Tough Guys*' rumble intercuts that dramatic turn in the score with the finger-snapping opening theme. This time it is not only the dandy-Jets who mime snapping to the recycled sound. Esmail Aqa Westside's gang snaps, too, but not the one-handed jazz snap of the Jets. Theirs is the *beshkan*, a two-handed snapping technique recognizable as Iranian. Dariush dubbed the sharp-toned *beshkan* of the toughs over the *West Side* score, while Madani, who cut the film, shows the parallel snapping in cut-ins as the two gangs advance toward each other. The film relays much of the music from *West Side*, again aided by the dandies as mediators, and again it sets up a contrasting group as a counterpoint. The dandies relay one of the most highly charted recordings of finger snapping in the history of popular music, and the toughs snap back. The distinct sounds of each created a gag that could work with or without its accompanying images. The gag could play just as easily when it was seen inside theaters as when it was heard over loudspeakers by fans listening outside.

In these scenes, media-obsessed subcultural types and cross-media performers create space in the modular narratives to integrate popular songs. They play off rival media and rival character types in comedic or melodramatic modes to direct a certain kind of knowing attention to the circulation of recorded pop music. Dandies perform choreography associated with these musical styles while rubes and toughs perform in counterpoint. Their comic dances and snaps gave a variety of points of affiliation with these songs. Audiences could enjoy their pop and their forms of distance from it, too. They could laugh with the dandies, and at them, as the dandies worshipped their gramophones and car stereos in bright, mismatched trousers. They could laugh at Haji Jabbar's take on the dancing from *Don't Knock the Rock* and still go back to tearful sentiment when the film returned to its melodrama with a switch back to "Tara's Theme." They could find humor in the Jahels' interruptions of a live performance of "Cerveza" or their out-snapping of the Jets and return to sincerity when Esmail Aqa Westside sang "Alef Beh," a serenade by the star singer Iraj Khajeh Amiri, in the film's final scene.

Pop songs occupied a space between recycled scores and Iranian songs, the binary that defined the musical alternations of midcentury productions. In an industry where some forms of craft and technical labor could still cross from one role into another, scoring and songs for films remained the work of distinct professionals, as it had in other industries with strong film-song traditions. Pop songs stood out in that they were still typically found sound, but they were brought into the diegesis, set apart from the underscoring or thematic music during action or heightened melodrama. Like the familiar scores, films used them to connect with a participatory culture around best-selling albums as they circulated globally. But unlike prestige themes from Hollywood history or big-theme hooks, which could be patched in almost anywhere in a film, these tracks involved additional framing. Media reflexivity and mediating types provided a way to authorize their extreme shifts in a film's tone and references. Scenes of relayed pop songs were not necessarily staples of studio production, but as spectacular supplements they turned up often enough to come with their own conventions. These musical interruptions, between the more common alternations of found score and café song, formed another part of a history of midcentury albums absorbed by an industry as they circulated.

The collage scoring in these films highlights the importance of reworking regional barriers in media history. It cautions against the ways our disciplinary formations may have, as Andrew Jones puts it, "reified the geographical region in question and avoided the complexities and inequities of the global historical processes in which these localities are necessarily involved."[43] How a recording travels, and how far, is an indicator of the political economy of media. To separate regional studies as if some kind of categorical barrier exists between the Iranian cinema and Hollywood, even if the goal is to address the imbalance of that categorical divide, is to potentially reproduce the imbalances of that political economy in one's own history. It is to miss the exchange that is a material and creative foundation for an experience of cinema. An analysis of *The Enchantress* can be both about the afterlife of *Spellbound*'s score and about the foundations of an industrial practice in Iran. Taking these elements as separate, bracketing one in pursuit of the other, is not a problem in itself, especially given the regional bias of sustained engagement with foundational figures. But taking their separateness for granted is a problem. It does not reflect on the political economy of media driving historiography. It ignores the exhibition context in which these films were screening simultaneously, and it tends to dodge the citational structures of these films. The category of the regional is clearly important for understanding film music in Iran, but as a vector rather than a foundation.

The scores patched into these films, however useful some of them originally were for classical narrative forms, were needed here for anticlassical purposes. The films made in Iran do not follow the narrative patterns of their source material. They move fluidly through genre conventions and comingle grandiose affect with intimate affect. They intersperse song and dance with drama and comedy. They are modular and intertextual. They borrow characters from previous films for cameos and contain interludes that make regular gestures to television, radio, and contemporary live performance traditions. A history of these traditions would overlook some of their most active interventions if it did not pursue the ways they incorporate characters from different worlds and make space for dissonant situational climaxes. They do all of this within a network of citation that jumps from one frame of reference to another with the help of authorizing devices.

The music editors for these films repurposed music to fit the films' modular and intertextual modes. Their craft would be out of place in a hermetic diegesis or even in a series of attractions configured with stable genre expectations. The recycled music in these films had trouble remaining polite and unnoticeable in the background. Even a distracted ear had to reckon with musical fragments, few of which were original to the film. Calls for originality, even if they had been possible to achieve, would have run counter to the energy of these compilations. Many of these scores were heard more than once, in their undubbed imported versions, as reworked within dubbed scores, and in local productions. While the overdubbed imports largely maintained their original function (as with the sonically altered but functionally comparable score for the Persian dub of *Psycho*), in these scores' new life in Iranian studio productions, they took on conspicuous functions their composers never expected them to take. The euphony and melody of classical film compositions gave way to creative interruptions. The sound was hard not to notice because it had a conspicuous provenance. In films with many influences, this is the only component that involved systematic duplication and re-editing. It is the most intermedial aspect of these films, and it is put to use in service of intermediality. What we see in film after film is a popular cinema that revels in switching codes. The collage score became an agent of this code switching.

I do not mean to imply that these films were constructed for their audiences as esoteric texts. Sound editors, motivated to develop a commercially effective craft on a budget, could hardly expect audiences to pore over and dwell in an occult knowledge of their musical sources (although I do sometimes worry that my own method of identifying the sources has verged in that direction). Nor do these films' citations necessarily reward specific knowledge about their context. They deliver few inside jokes that can only be understood if one knows the context of the reference. The many samples of "Tara's Theme" do not really wink at audience members with specific knowledge about the plot or characters of *Gone with the Wind*. But given the pattern of sampling earworms from popular film and television albums including such wideranging recordings as *Bonanza*, *The Bridge on the River Kwai*, *From Russia with Love*, *Peter Gunn*, *Spellbound*, *West Side Story*, and *Rock around the Clock*, neither should one discount the way these scores embraced familiar commercial soundscapes. Given the subcultural dandies who prided themselves on the memorization of songs cited in these films, a subculture whose caricature was no less a go-to within the films themselves when it was time for a particularly bold citation, it is not unreasonable to pursue the possibilities for affiliation introduced with this recycled material.

A study of a cinema attentive to the global political economy of the medium should not discount any form of intellectual labor, however removed from immediate visibility, that contributes to a vitality of the medium against its typical flows of property. The archive of relayed recordings in commercial features, positioned on largely unseen maps of circulation and managed by partly visible labor, can help to reveal such countercurrents. It offers one place to look for forms of reflexivity that expand the boundaries of modernist cinematic practice. These films' sound practices were reflexive, and they were uncontained. They served fans as fans, but they did not require encyclopedic mastery of their citations as a pretext for enjoyment of their reflexive aspects. The collage sound in these films did not necessarily remind viewers that "this is a film" so much as it emphatically declared that "this is cinema." It was a modular cinema, one that jumped from one mode of address or one medium to another, from private space to the street. Relayed music kept the participatory media culture at midcentury within earshot of the medium's monumental forms.

CHAPTER 4

The Anxious Exuberance
of Tehran Noir

As film studies warms to archives of theory and criticism that have not yet found their way into anthologies, the slow work of identifying patterns in film publications is accompanied by the pleasures of imagining which essays one could put forward for translation and why. What alternative principles of canon formation are possible? What might such writing tell the discipline about a local film culture, but also about the transnational circulation of ideas about the medium? For my own nomination from midcentury Iran, I would want something that showcases the eclectic energy of the period. It should address the potential of cinema in this period but also take a playful form. It might be meandering in topic, alternately polemical and practical, and alight equally on technical issues like tax reform and imagined scenarios written in a literary style. There would be much to learn about transnational intellectual history if the selections discussed well-known work in film studies: if the author knew D. W. Griffith, UFA directors, and 1920s Soviet film theory as well as contemporary genre cinema. Such a selection might also reflect the multiple roles taken on by Iranian intellectuals at the time. It might be the work of a filmmaker who wrote criticism or a critic who also worked in the studios. Such a wish list would not be too much to ask, as there is a wealth of material that would qualify. Commercial film production had been in place since 1947, but it had increased enough by the mid-1950s for audiences to expect regular releases and for critics to declare a shift out of the industry's experimental period. Studios were recalibrating their ambitions, and producers of genre films sought forms of stabilization and prestige. Regular film columns in newspapers and film review sections in arts periodicals had accelerated. Dedicated film magazines had found solid footing. It was time to get to work making films and producing film criticism, time to address practical needs and to reflect on the promise of cinema.

From this period, I might put forward "Can One Have Hope for the Future of the Film Industry in Iran?" and "This Living Screen: A Discussion of Cinema in Simple Language," two expansive essays of several thousand words, published in weekly installments in 1955 and 1957 in Iran's most successful film magazine, *Setare-ye Cinema.*[1] They were not written by one of the magazine's regular critics but by Samuel Khachikian, the most prominent director of a genre that we might call, following the title of the first retrospective of his work outside Iran at the Cinema Ritrovato in Bologna, Tehran noir.[2] In advance of the anthology in which these essays might appear in their entirety, I offer a passage from each as a way to begin thinking about the state of genre filmmaking and criticism at the time. Each passage takes on a distinctive mood, and the polarity of these moods characterizes much of the efforts by intellectuals to frame the possibilities of cinema in such an environment. There was much to be excited about, but even the optimists had to admit that local production was bound to be uneven given that access to film capital, infrastructure, and professional training were relatively scarce and would remain so for the foreseeable future: "Most of our films' subject matter, and unfortunately some of their inventions, creativity, and mise-en-scène, are imitations of foreign films. The situation has become so bad that filmmakers even 'nationalize' footage of foreign films, forcefully insert it into our own films, and sell it back to the public. These distinguished gentlemen are exactly like some of our music composers who, instead of using our plentiful native resources, use foreign themes and mix it with Iranian music in a way that has caused the folkloric Iranian music to completely lose its color and smell."[3] With a sly reference to nationalization at a time when the public was still coming to terms with the nationalization of oil and the subsequent CIA coup of Iran's elected leader only a few years earlier, Samuel Khachikian addresses concerns around a culture of copying in local productions. Concerns about copying imported styles would soon accompany Khachikian's own work as his noir style became more pronounced. I am drawn to these anxious refrains but also to the moments when they suddenly seem not to matter.

The dark of night covers this city symphony with its black curtain. One-by-one each of the instruments in this symphony fade until all that can be heard in the city's corners is the lullaby of the cabarets. The pale poet is out seeking inspiration from the moonlight, and a neighborhood drunk is sick behind a dirty wall. A beautiful new automobile pulls away from Shah Reza Street on the way to the winding dark roads in the hills of Darband outside the city. The laughter of its well-fed occupants is heard by the hungry woman of the street.[4] The heavy footsteps of the neighborhood beat cop, who wants to impose order, can still be heard. But the city is now asleep. The performers in the symphony, those who give and receive orders, the well off and the downtrodden, are all in their beds asleep.[5]

Here, Khachikian takes a brief break from an itemized critique of the film industry in Iran to present the magazine's readers with a treatment for a Vertovian city symphony. It starts with shutters blinking open and street cleaners bathing the built environment. Rhythmic labor shapes the sound of the city. When the sun sets, the setting shifts to a Tehran noir cityscape. It resembles the urban montage sequences found in his films and repeats motifs from other famous works of film noir. It bears striking resemblance to the opening of *The Naked City* (Dassin, 1948), with some almost identical sentences and similar shutters, street cleaners, and parallel juxtapositions of the ambient sounds of the rich and the poor. Dassin's fusion of noir modernism and city symphony even has a drunk man leaning on a dirty wall. Khachikian's noir treatment (casually embedded in a treatise on the industry) mixes citations, genres, and aesthetic traditions with a self-taught openness that seems to shrug off the very anxieties that pervade this essay and that had characterized much of the criticism of his cohort of filmmakers.

These two passages invite us to consider the tandem moods of vernacular modernism in midcentury Iran: playful and earnest, exuberant and anxious, optimistic and frustrated. On some occasions the forms of imported cinema are greeted with hospitable creative energy, and on others there is a marked cynicism about habits of imitation. The two passages bring together the phenomena discussed in the last two chapters, recycled footage and collage sound, with the subject of this one, the relay of genres and the labor of critics, as they express both anxiety and exuberance about the possibilities of cinema emergent under conditions of relative scarcity. While midcentury circulation worries have taken a material inflection in my previous discussions—the actual labors of maintenance required to mitigate the material wear and physically prepare imported prints to run through projectors in Tehran cinemas—I want to take time here to consider the intellectual labor that gave shape to circulation worries as an aesthetic issue. A sense of *anxiety*, a term sharper and more often associated with conflict than its cousin *worry*, seems more appropriate in describing some of the controversy surrounding the love of crime thrillers in midcentury Iran. Some experience love as careful worry, some as anxiety and excitement about an uncertain future.

Before art cinema emerged in Iran, there was greater uncertainty about definitions of cinema's aesthetic possibility. Critics and filmmakers were edging closer to the outpouring of critical attention to festival modernism that would arrive in the late 1960s and 1970s (some festival appearances began earlier, with directors discussed in this book). Proto-new-wave feature filmmaking would begin in 1965 with such films as *Khesht va Ayeneh* (*Brick and Mirror*, Golestan) and *Shab-e Quzi* (*Night of the Hunchback*, Ghaffary). These achievements were followed by signal ambitious films and a stream of prominent directors of world cinema brought to town by the Tehran International Film Festival in the 1970s. Before this period, those who sought to define prestige production looked to genre production, to a mix of Russian and French film theory, and to the successes of golden ages to navigate the possibilities of the medium in Iran. Film studies knows its global new waves. Global golden ages and prestige genre production it knows less, despite the fact that midcentury national studio production, too, was conceived in circulation. The currents just ran differently than those of the new waves. This is not to say that cinema in Iran experienced a proper golden age between the proliferation of studio production in the mid-1950s and the transformations of the 1960s. The window was too narrow, local production infrastructure still held too small a share of the capital flowing through the movie business, and critics were still reluctant to find value in, or even to review at all, many of the films made in Iran. While the possibilities of festival participation and a stable golden age of production were regular topics of conversation after the mid-1950s, it is probably most accurate to describe the period as one of possibility in which a wealth of compelling films and film criticism looked forward to a future that never materialized in the ways it had been imagined. And it is this framing of possibility that should be appreciated as such. If we follow Kaes, Baer, and Cowan's assertion that we should remain attentive to claims about the promise of cinema as much as the claims of its ontology, to the ways that the theorization of cinema "often occurred in the subjunctive rather than the indicative mood," then this period of cinephilia in production and criticism should compel our attention.[6]

The pages of *Setare-ye Cinema*, the longest-running film magazine read by fans as well as members of the trade, provide access to forms of cinephilia and modernist criticism with a sustained emphasis on the promise of cinema.

I should note at the outset that I make use of *Tehran noir* here as an evocation and not a hard taxonomic term. I am sympathetic to Lalitha Gopalan's call for understanding generic markers of global noir as "part of a promiscuous global cinephilia that has little patience for unitary terms."[7] One's patience for this cycle of midcentury films admittedly would be challenged, just as it was for some critics at the time, if one chose not to proceed with a recognition of the limitations of purist taxonomies. And yet it is valuable to locate the cinephilic allusions of these films in a history of distribution and film journalism that shaped which allusions were possible and successful. The debates around these generic markers in this period, which this chapter labors to trace, often hinged on claims of purist knowledge and accusations of counterfeit. *Setare-ye Cinema* favored certain types of films over others, which gives a sense of the formation of prestige at the time. The journal underrepresented the importance of Hindi and Egyptian films with audiences, and it reserved some of its greatest acts of dismissal for local productions themselves. Films made in Iran were routinely scapegoated by the country's critics as a means to articulate their own standards of aesthetic distinction. The appropriations of film genres from abroad were among the routine targets. I take this historical anxiety over the value of *filmfarsi* not as a position to be defended or proven wrong but as a phenomenon worthy of reflection. Even as one commits to exploring the premise that Hollywood offered a modern vernacular for global filmmakers, critics, and audiences, we should not ignore the wide variation in the types of attachment to it, which depended on distribution context, the resources of the local industry, and the formation of critical institutions in a given period. Circulation creates enthusiasm as well as suspicion, and an analysis of which productions and genres generated buzz in the journals offers a way to consider this ambivalence. The fascination with the crime thriller was among the most important phenomena of a midcentury industrial-critical complex that was in the process of defining, debating, and theorizing the possibilities of local production.

Tehran noir was not the only relayed genre of the emergent industry, but it had an imposing presence. What is remarkable about the status of the crime thriller in Iran in the 1950s is its balanced ambivalence. Crime films sometimes accounted for more than a third of the films made in

Iran annually during this period. At the same time, critics in Iran were following developments around the world pertaining to the careers of authors of crime fiction, the stars of their adaptations, and the directors who stepped up to adapt them. While the local productions in the genre were certainly not exempt from dismissal by critics, some of these films succeeded in making waves both with audiences and with critics. It was a form full of promise, a genre that stood at a charged intersection. Foreign crime thrillers played an important role as the industry sought to move beyond the experimental period of commercial production. Aesthetically ambitious productions in late-1950s Iran, which turned to visually stylized genres as a way to express their ambitions, strained the tensions of the critical binary that largely left local productions out of the discussion of the medium's promise. Because the aesthetic achievements of film noir had been nurtured in conditions of low-budget scarcity even in some of the wealthiest film industries of the world, the genre offered a way to engage with compelling films without the access to capital available to the tent-pole projects of those industries. It allowed assertions about aesthetic choices, authorship, and the development of a deliberate style. But with increased notice came greater scrutiny, which led to claims that some of these newly celebrated films were trading in counterfeit stylistic currency. The enmeshed world of the press and the film industry at this time heightened this anxious exuberance and gave it significant power in managing a public film culture. Noir presented a site of negotiation for these recurring challenges. Through discussions of films made in the orbit of the crime film, we can see the ways in which the industrial/technological challenges interweave with the intellectual/aesthetic ones. In other words, as a vehicle for modern style, one that turns the limitations of technology and production budgets into modernist virtues, noir's successes and failures brought infrastructure and aesthetics into a shared light. As a cycle that drew attention to film form within commercial filmmaking precisely by demonstrating fluency with borrowed forms, Tehran noir was perhaps bound to encounter ambivalence.

The first decade of Samuel Khachikian's filmmaking career offers a pathway through these questions. He was the standout director of crime thrillers in this period, one who had a significant influence within the industry and who fielded much of the criticism of mimicry of imported forms. He was one of several Armenian-Iranians who made the transition from theater to cinema and was a leading director for the foundational Diana Film and Azhir Film studios. Critics in the late 1950s referred to him using the language of world cinema before this was a reality for films

FIGURE 22. Samuel Khachikian. Private collection.

made in Iran. He was to some "the bright face of our cinema" who "one day not far from today will be counted among the players of world cinema" (figure 22).[8] He was referred to as "the Hitchcock of Iran" for both his interest in the thriller and his efforts to elevate the name of the director in an industry where many films did not emphasize authorship. Looking back at the influence of his work, film historian Massoud Mehrabi refers to him as the "avant-garde of crime cinema."[9] At the height of his noir output, Khachikian released the first- and second-highest-grossing films of 1961, *Faryad-e Nime-shab* (*The Midnight Cry*) and *Yek Qadam ta Marg* (*One Step to Death*). The success of these two films prompted a rush in crime thrillers, which composed fully half of the following year's productions. Emulations were layered upon emulations in this period. It was no minor phenomenon. One of the tasks for a period marked by so many degrees of active appropriation is to define and locate the phenomenon in processes of intellectual labor.

Khachikian himself took a proactive role in discussing labors of appropriation and reflecting on the state of the industry and its possibilities, which invites us to think *with* his work as well as about it. He not only reassembled currents in a way that reflected a deep knowledge of film history and theory but also took part in constant reflexive play with these influences. He wrote about the status of the film industry in detailed structural terms, but also in forms of writing that moved playfully between conversational, historical, and experimental literary modes. Suspicious critics accused his films of being counterfeit, films that were themselves about counterfeit and suspicion. The films borrowed and remixed a variety of visual styles and were filled with characters who called attention to their own borrowed styles of dress and interior design. Khachikian had many dandy figures in his films, and he was something of a dandy himself, with his ascot and pencil mustache. His own writing, while taking the topic of the possibility of an art of cinema in Iran seriously, is full of irreverent turns of phrase and ironic gestures of respect for those critics who either attacked his colleagues with personal vendettas or cooed over foreign productions with what he perceived as false adulation. He offered journalists visiting his studio a bright red infusion of sour cherries that he called "Technicolor tea." [10] In this period he took great care and, it seems, a degree of mischievous pleasure in constructing a public face for his work. The citations of film noir (by a director who also knew his German expressionist films and Soviet film theory) are legion in Khachikian's films from this cycle. What does it mean to consider the work of an assembler as the avant-garde of the crime thriller in Iran? Such questions not only are a necessary step toward making sense of an underexplored body of studio films in midcentury Iran, an archive that has only recently become widely accessible; they also expand our understanding of what Jennifer Fay and Justus Nieland describe as central to the consideration of film noir as it was taken up around the world: "noir cinephilia as offering a different, idiosyncratic type of global film history, one that proceeds through loved moments, iconic gestures, and transportable fashions." [11] Khachikian's films reassembled gestures from noir's ever-intermedial existence in order to announce a promising form of cinema. The form of cinephilia at work in his films can be characterized by its concentrated allusions, its modularity, and its play with mixed signals. In a media environment in which there was plenty to fret about, Tehran noir provided a target for anxieties about the industry. It also presented one possibility, for a time, of a cinema worthy of a kind of love.

THE CRIME THRILLER AS CURRENCY IN THE PRESS

A director of crime thrillers who planned out his sequences with detailed shooting scripts, who storyboarded scenes, and who even included director cameos would have a hard time avoiding associations with Hitchcock in Iran, but Khachikian had good reason for not appreciating this ambivalent marker of prestige.[12] While such analogies are often created in the spirit of drawing connections and highlighting aesthetic trajectories (a task shared by historians of these genres), they also reduce an audience's ability to encounter the work as something unique and unfamiliar. They set up dissimilarities from the point of comparison as inconsistencies or failures. We might see Khachikian's distaste for his comparison to Hitchcock as part of a history of defining one's creative process and intellectual property in relation to such global currency. Even when these comparisons increase recognition abroad (one of the stated ambitions from this period), there remains a concern that global arts institutions might use an easy frame of comparison to welcome work from the world with a false hospitality.[13] Media historians, in turn, should avoid a historiography that reproduces the forms of power at work in such comparisons: Khachikian as the "Hitchcock of Iran," Atef Salem as the "Hitchcock of Egypt," Raj Khosla as the "Hitchcock of India." In doing so, however, we might also use such comparisons to examine why and how they stick in a particular context. Hitchcock's functions in the film press of the 1950s, when each of these directors were active, were not the same everywhere. At a time when it was the norm for critics in Iran to celebrate globally recognized filmmakers and reserve withering tones for local productions—particularly, it seems, when those films had aspirations to artistic achievement—Khachikian was one of the few commercially successful directors who fared well with certain critics. Working through the stakes of his comparison to Hitchcock and the critical reception of the crime thriller can help to put this anomaly in context.

Setare-ye Cinema gives some indication of Hitchcock's central role in the framing of the crime thriller during the postwar growth of cinema institutions in Iran. While Hitchcock is not the only prominent figure in the pages of the journal, his interviews, his films, and critics' engagement with those films do stand out. In the period I examined, 1953 to 1959, each of his new releases was advertised and reviewed. Photographs and illustrations of Hitchcock's face appear with frequency, sometimes cut-and-pasted onto posters or lobby cards reduced on the page so that taglines, exhibition information, and praise for the actors could be oriented in Persian text surrounding the original English text of the graphic. In one "photo corner" feature of the journal printed alongside an interview about *I Confess* (1953), Hitchcock's face is

مولن روژ ـ مهتاب
کریستال ـ برلیان ـ زهره

آنتونی پرکینز
جانتلی
جان گاوین
دوبله فارسی در
استودیو مولن روژ

PSYCHO

فیلمی که باید حتماً از ابتدا به بینید و پایان آنرا
برای کسی تعریف نکنید درب های سالن

FIGURE 23. Advertisement using torn and cut-out images for the release of studio Moulin Rouge's dubbed version of *Psycho* (Alfred Hitchcock, 1960). Courtesy of Ehsan Khoshbakht. Viewers are instructed to see this film from the beginning and not to reveal the ending to anyone who has not seen the film.

pasted over Montgomery Clift's belly, emerging from the layout of the original source poster in a sort of collage cameo, and in an advertisement for *The Wrong Man* (1956), a production photo of the director with his arm extended is combined with a scene from the film in the illustration. Suggestive of an act of conjuring, a dark cloud extends from the director's hand and envelops Henry Fonda's head and torso, which is superimposed over a police lineup.[14] This collage using the director's image as a kind of paper puppet continues into the 1960s, with his face and extended hand appearing in ads for screenings of *Strangers on a Train* and *Psycho* (figure 23). Among this steady stream of advertising and critical publicity that showcased Hitchcock as a public figure in the Iranian press, translations of interviews with the director were published, as were translations of synopses and original story material for films including *Rear Window* (1954) and *The Wrong Man*.[15] *Vertigo* received special treatment, with portions of Boileau and Narcejac's original source novel, *D'entre les morts*, translated and serialized in seven installments over two months beginning in July 1958.[16]

In the pages of *Setare-ye Cinema*, then, "Hitchcock" was pieced together through the sustained intellectual labor of editors, translators, critics, and graphic designers. They used the director's name as one way to frame the crime thriller as an object of critical interest, global prestige, and aesthetic sophistication. Much of this critical discussion from the 1950s often took on effusive tones. This was the case for most of the writing on figures whose names had global currency, but Hitchcock's releases had an advantage in their ready-made publicity. *Undisputed master* accompanied the director's name in article titles and advertisements alike.[17] Instances of *Setare-ye Cinema*'s excessive praise might rightfully appear disingenuous or thin. It certainly did to some critics at the time and was, in fact, a topic of continual debate in the pages of the magazine. Critics were ever ready to call out their peers' puff pieces, and the magazine made room for rowdy disagreement. Other threads of discussion in the magazine in the 1950s even looked ahead to the focused auteurism in intellectual circles of the late 1960s, in which critics translated canonical pieces from *Cahiers du cinéma* and *Movie*.[18] Regardless of which side a critic may have taken in these discussions, such positions constituted the labor through which the magazine helped to build and manage cinema audiences. Reviews and advertisements occupied publication space alongside longer translations of interviews in which Hitchcock discusses the production context of his films, his relationship to art cinema, or the difference between mystery and suspense.[19] To understand the splashy celebrations of a global name as fundamentally distinct from more discerning forms of critical labor might overlook their interconnected functions in film publishing in 1950s Iran.

Of course, Hitchcock was only one component of an archive that includes hundreds of items related to the crime thriller in this midcentury publication run. Taken together, these items reveal patterns about terminology, publicity strategies, critical ambitions, and intellectual influences. Although *film noir* was in use elsewhere in the 1950s, it did not emerge in the pages of this journal until the following decade. The most common terminology critics used to describe the genre was *police and crime* (*polisi va jena'i*), but those who read French also used the cognate *policier*. There were mentions of the *Série noire*, the French imprint that circulated mostly Anglo-American hard-boiled fiction, but the instances I found from the 1950s do not use *noir* as a cognate (*serie siah*). Film marketing appears to have been drawn to film-noir graphics and retitling. For example, Cinema Moulin Rouge regularly applied a banner graphic titled "Along the Sidewalk" (*Kenar-e Piadeh-ro*) to their coming attractions advertisements. The banner included a corner sketch of a woman leaning on a lamppost at night with a cigarette in her mouth. This film noir iconography accompanied advertisements for urban thrillers including *Diary of a Bad Girl* (Moguy, 1956) and *Down Three Dark Streets* (Laven, 1954), but it was also used for adventure films such as *Desert Sands* (Selander, 1955). The noir signifiers of films were regularly accentuated in their translated titles, and some even changed over time. *Dark City* (*Shahr-e Tarik*) was preferred over *Crime Wave* (De Toth, 1954).[20] *The Pushover* (Quine, 1954) became *The Traitor Detective* (*Karagah-e Kha'en*) and then became *The Misguided Detective* (*Karagah-e Gomrah*) for its run at another cinema nine months later.[21]

Alongside these advertisements and short reviews, critics made extensive efforts to engage with film noir in the pages of the magazine, which took the form of encyclopedic filmographies, histories, and long-form translations. There are three elements that I want to highlight in this material: the critics' and editors' attention to intersections between literature and film, their specific periodizing interest in the genre as a transnational postwar phenomenon, and the way the genre offered them a means to disentangle cinema's social or moral value from its aesthetic value. The vital intermedial connections between literature and cinema have been mainstays of the scholarship on film noir since the term's establishment by critics. These foundational aesthetic crosscurrents and tie-in opportunities notwithstanding, one might not expect the degree to which the literary aspect of the genre was discussed in a magazine called *Cinema Star*. The magazine contained extensive discussion of the serialized stories from which the films were adapted. This discussion spanned from the advertisements to translated material to the writing of its regular film critics. The full-page advertisement for *Crime Wave* is composed of three lobby card images surrounded by several lines of text that mention the prestige of the Warner Bros. company (twice) along with an explanation that the story was originally serialized in the *Saturday Evening Post* and "remains one of the best crime stories published in that magazine."[22] Stories of crime films were regularly included as entertainments in their own right, sometimes in single-issue synopses of no more than a couple thousand words, as was the case with *Rear Window* and *The Big Heat* (Lang, 1953). Other times, original story material for a film was translated and serialized as more substantial reading material. This was the case with *The Wrong Man* and *Witness to Murder* (Rowland, 1954).[23] The serialized story of *Vertigo* took up considerable space on the pages of the journal during the summer of 1958 as the film, which had its American release that January, made its way around the world. This serialized fiction was useful at a time when dubbing was still an intermittent and experimental process. At a time when disruptive intertitles were still common for undubbed sound films, even complete titling received special mention in advertisements. The ad for *I Confess* (Hitchcock, 1953) specifies, just below the title, that the film will screen "with complete Persian subtitles," presumably to distinguish this quality translation from other films with incomplete titling.[24] Synopses and story translations were special features presented for enjoyment as attractions on their own, but they could also be used as screening guides in situations with no dubbing and suboptimal titling. Those who made use of these serialized film noir stories as supplements to moviegoing encountered the genre in its full intermedial fashion.[25] Not only did cinema fans have access to more complete translations in the magazine, they sometimes had access to hard-boiled prose translated directly from the *Saturday Evening Post*, or from French source material two translations removed from the American screenplay. Such was the case with *D'entre les morts*. Historians of film noir have stressed the importance of moments in which modernist film critics fostered linkages between the print culture of postwar crime fiction and cinema audiences. The work of translation and curation in magazines like this one thus shows how widespread this process had become by the late 1950s.

The currents of transnational circulation of postwar crime fiction and cinema were not only demonstrated by *Setare-ye Cinema*'s style of compilation. They were explicitly discussed in its articles, where authors and editors made distinct efforts to consider the genre's aesthetics in a postwar historical context. Regular subscribers to the magazine in the 1950s had opportunities to read features about prominent figures in the creation of crime thrillers by émigrés in Hollywood including Fritz Lang, Otto Preminger, Ida Lupino, and Peter Lorre. They could read about Americans making crime films in France, including Jules Dassin and Eddie Constantine. They had access to articles about the prominent novelists of the genre, in which they could read about the stylistic differences between Mickey Spillane and Peter Cheney as representatives of American and British crime fiction.[26] These articles did draw links to crime films and detective fiction from decades past. They mentioned 1930s gangster movies, Hitchcock's early features, and Arthur Conan Doyle, but they also highlighted the specificity of hard-boiled fiction and postwar cinema. "These days, works about secret agents and detectives have changed dramatically. The modern, atomic world requires a different approach than the one offered by Sherlock Holmes with his curved pipe and special cap."[27] In this article on "cinema and crime films," the brutality and cynicism of Bulldog Drummond, Mike Hammer, and Lemmy Caution are held in contrast to the "démodé film detective" represented here by Holmes.[28] This discussion of the tensions of atomic-age modernity continued through subsequent essays published in the magazine, including a translation of an essay by BBC critic Gordon Gow in which he discusses the postwar crime film as a symptom of "our world of excitement, anxiety, and nervous exhaustion."[29] The essays and translations by these critics demonstrate how much of the archive of film noir criticism is distributed around the world.

The third pattern that stands out in the critical writing about film noir in the magazine is the tension between two forms of critical prestige: a tradition of film criticism concerned with social uplift meets an emergent interest in cinema aesthetics. Such tensions have accompanied the medium of cinema since the origins of the feature film with American organizations like the National Board of Review advocating for "aesthetic, not moralistic censorship" in the 1910s. The crime thriller, particularly in its morbid postwar varieties, was less amenable than other genres to narratives of cinema as a vehicle for social uplift. It thus gave cinephile writers in Iran an opportunity to distinguish their work from other cultural critics who may have been less concerned with possibilities of cinema as a medium of modern aesthetics. Cultural critics warning of the moral dangers of the crime film were, of course, common almost everywhere. Their work spanned the American press discussing its own national products, French writing on the crime film as a threat to versions of national culture, and concerns of British colonial powers that American crime films would undermine their legitimacy among moviegoers in the colonies. What is worth stressing in this case is that film critics who were writing about crime thrillers in *Setare-ye Cinema* did see debates about aesthetic or social criticism in local terms. "A Little Bit about the History of the Crime Film," from 1956, offers an extensive discussion of the filmography of artistically notable noir directors and actors of the postwar period, but the material is framed by a partial turn away from censorship based on the perceived social value of films. The author discusses the prevalence of the "misconception that crime films cause moral decadence and corruption among viewers," an idea that is "prevalent in improving countries (for example, our own) where it is applied with even greater dogmatism," whereas in "prominent countries of the world such as the US, UK, France, and Italy, crime films are not only marketable, they receive a surprisingly warm welcome."[30] In order to understand these films as artistic achievements, evidenced by their ability to circulate and gain international attention, the author brackets questions of morality and social uplift in favor of questions of aesthetics. It is this dandyish turn toward style, in which aesthetic sophistication peels away from fears of social decay, that makes it possible to understand the appeal of postwar crime thrillers, which "have emerged from their dry and monotonous past to become an international phenomenon."[31] The issues of transnationalism and periodization of film noir appear here in the context of an essay that seeks, if not to eschew questions of social uplift entirely, to switch over to aesthetic questions central to a definition of the medium. This tension would become a recurring element in local noir productions in the years to come. The crime film attracted filmmakers interested in the aesthetics of the medium, and these stylists placed questions of aesthetic value on the table for cultural critics in the habit of discussing the medium of cinema in terms of its social value. The critical life of Hitchcock and other stylists of foreign crime thrillers provide context for the markers of prestige, disputes about originality, and excitement about genre cinema that accompanied some of the most successful films made in Iran of the decade, for which production climbed and which finally found their way into some of the first-run theaters that typically only showed imports.

Setare-ye Cinema's preoccupations demonstrate the global currency of the crime thriller and its stars for an emergent industry hard at work on establishing codes of authorship and a sense of the aesthetic traditions of the medium. The magazine took several turns through the decades of its successful publication, but it cut its teeth in this milieu—a collaboration between a group of young 1950s cinephiles and a bookseller who happened to own a shop in the arcade across the street from Cinema Metropole, where they liked to hang out.[32] It is significant that a single publication was functioning to circulate noir fiction, advertise the adaptations of this fiction for Tehran cinemas, review these films for fans, and write histories of this fiction as well as the films. For this reason, I see a benefit in examining patterns of exploring modern literary traditions, atomic-age periodization, and cinema aesthetics through the socially cynical genre of film noir as part of a coherent body of work within the magazine.[33] The magazine, as a critical institution and one of the most coherent archival sources available, provides a sense of what it could mean for local productions to recycle film noir plots and to sample fragments of their scores. One of the most compelling features of film noir is that it is a form of modernism derived from a combination of pulp (which is an index of circulation: pulp can outrun rag) and extraterritorial critical attention (a generative attention from modernist critics fascinated by this work that came from somewhere else). The intellectual labor of a magazine like *Setare-ye Cinema*, therefore, is film noir in action. Noir is a genre in which the signal is dependent on its points of relay. There is something misguided about conceiving of the global archive of noir as echoes of a genre invented elsewhere when the very idea of film noir came into existence through global circulation and through critical curiosity about its elsewhereness.

CURRENCY DISPUTES

"Ultimately, *The Midnight Cry* is a counterfeit film about counterfeit dollars."[34]

Houshang Kavousi, *Honar va Cinema*, 1961

"It is the dollar that makes films by Cecil DeMille, not his imagination or his labor. It is the dollar that makes those spectacular crowd scenes in *Desires of the Emperor*. It is the dollar that carries talentless actors like Esther Williams and Errol Flynn to the pinnacles of wealth and fame while the Iranian actor that you see on the screen has worked tirelessly day and night, has not slept, and is thirsty and hungry."[35]

Samuel Khachikian, *Setare-ye Cinema*, 1955

However generative the elsewhere of film noir may have been for the critical establishment in 1950s Iran, critics' interactions with their own industry's noir productions took an entirely different path. While some took notice of the crime thriller as a genre with promise, even ambitious crime films faced a long-standing tendency to dwell in the inadequacies of local productions. The two-part takedown of a new *filmfarsi* release was a regular sight in film reviews, that is, when critics bothered with local productions at all. A review would begin with a few paragraphs about the technical failures of its lighting, framing, editing, and sound and then follow with a few more about how the film in question was artistically derivative. Because the early studios were configured around material scarcity, a robust dubbing culture, the collage score, and the circulation of generic types from abroad, disagreements about what constitutes intellectual ownership of films were the industry's inheritance. A community of film critics with an interest in cultivating knowledge of

FIGURE 24. Counterfeit dollars in *Faryad-e Nime-shab* / *The Midnight Cry* (Samuel Khachikian, 1961).

film history could readily generate suspicion around its processes and patterns of recycling genres. Ambitious productions were not spared. Even better crime films received backhanded compliments, as with Parviz Davaii's review of *Sodagaran-e Marg* (*Merchants of Death*, Malek Motie'i, 1962), each paragraph of which points out a different element of the film as essentially "not bad for *filmfarsi*."[36] Such suspicions were in fact more likely to be taken seriously once those who worked in the industry sought to establish the standards of their professions and some filmmakers began to actively manage their careers in a public forum. The question is less about whether these claims of technical or aesthetic inadequacy were correct. I am more concerned here with where authors directed blame for problems and how they reserved praise for promising forms. The global currency of modern genre filmmaking, especially the crime film, attracted significant attention. Each faction in the disputes about the genre's global currency prescribed a correct way of operating within the industry and a method for fostering its sustainability.

To see how film noir functioned for these recurring disputes, let me turn to one of the most dramatic points of tension: a public feud between Khachikian and Houshang Kavousi, the film critic and quondam director of film noir who coined the pejorative term *filmfarsi*.[37] Khachikian did publicly feud with others, but whereas those were mainly business disagreements, Kavousi attacked his films on artistic grounds. The two had overlapped briefly at Diana Film studio in its early years. Khachikian's career took off with a few successful productions, leading to the cofounding of Azhir Film in 1957.[38] Kavousi pursued the path of critic and programmer, although he did take on a few film projects. While there certainly were films that dealt with crime, detection, dark urban themes, and fatal love before Kavousi took on the role of director, he considered his most notable work, *Hefdah Ruz be E'dam* (*Seventeen Days to Execution*, 1956), the first true policier made in Iran. The lack of critical and commercial success of this original film noir surely fueled this particular feud throughout the period of Khachikian's successes as a director of film noir.

Kavousi's assessments of Khachikian's work are summed up in the title of his review for Khachikian's *The Midnight Cry*: "a counterfeit film." He attacked the film because it "exudes a foreign smell in the movie theaters."[39] Most of Khachikian's films from this period included some form of cynical brutality, gramophone jazz, a criminal underworld, femme fatale characters, and location shooting of Tehran at night, but *The Midnight Cry* is saturated with all of these. As a film full of allusions, and the top-grossing Tehran production of the year, it made for a large target. The film's central character configurations bear strong similarities to *Gilda* (Vidor, 1946). One of its triangulations centers on the character Zhila, who is married to a crime boss (a counterfeiter of US currency himself) and attempts to seduce his young bodyguard, Amir, with whom she had been previously acquainted. In his review of the film, Kavousi told his readers that he learned by accident that Azhir Film had the only Tehran print of *Gilda* in its possession, presumably to copy it in detail, in the months during which *The Midnight Cry* was in production (figure 25).[40] Khachikian's title, too, may have been borrowed from a recent crime film in circulation. I have not found an export record for *A Cry in the Night* (Tuttle, 1956) in the Middle East material in the Warner Bros. archive, but the film played in Tehran at the Warner-affiliated Cinema Rex in October 1958. It was billed as a new release in *Setare-ye Cinema*, "the latest production about crime and passion by the Warner Bros. Company."[41] Its translated title, *Faryad-e Nime-shab*, was identical.[42] Even decades later, Khachikian appears to have been sensitive about the accusations of imitating *Gilda* and other crime films, claiming that his screenwriter had seen *Gilda* at that time

FIGURE 25. Advertisement promoting the classic status and the global simultaneity of a 1959 screening of *Gilda* (Charles Vidor, 1946) at cinema Radio City in Tehran. Courtesy of Ehsan Khoshbakht. The ad copy indicates that on the occasion of Columbia Pictures' thirty-fifth anniversary, a new print is being shown simultaneously in fifty-four capitals of the world.

but he himself had not. Rather than taking a purely defensive posture in this response, however, he noted these affinities as evidence of his success as a stylist: "I take pride in the fact that the shots of my films are likened to others. . . . My shot selection and camera angles were so successful that critics thought they must have been copied from other films."[43] In these ongoing discussions, in which the intellectual ownership of an aesthetic tradition is at stake, it is significant that Khachikian claims his choices as evidence of his knowledge of the medium and as constitutive of his standout style.

Kavousi's film was, itself, just as enmeshed in the fabric of crime-film citation, and he was ultimately taken to task by his own colleagues for this very reason. *Seventeen Days* was not an original script but an adaptation of Cornell Woolrich's *Phantom Lady* (1942). The appeal of Woolrich makes good sense for a critic aspiring to make what he believed to be the first policier in Iranian cinema history, but it also created problems not faced by films that borrowed from multiple sources. Woolrich was one of the most widely adapted writers of hard-boiled fiction inside and outside the United States. His biographer notes the translatability of his work in Argentina, the USSR, Japan, France, and Germany.[44] His presence in Iran fits within the context of this broader adaptation of his work into films around the world. At the time that

Kavousi was working on *Seventeen Days*, the most famous film adaptation of Woolrich's work, *Rear Window*, was making top ten lists in journals such as *Cahiers du cinéma*, which were read by critics in Iran. Woolrich's writing was not always credited in publicity material, but Paramount's posters and the full-page advertisement that circulated in the film magazines of the late summer of 1954 in Iran featured the author's name.[45] *Setare-ye Cinema* itself published a five-page translated summary of the film in the summer of 1955 and credited Woolrich with the story in the title material for that piece.[46] *Phantom Lady* had been adapted ten years earlier by Universal Pictures and Robert Siodmak. Kavousi may have known Siodmak's version.

While Woolrich was a reasonable author to adapt, critics noted that the specific plot of *Phantom Lady* presented problems for an adaptation in Iran. A man goes out into the city after quarreling with his wife and spends an evening at a cabaret show with a woman he meets in a café. The two never exchange names and part shortly after the show. When he returns home, he finds a detective in his apartment, who reveals to him that his wife has just been murdered. The phantom lady from the café becomes his alibi, but neither he nor the detectives can locate her. The plot flips the usual process of detection and conviction. The detective's work establishes the paranoid premise, and the courtroom scene is over, with a death sentence, by the end of what would become the screenplay's first act. Kavousi's title references the fatalistic plotting in which each of the novel's chapter titles counts down to the day of his execution. A second detection plot is initiated by the man's paramour, whose relationship with him had provided the prosecutor with a motive. It is a wrong-man plot combined with a gaslight plot, with its typical climactic scenes presented out of order. A fan of hard-boiled fiction might find its reversals and restructurings of detection plots inventive, but without such context, it is an odd text even before being translated. The negative review of *Seventeen Days* in *Setare-ye Cinema* mentions specifically that this aspect of the plot pushes the limits of suspension of disbelief.[47] It also questions the love relationships in the film, struggling to make sense of how the hero of the story managed relations with three women simultaneously: his wife, his lover, and the stranger at the café. These relationships were implausible to reviewers, especially considering that the story was meant to portray the main character as a vulnerable and precarious investigator. The circumstances of the protagonist misaligned with forms of masculinity readily at hand in popular genre films made in Iran.

FIGURE 26. *Hefdah Ruz be E'dam / Seventeen Days to Execution* (Houshang Kavousi, 1956). National Film Archive of Iran.

The adaptation might have been more effective had it emphasized this sense of dread and vulnerability, but it was directed as a straightforward procedural. I had the opportunity to watch a print of this rare film on a Steenbeck, on a hot summer day during Ramadan, at the National Film Archive of Iran. This viewing, even after correcting for how it may have been influenced by a lack of hydration, did confirm that the film's artistic choices lean toward a demonstration of by-the-book mastery. *Seventeen Days* at times feels encumbered with demonstrations of knowledge. Its most conspicuous shots align with iconic scenes from cinephiles' favorite crime films. The recurring image of the protagonist's head, wearing a noose, superimposed over a clock (with skulls for numbers) signifies fate in the manner of a Fritz Lang film (figure 26). Critics listed this repeated image, alongside Kavousi's cavalier use of unusual camera angles and pacing, as nonsensical (figure 27).[48] These images are layered with references to film noir that the director would have known from his work as a critic. But their perceived heavy-handed citations failed to land with Kavousi's colleagues or with audiences. These elements were thoroughly critiqued when the film was released:

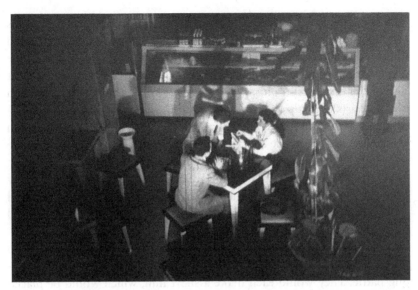

FIGURE 27. *Hefdah Ruz be E'dam / Seventeen Days to Execution* (Houshang Kavousi, 1956). National Film Archive of Iran.

"It appears that Dr. Kavousi wanted to jam into his film anything and everything he has seen and read. Because of this, his film is just a series of moving theories of filmmaking."[49]

Much of the criticism in the review followed a familiar form. It was directed at failures in the craft of the film: its unimaginative camera work and editing, its inappropriate scoring, its failure to create a truly sadistic villain resulting in an awkwardly likeable murderer, and its inability to create suspense due to a failure to generate the psychological intensity appropriate for a race against a deadline at the gallows. These observations about the film's uneven craft are not inaccurate, but they are perhaps ungenerous and not exclusive attributes of this film. The film was not exactly an inept film. It was an ambitious critics' film that creaked under the weight of its ideas rather than engaging its viewer with them. The author's identity is not listed in this particular article in *Setare-ye Cinema*. According to film historian Ahmad Amini, Kavousi believed that this article was written by Hajir Dariush, who wrote a regular column for the magazine.[50] Dariush had written a similarly harsh review of the film in the journal *Omid-e Iran*. Other accounts suggest that the article was written collectively by the editorial staff at the magazine and possibly by the editor in chief at the time, Robert Ekhart, which may have led to an act of retaliation in which Ekhart's name was forcibly removed from the magazine's credits (he was under thirty and therefore technically ineligible to run a magazine).[51] This collaborative explanation makes sense given the modular nature of the long article, its use of the first-person plural, and the regretful tone at the outset when the author(s) explain the awkwardness of taking one of their own colleagues to task. Like much of Kavousi's own critical work, the criticism of his film illustrates the charged internal politics that characterized the scene of Iran's film intellectuals at the time.

The rivalry between Kavousi and Khachikian in the press occasionally took on the almost playful dimension that one hopes to find in a good public feud. Uplift of the industry was a value that both of them shared despite having opposing prescriptions for what was necessary to accomplish it. In 1958, the filmmaker and investor Said Neyvandi attempted to create a forum in which they might settle their grievances in a filmmaking battle. They would each make a short film, which would be placed in competition and judged by a panel of experts. The press around this battle took on an almost comic dimension, with Khachikian immediately agreeing to the competition. Kavousi treaded more carefully and, verbose critic that he was, wrote a series of lengthy conditions to his participation in the competition. He first dismissed the competition and Khachikian's status as an intellectual. "As we know in athletic competitions . . . the two sides usually do not face each other unless they are in the same weight class, and so it would be better for Mr. Khachikian to find a competitor at his level of taste and knowledge."[52] Not wanting to be the one to run from the challenge, however, he accepted it provided that he would only be judged on the merits of *Seventeen Days* (not a new short: "I do not have this kind of time to waste"), and that the panel must be composed of film critics in France (not Iran).[53] He agreed to serve as translator for this enterprise, due to what he indicated were his superior language skills, but refused to pay the costs. When Khachikian casually agreed to accept the costs of transporting their prints to France and back, Kavousi decided that Khachikian should also pay for the costs of a new print of *Seventeen Days* from the camera negatives. This new condition finally made the competition impossible, and the matter was dropped.[54] The saga of this competition, which over several issues of the magazine had begun to resemble a comedy plot with Kavousi as straight man, recalls familiar debates about originality and its anxieties. Kavousi felt that the cold reception of his film would be redeemed by French film critics' ability to distinguish true *film noir* from mere *filmfarsi*.

While it is hard to imagine that this performance of conflict did not have a tongue-in-cheek aspect to it, Khachikian did take these debates to heart. As a filmmaker who had been working to establish a sense of authorship within a largely authorless industry, one who framed his films as authored works despite being continually attacked by certain critics, it would not be unexpected for him to dismiss the critical establishment outright. But Khachikian took a generous view of the possibility of critical labor. Not only did he see an essential value in sustained criticism of Iranian films, but he defended the separation of disciplines. He held that a critic should not be an experienced maker in the industry and should focus on the profession of writing as its own sphere. A critic's technical understanding was less helpful to the industry than an ability to serve as an interlocutor. Even in response to rather personal attacks from critics like Kavousi, Khachikian was able to separate out his assessment of the profession and consider the work of the critic in institutional terms. Rather than point out instances of counterfeit as individual failings, the critic might work with the other film institutions to shore up an industry against "the dollars that make DeMille films."

AESTHETIC STANDARDS AND SCARCE RESOURCES

Khachikian's writings discussed critical labor on the same list as tax subsidies, festival structures, censorship boards, and unionization. The structural comparison of industries, of imagining celebrated directors of the moment (or of the past) operating within the system in place in midcentury Iran, was something of a refrain in Khachikian's writings. He mentioned this in both of his long, serialized essays in *Setare-ye Cinema* and in multiple interviews. "Their Excellencies Elia Kazan and Cecil DeMille, if placed in the current conditions in Iran, would be able to accomplish nothing. . . . Foreign film companies are well equipped and carefree whereas the Iranian producer has to go door-to-door in search of raw stock, often paying inflated prices for it without even knowing if the stock's shelf life has expired."[55] A later interview with the director was titled with this refrain: "Our Working Conditions Would Bring Charlie Chaplins and De Sicas to Their Knees."[56] For Khachikian, cinema production in Iran could and should have an organic connection to the acclaimed works brought in by importers. In other words, while filmmakers and critics would have been unrealistic to have not acknowledged the real infrastructural disadvantages of the local industry, he claimed that they should not place these productions in an entirely different category from those imported films that commanded high ticket prices in first-run Tehran movie houses. When local critics inflated their praise for Hollywood and European cinemas, they flattened their analysis and thus countered the very awareness of currents in global cinema that they sought to cultivate. Instead, Khachikian repeatedly claimed in his writings, critics should develop professional commitments that would reliably lead filmmakers in Iran to the same high standards these critics claimed to support when they trashed *film-farsi* and lauded the craft of wealthier production contexts.

Khachikian's prescriptions for the uplift of the national industry were systemic. Key for him were tax reform, professionalization, technical training, an organized division of labor, and a reliable supply chain. Institutions of film criticism would need to share his holistic approach to the industry and stand firm in their ethical commitment to holding him and his colleagues accountable for their work within this system: "Our film critics should not complain about the tastelessness of our native Ginas [Lolobrigida] and Ava Gardners, because they are the very people who are publishing full-color pictures of these 'artists' on the back of their magazines."[57] Imitative tastes, the argument goes, derive not only from a lack of imagination but from publishing norms. Khachikian called out critics and editors for a lack of responsibility, producers for backing shortsighted cash-grab projects, audiences for resisting quality films, and the government for not protecting local productions and not establishing formal training in film as it had in many other crafts. Statements like these point out underlying factors driving currency disputes. However personal and idiosyncratic arguments over cheap imitation could become, these quarrels had structural causes.

Beyond cultural institutions, Khachikian points out the necessity for reform in even the basic material systems necessary for a studio to function properly. The problems with the systems of acquiring raw stock are compounded by the unreliability of the infrastructure needed to expose it properly. The studios had to buy stock from intermediaries who engaged in price gouging with questionable stock, which had already been unreasonably taxed during import. Without institutions of quality control, stock was a liability for a studio that was already under budget constraints that prevented it from reshooting scenes. And even perfect stock depended on a reliable electrical grid for proper exposure. "The lighting for our scenes is dependent on the electricity office. We sometimes have to stop shooting abruptly in the middle of our work day. Because of this, using color film stock is impossible. We cannot count on having enough light for proper exposure."[58] Mehdi Missaghieh, the influential producer who worked with Khachikian in the late 1950s, offered a similar assessment of the challenges faced by unreliable access to electrical infrastructure. He complained that even when he went through all of the proper channels to procure permits for electricity necessary to shoot essential scenes for their films, they were still denied power at the last minute. For *Shabneshini dar Jahannam* (*Party in Hell*, an ambitious production of its time) they had to rely on American institutions in Tehran to share their private electricity. "We have energy permits, and still we must beg for electricity from foreigners. Is this something that an industry in our country deserves?"[59] Both Khachikian and Missaghieh note the aesthetic impact of such conditions. The studios could certainly adapt to unreliable stock and electricity, but such flexibility affects choices about shooting ratio, film speed, lighting schemes, and color. For directors and producers with aesthetic ambition in a film industry moving out of its experimental period, reliable production standards would open up possibilities, even without a significant increase in access to capital. Professionalization of institutions and standardization of resources would allow them to focus attention on developing aesthetic fluency with the tools at hand.

When film critics addressed technical flaws in local productions, they often framed their prescriptions in simple developmental terms. Better tools, more expensive and updated cameras, lighting, editing, and sound equipment, would lead to better films. By contrast, while Khachikian complained about conditions of scarcity in the industry in Iran, he did not take a deterministic view of available technology. He was careful to avoid assumptions that had led other writers to either a fatalistic condemnation of the industry or a false confidence in better equipment as a panacea. He recognized scarcity in all of its details, from the ability to professionalize actors to the ways the electrical grid and film stock limited lighting choices. In his "Hope for the Future" essay, Khachikian took issue with others' inability to see the aesthetic possibility in scarcity.[60] He argued instead that the problem was not lack of technology or equipment but lack of artistic commitment and knowledge of cinema history. He took the datedness of studio equipment as a fair point but pointed out that this equipment equaled the technology available to Hollywood or European filmmakers twenty years earlier, and there were numerous masterpieces made in these cinemas before that time. Khachikian mentions Stiller, Seastrom, L'Herbier, Gance, Griffith, German silent cinema, and Russian cinema before and after the revolution. He quotes Pudovkin multiple times and mentions those aspects of Griffith's and Chaplin's work that would have also been relayed by Soviet film theorists.[61] Working within conditions of scarcity, Khachikian argues, was part of the production realities, and the aesthetic theories, of each of these figures, so there is no need to wait for a certain threshold of technological capital before taking the medium seriously. The industry should, instead, identify its own future in the canonized achievements of the past, which offer a contemporary director in Iran an education in how to do more with less.

Cinema studies is acquainted with aesthetics of scarcity in non-Western cinemas primarily through the generation that followed this one. Manifestos of aesthetics of hunger have, as a result of a generation of scholarship on these cinemas, found their way into surveys of world cinema. Longer histories of aesthetics of scarcity, histories that reach back into commercial and genre filmmaking in small industries that bear little resemblance to the films that would later succeed at festivals, are only beginning to emerge. These histories constitute a crucial part of the imaginary of modern world cinema. Khachikian and Kavousi both contributed impassioned critical commentary on the possibilities of their industry in the context of cinemas of the world. Khachikian's writing in the late 1950s contains practical prescriptions, aesthetic knowledge, and a structural sense of the industry's division of labor. Writing and studying cinema history when he was between films, he articulated a commitment to aesthetics within a small commercial filmmaking operation. Kavousi's critical assessment of *filmfarsi* was itself elegant in its takedowns of films and continues to influence the understanding of these films today. Both of these writers, along with several others that I have cited only briefly, contributed to a discourse of modernism in world cinema before the better-known new wave modernisms. They both looked to festivals and foreign awards as possibilities (*Party in Hell* did screen in Berlin, Kavousi did push for a French jury for *Seventeen Days*, and *The Midnight Cry* played in Italy), but they remained active for some time without relying on these festivals.

The prestige crime thriller offered one way of framing the possibilities for this small film industry in relation to world cinema. In Missaghieh's words, "I vow before the people of Iran that, as long as the government offices cooperate and do not obstruct my work, my films will be equal to the best American and European films on the market. If not, our society can feel free to condemn me."[62] He made this proclamation at the start of his collaboration with Khachikian on the crime-film focused

Azhir Film. Kavousi's adaptation of Cornell Woolrich had been released a year earlier. The crime film created contentious disputes. Filmmakers and critics feuded over which sorts of engagement with noir's global currency were correct and which were counterfeit. But for many in this period, the genre could offer an effective means of aligning the interests of film audiences, critics, offices of government regulation, and ambitious studio expansion.

MODULARITY AND FLUENCY

Turning to the craft of the films in Khachikian's Tehran noir cycle raises new questions that complicate disputes over counterfeit and imitation. Resemblances to imported film noir drew significant debate, but some elements of the six films in the cycle—*Tufan dar Shahr-e Ma* (*Storm in Our City*), *Faryad-e Nime-shab* (*The Midnight Cry*), *Yek Qadam ta Marg* (*One Step to Death*), *Delhoreh* (*Anxiety*), *Zarbat* (*The Strike*), and *Sarsam* (*Delirium*)—present as more invested in film noir than others. This was a recurring conversation when four of Khachikian's films screened at Il Cinema Ritrovato in Bologna in 2017. What to do with the ways in which the genre is intermittently evoked and altered, sometimes testing the limits of recognizability? The task of accounting for the patterns of these resemblances and dissimilarities is part of identifying the kinds of work the genre was able to perform globally in the 1950s. And these tasks are not exclusive to Tehran. They align, for example, with Corey Creekmur's observations when he argues for understanding 1950s Bombay noir as "resembl[ing] Hollywood noir on its surface but not at its heart."[63] What are some of the most salient elements of a cycle of genre films that is so full of allusive style and yet also sends mixed signals? How might we understand the patterns in this cycle as responses to pressures of local conditions of scarcity as well as to the pressures of scrutiny as the films engaged with the global currency of modern cinema with some success?

The films from Khachikian's noir cycle lend themselves to two approaches to these questions. First, an analysis of the films should attend to the modular intensity of their construction. That is, some attention should be directed to the relationship between part and whole within and across these films. Modular sequences have a relatively high degree of stand-alone stylistic or generic integrity that, while often incongruous from one scene to the next, are highly planned and repeated across multiple films. The second approach, discussed in the next section, addresses the forms of code switching at work sometimes within a single scene, particularly around themes of kin, love, and home. Both approaches highlight the fluency of dissemblance in the films. As Khachikian's strongest critics made clear, if a film looked like film noir, it would not do to simply be a provincial film in a counterfeit wrapper. It needed to have comparable functions: to take up noir's forms of expression, to generate anticipation and expectations upon its release, and to encourage cinephilia. But placing local genre production in conversation with noir from elsewhere was easier said than done. The fate of *Seventeen Days* pointed out that adhering tightly to a formula or to-the-letter adaptation, no matter how pedigreed the story or knowledgeable the filmmaker, was hardly a guarantee that a production would come closer to the returns or critical praise of imported films. Purism did not seem to define a sustainable or effective way to reject the perceived sloppiness of *filmfarsi*. What stands out in Khachikian's craft is a dandyish enthusiasm for juxtaposition, combined with a commitment to professionalized control of these elements. The most successful iterations of film noir, as anxious as they may have been, demonstrate a nonpurist fluency.

Most productions at this time interrupted formulas as much as they repeated patterns. The well-made ones demonstrated fluency derived from sources ranging from Persian or Armenian folklore to the staples of melodrama found in Hindi and Egyptian films that screened in Iran. Khachikian's films were particularly omnivorous. His films switch from film noir situations, to rock-and-roll comic dance performances, and then again to cityscape montage sequences. Sequences such as the one he describes in "This Living Screen" became a hallmark of his work during this cycle. The Fireworks Wednesday city symphony sequence in *Storm in Our City* links spaces of the "Mambo Rock" dance in the hills outside of the city, through the downtown bustle, and then through the speakers of an RCA console stereo into the home of the film's privileged family. The sequence traces the labor and energy that drive the city. Bricklayers, furniture makers, and blacksmiths exercise their craft in a rhythm that makes it unsurprising that Khachikian quotes Soviet theorists of montage in his writings. The montage links electrified streets with the factories that use the same power. The multisensory linkages of *Man with a Movie Camera* (1929)—its cuts between pungent film splicing solution and acetone nail polish remover in a beauty salon—find a place in this Fireworks Wednesday sequence. Images of steam rising from a press around workers in a professional laundry are intercut with images of a street kabob vendor fanning vapors on his grill. The sequence, like the one before it, works as a stand-alone attraction full of allusive play with film styles. It also functions as a bridge. It links different modules of the film—the main characters arrive back at their homes before the next act—and it links themes of labor and recreation in a series of images that momentarily demonstrate fluency with forms of nonfiction montage.

The films' modularity made it possible for them to refuse purist restraint (a mark of their exuberance) without giving up aesthetic control (a problem when working under the dual challenges of critical scrutiny and scarce resources). Khachikian's shooting scripts illustrate how bureaucratic function and aesthetic ambition could align in the industry at the time. One would miss important aspects of these films' construction if they took the lack of resemblance to a stable model as evidence of the filmmaker's lack of deliberate craft. A filmmaker could count on a level of unpredictability that would bring world directors to their knees, which increased the stakes of realistic and practical preproduction. Khachikian and his colleagues referred to his method of sequencing and planning, excessive compared with other filmmakers of the time, by its French cognate: "In my découpage . . . I described every scene so meticulously that if, for some reason I was unable to make it to the set, my assistant director could shoot the scene according to my detailed descriptions."[64] Shooting scripts offered several practical advantages for working with scarce resources, unpredictable production schedules, and a diverse group of technicians. Meager budgets and limits on stock and electricity tended to favor straightforward artistic choices on set. For a director interested in deliberate camera movement, dramatic variations in lighting, and precision staging in depth, tight control over shooting ratio and technical labor was a necessity. Shooting scripts allowed Khachikian and the studio to budget raw footage and electricity for his relatively complicated work on set. On each of his découpage worksheets, he typically accounted for every second of exposed film and noted whether a scene required "high" or "low" quantities of light. The language choices of these detailed descriptions reflect the division of labor and give clues about the training of technicians. Beginning with his work at Diana Film, Khachikian developed long-standing working relationships with a handful of Russian lighting designers and camera operators, who preferred English to written Persian. There were also technicians from India and several Iranian crewmembers for whom Persian was not their first language. The portions of the découpage that pertained to camera movements, framing, and lighting were in English as a written lingua franca, while those relating to sound, dialogue, costume, and performance were usually written in Persian. Technical terms were usually written in English but can also be found in Persian and French in the shooting scripts. Such adaptive studio paperwork, something Khachikian introduced with his early films, was what control looked like in an industry in which one had to work within a system that made control and resources unpredictable.

Tight planning of shots and music in these films complemented their modularity. The pretitle sequences of Khachikian's noir cycle led with some of the films' most overt genre coding. There would be time later in each feature to fold in the gags of popular comedians, the voices of radio singers, or the situations of family melodrama. A few other respected directors at the time experimented with similar opening citations. Nasser Malek Motie'i began his Persian Gulf drug-trade policier with a sequence that resembles the famous heroin withdrawal scene from *The Man with the Golden Arm* (Preminger, 1955), a film noir that received significant attention in the press when it played in Iran.[65] Khachikian's films from this period show a consistent pattern of attention to pretitle sequences. Each of the six films from his noir cycle begins with some combination of gunfire, police sirens, corpses, heels, fedoras, blond wigs, empty streets at night, gloved hands emerging from off-screen, and guns pointed at the camera. The music editors sampled music from Henry Mancini, and the title designers, especially Abbas Mazaheri, borrowed styles of title animation from Saul Bass. Four of the six films begin with murders. The other two open with a robbery and a police chase. They are lit like noir sequences, they conceal faces in shadows or with cameras positioned close to the ground, and they make use of elaborate camera movements.

The two most commercially successful films made in Iran in 1961, arguably the most immediately influential films of Khachikian's noir cycle, possess the most concentrated set of film noir allusions in their pretitle sequences. In the opening sequence of *The Midnight Cry*, Afshar the crime boss quietly kills a man in the dark backseat of a taxi. The driver's radio conceals the sound of the murder. It starts with a few bars of "Blues in the Night" and, after Afshar orders the driver to increase the volume, transitions to a scene from a radio drama, which picks up the song's (and the film's) theme of an unfaithful partner. Afshar, his identity still concealed by low-angle and low-key shots, gets out of the car and instructs the driver to deliver the man to his home. The driver

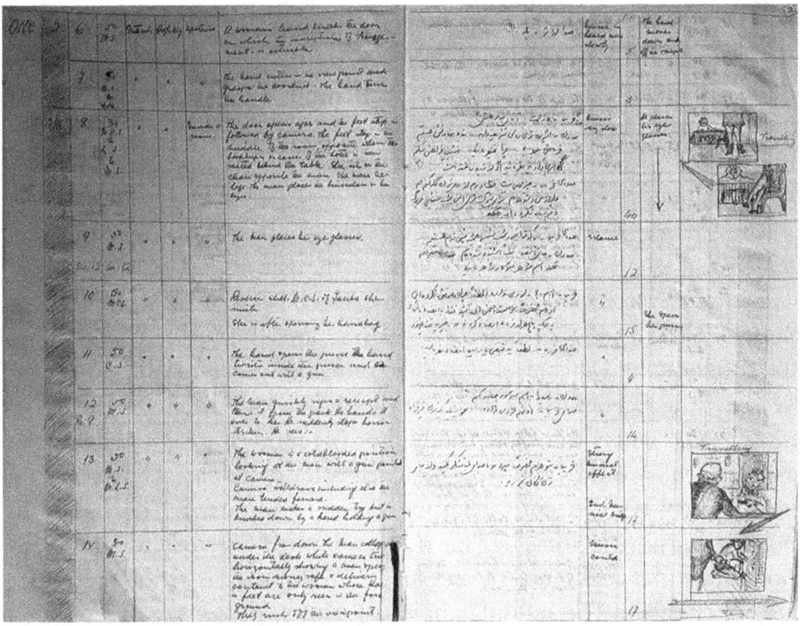

FIGURE 28. Découpage for *Yek Qadam ta Marg* / *One Step to Death* (Samuel Khachikian, 1961). Museum of Cinema, Tehran.

stops making small talk only when he turns to see the occupant in the back seat, whose face finally falls into the light. As the driver screams, the title of the film appears over the corpse's face. The sequence compresses the midnight street scenes, costuming, lighting, and cigarette consumption of film noir into a compact bundle that has little to do with the film's plot. *One Step to Death* opens with a couple robbing the safe of the Hotel Atlas. In one take accompanied by a Latin-jazz rendition of "Guaglione," the camera tilts from the neon hotel sign to reveal its facade as a late 1950s Chrysler passes and then backs into the frame. A woman, shot from the waist down with the camera positioned near the ground, emerges from the back seat and enters the hotel. Seven brief shots follow her and her accomplice, still cropped by the low camera, through the corridors and up the stairs to the assistant manager's office. We only see her face after she is framed "in a coldblooded position looking at the man with a gun pointed at the camera" (figure 28).[66] Most of the shots in the sequence are lit low-key, and they incorporate several quick and precise reframings, which were hallmarks of Khachikian's work at Azhir Film with cinematographer Ghodratollah Ehsani.[67] Each of the traveling shots is sketched as a before-and-after image in the shooting script with arrows to denote camera movements. The scene follows the shooting script in precise detail. It includes not just one low-angle shot but an entire sequence planned with each camera movement noted in the découpage. Each of the opening sequences offers a condensed choreography of noir attractions.

The pretitle sequences of the films in Khachikian's noir cycle prepared viewers for the overt gestures to the genre and borrowed plot elements interlaced through these films, which arrive with a pronounced modularity, as a series of stand-alone attractions. Pretitle sequences were not common, and this level of condensation of genre motifs stood out. Next to other scenes in the films, they look like film trailers. Khachikian himself took pains to create trailers for his films at a time when trailers for local productions were practically nonexistent. Theaters were lucky if they could secure them for valuable imports.[68] The stand-out modules within his films, like his trailers, framed his work in relation to those films that continued to outperform Iranian films at the box office and with critics. The modular noir sequences, possessing the concentrated elements of style for which Khachikian became known, worked together with the marketing media and the discussions in the trade press. They promised a commercial cinema in Iran fluent in the modern idioms of postwar genre cinema. This imagined possibility for studio film production in Iran did not last long, and it was not without critics, such as Karim Emami, who saw such allusive style as a dead end.[69] But it did yield record-breaking box office returns in 1961 and led to a shift toward the production of crime films, and to Khachikian's *Anxiety* outselling the twenty-six other releases of 1962 (figure 29). Modularity provided a method, a frame for cinematic allusion, and a space for an exuberant variation in style and tone within a single film.

MIXED SIGNALS OF KIN AND HOME

Anyone interested in tracking this cycle in relation to canonical works of film noir will have to come to terms with the way they forcefully, but only intermittently, take on the genre's stylized cruelty and profound cynicism. Contemporary critics' accusations of excessive imitation notwithstanding, one must account for ways in which the femme fatale characters of Tehran noir toggling in and out, often abruptly, of their expected destructive roles. The young recruit into a Tehran criminal organization may not be as death driven or paranoid, or at least not for

FIGURE 29. Lobby card for *Delhoreh* / *Anxiety* (Samuel Khachikian, 1962).

long. He often seeks only to earn enough money to get married. Mixed signals complicate resemblances. Even the modular opening sequences, as stylistically allusive as they may have been, sometimes switched codes. The pretitle shots of *The Strike* show the young Shirin looking out of her window at night. The view out of this window reveals a noir street scene. A man in a fedora and trench coat walks over puddles in a dark alley preceded by his long shadow. But, as the découpage notes, he is singing a "folkloric song" incongruous with the style of the shot (figure 30).[70] The soundtrack layers the voice of Shirin's sick mother over this point-of-view shot out of the window. Its iconography, appropriate to the opening of a crime film, is interrupted by a melodrama about the labors and economics of multigenerational care. Rather than directly reciting genre cinema, these films continually switch codes between, and within, scenes.

Elaborate kinship structures, with pronounced dramas of care, devotion, and sacrifice, find their way into films that otherwise engage a genre driven by a no-future dissolution of traditional kinship. The films in Khachikian's noir cycle are urban but without the urban anonymity

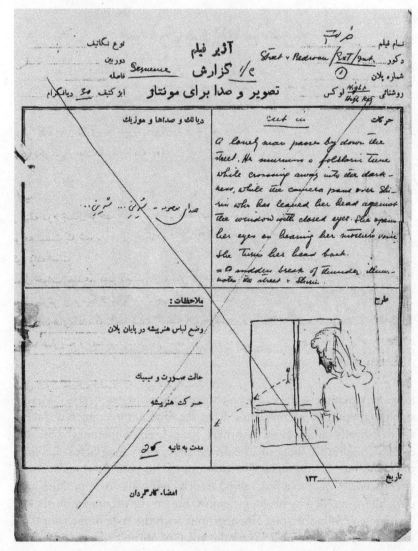

FIGURE 30. Découpage for *Zarbat / The Strike* (Samuel Khachikian, 1964). Museum of Cinema, Tehran.

and isolation that one might expect given their visual style. Instead of the marked absence of family networks often found in film noir, these films reach into dramas of aging uncles, adult siblings, and children. They still point to trouble with kinship, but not in the American form of a meltdown of the promise of the nuclear family.[71] The favored devices to create some degree of wanderer status in these films were orphan and widow plots. There are many orphans in the films from this period, and these characters run up against familial structures and their plots that detour from a noir script. As Pedram Partovi argues in his carefully researched study of Iranian popular cinema, the orphan figure's liminality in Iranian cinema, at once lacking family status and liberated from the more oppressive aspects of social life, made the male orphan an effective agent for heroic acts of devotion.[72] These forms of heroism, at home in Iranian tough-guy films that hinged on masculine sacrifice, made for strange guests in stylized crime thrillers. *Storm in Our City*, with a plot that opens by suggesting a triangulated rivalry between the orphan Said and dandy Houshang, expands into a multifaceted family drama involving Said's sister Pari, whose love for the cinema (her room is full of photographs of Elizabeth Taylor) and rock music (she dances to Bill Haley in the park) puts her into a parallel formation with Houshang's sister, whom we see on a divan listening to jazz on the radio so loud that it can be heard throughout her family's home. Because Pari is working class, with absent parents, her interest in cinema and pop music puts her in harm's way with Houshang and his gang. Said assumes a protector role with her and with the impoverished widow Simin. Simin and Pari's only connection to each other is that they wind up in the same uncanny vacant building in the film's climactic fight scene—a temporary home for all the socially marginalized characters in need of protection. To viewers well versed in Iranian tough-guy films, the film's stylistic resemblances to 1950s Hollywood might define its overarching impression. Those steeped in film noir style might overlook this impression as they ponder the film's comparatively elaborate uses of the melodramatic mode in its acts of familial devotion.

The Midnight Cry's romantic entanglements can likewise be understood in this context of code switching around kin. The protagonist, Amir, moves between two love triangles. The first triangulation of Amir, Afshar (the leader of the counterfeiting organization), and Zhila (Afshar's wife) follows a similar format to *Gilda*. It involves seduction attempts, gramophones playing jazz, and questions of loyalty within the criminal organization; each of these noir motifs puts the blame squarely on Zhila. The second triangle sets the noir plot of *Gilda* against a melodrama of family formation. Amir, an orphan, is also triangulated between Zhila and Mehri, whom he intends to marry. He does not possess the family wealth that he believes is a necessary prerequisite for marriage, and he will not hear Mehri's assertions that poverty is preferable to ill-gained wealth. Mehri's role in the plot feels cut from a family melodrama and pasted onto the noir armature, not unlike noir productions made in Bombay. She waits in the wings of the hard-boiled world in which almost all the film's action takes place. But despite this separation, she remains structurally essential to that world, as she is the reason Amir enters it as well as the reason he leaves it. Mehri and Zhila never meet, but they parallel one another in the film. Seduction scenes with Zhila bracket both of the scenes in Mehri's mother's apartment, highlighting the comparison between a spectacle of toxic attachment that film noir brought to screens around the world and an alternative spectacle of attachment common in global melodrama. Versions of this virtuous betrothed, who pull orphan protagonists away from criminal substitute paternal figures, were not absent from Hollywood crime films, but they were a mainstay of the products of film industries in the Middle East and South Asia.

The film's interlocking triangles brings familiar binaries of the melodramatic mode into play, but with subtle shifts in style that suggest that moral clarity was not the creative priority. While the split between the two female characters promises a Manichean moral frame, the performances send mixed signals. Before assuming a simple split between Hollywood eroticism/romance in one triangle and conservative virtues of family melodrama in the other, the viewer must make sense of Zhila's multiple acts of ventriloquism. Parvin Ghaffary's performance as Zhila switches from portraying an almost abstract noir icon to incongruously making earnest declarations of love to singing a song sequence in which her embodiment is doubled with a canned voice. And Amir's scenes with Mehri, perhaps taking advantage of the talent and range of Vida Ghahremani as Mehri, occasionally take on a form of classical Hollywood romance that cuts against the grain of her simple role in the plot as a virtuous placeholder. Looking back at her films from the late 1950s and '60s, Ghahremani discussed the influences of evergreen films like *Gone with the Wind*. This makes sense, given that just months before Ghahremani began working with Azhir Film and Khachikian on *Storm in Our City*, *Setare-ye Cinema* promoted ongoing screenings of *Gone with the Wind* with reviews by critics and lengthy discussions by film fans focusing primarily on the performances of Clark Gable and Vivien Leigh.[73] Ghahremani suggests that her scenes with Fardin in *The Midnight Cry* were modeled on the staging and performance style in these love scenes.[74] The two scenes in which Mehri appears with Amir register such shifts into this allusive performance. Their relationship switches from static purity to dynamic argument. The staging showcases Fardin's imposing form of masculinity as not far from Gable's as he leans into a series of low-angle shots of turning and pointing and tight two-shots that frame exchanges of sarcasm and set up dramatic exits. The codes of performance and staging in this peripheral scene shift into a cinematic register that gestures to Hollywood's leading romantic scenes, which critics and fans had discussed at length in the press. Ghahremani and Fardin thread their citational performance through situations that are misaligned with Hollywood screen romance. The choreography of iconic Hollywood romance could not be expected to play seamlessly. Such a feat would be a challenge when set in the back room of a multigenerational household while Mehri and Amir argue about the honor of the financial obligations of marriage while waiting for Mehri's mother to bring them tea. Nor should a viewer of this film expect seamless switches between the scenes of family melodrama in this bright and humble apartment and the parallel violent, death-driven thriller plot that plays out in the home of Zhila and Afshar, with its secret passages, winding staircases, and rooms stocked with conspicuous art objects, whiskey, and jazz records.

Given this free play with the codes of domestic relations, it is not surprising that Khachikian's noir cycle would give special attention to stylized and coded domestic interiors. The homes in these films are carnivals of inhospitality. Khachikian's interiors amplify what Jennifer Fay calls "the hostile animism of noir's environment," as such hostilities clash against historically idealized and formalized traditions of hospitality that suffuse everyday social life in Iran.[75] The domestic spaces in this cycle, whether indicative of wealth or poverty, often defy habitability. They are unwelcome places in which codes of hospitality have been fouled. The main home in The Strike is a dilapidated structure with a leaky roof and a dead tree in the courtyard. Still, its inhabitants cannot make rent. With its environment of thunderstorms, chiaroscuro, and rainwater always threatening to reveal where the bodies are buried, this home is representative of the gothic current in Khachikian's thrillers, which is also evident in the vacant squat in Storm in Our City and in the ancestral home in Delirium (1964). These dwellings evoke the uncanny of psychological horror while still providing a setting for the professional activities of criminal gangs and detectives.

While the interiors of the poor in this cycle depict vulnerability in a gothic style, the dwellings of the rich are modernist and often the point of origin of criminality. At least as common as the haunting, decrepit spaces of the socially marginalized are the suspicious dwellings of the nouveau-riche dandies who commit crimes. In The Midnight Cry, art

FIGURE 31. *Faryad-e Nime-shab / The Midnight Cry* (Samuel Khachikian, 1961).

director Valiollah Khakdan packed the home with markers of modernist excess (figure 31). The framing and staging draw attention to these curiosities of decor, and they are mentioned in the dialogue when Afshar points out to Amir that they were all selected by Zhila. The salon, with its dramatic curved staircase, is the main space of the home. The central staircase creates a range of possibilities for Khachikian's love of steep angles and elaborate camera movements. A crane shot follows Zhila's grand entrance as she descends the staircase to the tune of "Blues in the Night," a callback to the taxi radio in the pretitle sequence. Although Khachikian has said that he had not seen *Gilda* before making the film, the staircase in the boss's home serves a similar function in both films.[76] When Ballin/Afshar (re)introduces Johnny/Amir to Gilda/Zhila, the dramatic staircase stands as a display of wealth and a threshold across which, to the tune of a jazz song about a heartbreaker, the characters with a shared secret past become reacquainted. It is in this living area that *The Midnight Cry* ends, having traveled far from *Gilda*'s plot by this point, in Grand Guignol style: Zhila and Afshar murder each other, and their suitcase full of counterfeit US dollars is scattered across the floor, soaked in blood. The film leaves the viewer at this house, a center

FIGURE 32. *Faryad-e Nime-shab* / *The Midnight Cry* (Samuel Khachikian, 1961).

of gravity that has proven difficult to escape. Instead of reuniting with Mehri on screen, Amir makes a quick call to her from the living room. He says, "You were right; this money smells of blood" while seated in the background of a deep-focus crane shot (figure 32). The contorted bodies of Afshar and Zhila in the foreground, the cash on the floor, and the conspicuously modern decor surrounding them overwhelm the film's half-hearted telephonic gesture toward recuperation in the hospitable elsewhere of Mehri's bright apartment.

Khachikian's most explicit use of the modernist excess of the domestic interior came a year later in *Anxiety*. Centering on the recently married Behruz and Roshanak, the film comingles plot elements from at least two perfect-crime thrillers that had premiered in Tehran a few years earlier. Gesturing to *Dial M for Murder* (Hitchcock, 1954), Behruz is a writer of crime fiction, and Roshanak is blackmailed with old love letters.[77] Gesturing extensively to *Les Diaboliques* (Clouzot, 1955), Roshanak is tricked into believing she has murdered her blackmailer next to a fireplace in his home.[78] She is haunted by his "corpse" (a performance that resembles Paul Meurisse's in *Les Diaboliques*) in a plot orchestrated by Behruz to scare her to death so that he and his paramour can make off with her inheritance. The key scenes of this story of a poisoned marriage, from the early introduction of the blackmail letters to the final

If you're done with your job, beat it.

FIGURE 33. *Delhoreh / Anxiety* (Samuel Khachikian, 1962).

shift from restricted to unrestricted narration as the false murder plot is revealed, take place in the couple's expansive midcentury modern living area. Like the grand living area in *The Midnight Cry*, the space is cluttered with modern decor and defined by an imposing architectural feature that enables dynamic staging and camera movement. This room showcases a double-sided brick fireplace with the "rhetorically exaggerated massiveness" that Mark Jarzombek has identified as an "obligatory" feature of "Good-Life Modernist" dwellings.[79] Khachikian uses the open fireplace to frame characters, as an obstruction, and to create layered space in the sequences he stages there (figure 33). Roshanak's feet are framed by its opening in one of Khachikian's trademark low-traveling shots as she walks around it into view. Seconds before her apparent death by fright at the end of the film, when she sees the reanimated body of the man she believed she had killed (at the typewriter, another nod to Clouzot's film), his hand is shot from her point of view as she clings to the fireplace. The climactic fight scene between Detective Jamshid (Arman) and Behruz's heavy (Reza Beyk Imanverdi) also winds its way around and through the fireplace. In a cynical dismissal of the hearth worthy of Douglas Sirk, the thug grabs a log from it to use as a weapon. The fight ends when Jamshid throws him through the fireplace at the camera. Following Paul Guth's quip that "the two main characters in *Les Diaboliques* are a swimming pool and a bathtub" (the two conspicuous water features where Clouzot stages the film's terror), *Anxiety*'s main characters may be its fireplaces.[80] Roshanak's final scene appears to tease Clouzot fans with a premature jump scare of running water in an empty upstairs bathtub. The real scare comes moments later in the salon. Khachikian's film trades water for fire as the film's violence concludes in, around, and through the modern stone monument to consumerist domesticity in the center of the room.

In the living rooms of *The Midnight Cry* and *Anxiety*, modernist decor links character desires with a bad modernity of rapidly circulating wealth in contrast to spaces devoted to stable kith and kin (if such spaces ever exist for long in Khachikian's films). The domestic gathering spaces and hearth fires promising a version of the good life are the sites where life comes apart. The spaces are coded as conspicuously modern with their architectural details, artworks on display, and devices that play pop songs. The films place these artifacts of postwar globalized consumption within a frame of suspicion by criminalizing them even as these artifacts remain objects of fascination in the films. Such ambivalence offers one possible answer to critics' continual claims of counterfeit that dogged these otherwise well-received productions.

Still, it is not entirely satisfying to place these films along an axis of simulation-rejection: simulation on the surface but rejection at their social-critical core. Such an attempt at recuperation could downplay the films' preoccupation with style. There were other films, such as *Merchants of Death*, made with ambitions to ground the crime film in social problems. That film takes a comparatively sober approach to staging, lighting, and camera movement. The films in Khachikian's noir cycle, even as their ambivalences stand out next to the films from which they borrow, give their primary attention to the global stylistics of noir. The toxic home is, after all, one of the calling cards of the genre. The domestic spaces in Khachikian's noir cycle demonstrate fluency with a topos illustrated by Thom Andersen in his section on film noir in the documentary *Los Angeles Plays Itself* (2003): "the architectural trophy house as the modern equivalent of the black hat or the mustache."[81] For Khachikian, to dwell on modernist interiors as sites of alienation, criminality, and failed masculinity is to speak in the idiom of the genre.[82]

This idiom found some of its most exuberant forms of expression in neighboring film industries around the same time. I mentioned Atef

Salem's noir productions in Egypt at the outset of this chapter, and an analysis of the polished, modern domestic interiors in films like *Ma'wed Ma' el-Maghul* (*Encounter with the Unknown*, 1959) would yield a fruitful comparison. The affinity is even more pronounced in some of the contemporaneous Navketan noir productions in Bombay. The new home of Raghuvir, the black-market leader in *Kala Bazar* (Anand, 1960), is full of excessive modern decor and marks his full embrace of the fruits of his illicit labor. At the same time, the patterned, concrete room dividers in the center of the living area offer the filmmakers an opportunity to explore the space and play with long unmotivated camera movements. The tracking shots reveal actors' faces through the spaces in the screen in a rhythmic pattern. This happens three times in the film. In each case the space switches back and forth from an anchor of the location of domestic care to a site of stylish surfaces shaped by choreographed camera movements. These interiors are simultaneously spaces of contamination and of dynamic modernist visuality. The filmmakers activate the genre through their attention to domestic surfaces.

These scenes offer a rejoinder to anxieties about delay. Despite all the discussion in the Tehran film press about the industry falling behind, about its directors being lagging imitators, when it comes to situations in which "modernist architecture represents epicene villainy," Tehran noir was not at all late to the party.[83] The Azhir Film crime thrillers, in conversation with noir productions made around the same time in Bombay and Cairo, are actually on the early side of the phenomenon that Andersen describes. While he cites some early intersections of noir and modernist design such as *The Damned Don't Cry* (Sherman, 1950) and *The Night Holds Terror* (Stone, 1955), most of Andersen's examples come from the neo-noir of the 1970s through the 1990s.[84] The interregional use of the genre to express a grim fascination with the global flows of capital and consumer goods in postwar urban life look prescient, for example, when compared with the period in Hollywood neo-noir when Japanese crime bosses figured prominently in California's modernist interiors. In this later wave of noir, art directors dressed up modernist architecture in Orientalist style to help the American film industry spin its reaction to the entanglements of Pacific capital in 1980s Los Angeles. In each instance, the genre's current of fascination with a global elsewhere runs through private living spaces at a moment when new movements of wealth had amplified anxieties about, and aesthetic fascination with, a particular elsewhere. Noir's spectacular textures, at least as much as melodrama's spectacles of moral clarity, lend an aesthetic idiom appropriate to such anxious exuberance. In 1980s Los Angeles, just like they did in midcentury Tehran, Bombay, and Cairo, waves of noir seem to accompany, to haunt, the global itinerary of modern design.

Khachikian's career continued long after his generic preoccupations shifted away from crime thrillers, but as compelling as some of these later films were, they no longer served as leading indicators for trends in the industry. This shift helps to delimit the period of promise between the end of the experimental period and the changes of the mid-1960s. New possibilities of Iranian melodrama did manifest alongside a new energy for intellectual filmmaking. Neither the love of dance sequences and class-conflicted romance, exemplified in the record-breaking *Ganj-e Qarun* (*Qarun's Treasure*, Yasami, 1965), nor the developments in art-film cinephilia cinema fit exactly with the possibilities of the crime film in the early 1960s. However frustrated as he may have been by the new working conditions, Khachikian remained the same advocate for strengthening guilds and trade unions that he had been in the 1950s even as the possibilities of that fertile period had been redirected by later developments.[85] Directors in the 1970s still complained about "contract work" that limited their ability to make choices and develop a consistent body of work. Because the director of a commercial film must essentially serve up a film ordered by investors, and because the director must personally take on all of the practical roles in making a film that should be taken on by other professionals, many held that quality cinema was a Sisyphean task. In an interview with several filmmakers in 1970, the director Jalal Moghaddam described the situation by joking with his colleague Khachikian, whose hair had gone completely white by this time. "If, somewhere in this process, a spark of creativity finds its way into the film, then such a spark will come at the cost of four strands of the director's hair turning white. Just look at the head of Mr. Samuel."[86]

It would take an entire monograph to adequately account for more than a small section of these strands. Even a thorough interpretation of the films of Khachikian's first decade would require a different kind of chapter. By highlighting a few moments of particularly intense or perhaps unexpected affinities with film noir, I have focused on some of the impasses in the conceptions that often seem to accompany stylized work created in conversation with the circulation of genres. To refer to the style of these films as a kind of imitation would be misleading if such an assessment meant that the affinities were vague or compromised. As André Bazin argued in his review of *Les Diaboliques*, "The style is the genre."[87] These films' chiaroscuro and trench coats were not there as packaging for a different kind of film. Hard-boiled setups are undone by unexpected domestic turns just as moral clarity is interrupted by a subtle shift into an allusive performance style or a sudden shift to Grand Guignol. The plotting and the citations within a given scene are not imitative in the sense of following a preformed script. They follow a modular pattern and code switch using film noir as a global idiom. There are phrases of Hollywood performance at work in orphan dramas. Phrases of tightly constructed pretitle sequences, camera movements, and lighting schemes highlighted genre affinities intermittently. Each of these elements in Khachikian's films were often anchored in a mise-en-scène of modern inhospitability tuned to suspicious flows of global currency. The films from this cycle used style to build a local prestige genre cinema, not as a ruse to make viewers believe they were watching a foreign movie. Imitation conceived as passive labor or failed purism makes it difficult to identify the films' active phrasing and dandyish recombination of elements. The result would keep the study of global noir at arm's length from so much of its available archive. Studies of cinema as vernacular modernism can be especially effective when they go beyond pointing to its possibility and instead outline its wavering forms of fluency in a given period of cinema history.

Addressing the global operation of genre in this way means identifying intellectual labor not only within the films of the cycle but also in the press. Canonical crime thrillers were key in establishing an ephemeral possibility for cinema in Iran, and the critical discussion of that possibility forms a key part of that history. Imitation can imply a lack of reflection, and reflection is one thing that the critics, business operators, and prestige filmmakers in Iran were definitely not lacking. From the 1920s through the early 1960s, rather robust forms of reflection were made possible, and were sometimes required, by the peculiar structure of the film trade and exhibition in Iran. The extensive discourse around the crime thriller in the press, and its intersections with the decisions of studios and the labor of filmmakers, demonstrates such reflection in some of the most direct aesthetic language so far. The film community in midcentury Iran was a small world—a pressure cooker stocked with young critics whose careers sometimes brought them behind the camera and with filmmakers who took an active part in critical debates when they were between films. It was an environment of personal feuds and tactical adaptations to resources. But the knowledge base in this close community engaged with, and took part in constituting, the global vernacular of film noir. The genre offered a field in which to engage the promise of cinema, sometimes with playful enthusiasm about its possibilities and sometimes with a cynicism or anxiety about broken promises.

CHAPTER 5

Eastern Boys and Failed *Heroes*

No one ever makes it into a movie theater in Masoud Kimiai's *Pesar-e Sharqi* (*Eastern Boy*, 1975). This detail is hard to miss in an auto-biographical film, by one of Iran's most famous directors of the 1970s, about a group of children from Tehran obsessed with cinema. These neighborhood kids have to settle for a spot on the curb in front of their local single-screen venue, the soundstage of its outdoor loud-speaker, and their own collections of scraps from the projection booth (figures 34a–34d). They have spent their day playing with frames of 35 mm film gleaned from projectionists or bought from street vendors. Parroting the tough-guy language they have absorbed from neighbor-hood melodramas made in Iran, the boys gamble their loot in a game that involves throwing a single frame of film on top of an opponent's.[1] The most ambitious member of the group, called "Zorro" (Kiumars Nuri) because he rarely takes off his Zorro mask, tries to be an effec-tive leader—tries to make his fascination with cinema amount to some-thing—and mostly fails. A cashier turns the boys away from the local cinema, a group of rivals challenges them on the playground, and Zor-ro's father (Kiumars Malek Motie'i)—a traditional performer in passion plays—trashes their makeshift basement cinema. These scenes return to established themes from Kimiai's work, but they also stand out. At a high point in his career, right at a moment when this founding director of the 1970s would have been able to command his largest budgets, he made his smallest and most personal film, which reflects on the film

FIGURES 34A–34D. Frames from *Pesar-e Sharqi / Eastern Boy* (Masoud Kimiai, 1975). Above: inspecting and playing with collections of film fragments. Below: sitting outside the cinema under a *Rio Bravo* marquee.

culture of the previous generation with melancholy and uncertainty. This origin story follows children and their junk celluloid collections as a way to look back, after the emergence of local film festivals, robust traditions of film scholarship, and the new wave, to the film culture in which these transformations in Iranian cinema were incubated. The film reckons with the archive of foreign films in Iran, but how that archive functions, to what effect, and with what political valence, it treats with ambivalence.

Taking this ambivalent origin story seriously presents at least three questions that move the themes of this book into the better-known period of the late 1960s and '70s. It opens onto a pivotal but obscured moment in Iranian cinema history, one that has framed the contemporary moment. It foregrounds the role of circulating films in this period's transformations, requiring one to consider the methods that might be appropriate to address circulation during this globalizing phase. And as a personal film, *Eastern Boy* foregrounds the odd position of a director whose career can shed light on the roles directors have played in the global footprint of this cinema. The Iranian cinema that is known and celebrated around the world is, of course, the postrevolutionary, post–Iraq War festival cinema. It has engaged clearly with other global new waves and continues to work (and teach) well alongside contemporaneous traditions in film theory. It has thus achieved a deserved special status in scholarship, in cinematheque programming, and in college classrooms. But if, as a result of a collective scholarly reception that had to rush to catch up with festival recognition in the late 1980s and 1990s, a handful of brilliant art films seem to hover over their broader media landscape, then work toward a more expansive historiography is in order. The events of an earlier period, some mythologized and some swept under the rug, can provide a position from which to consider the films that are already well known. In other words, as some new scholarship revisits major shifts that occurred before the revolution, perhaps it might also draw attention to the enthusiasm for postrevolutionary art films as itself something to be periodized. The scholarship on Iranian cinema grew intertwined with the history of its boom in festival visibility in the 1990s, that is, with one phase of circulation in the history of the globalization of Iranian cinema. To engage and situate that history here, I consider counterglobalizations that manifested around 1969. It was a prolific environment that indeed influenced the celebrated work of the late 1980s and 1990s but within which competing ideas of prestige, and failure, were also under construction.

These interventions could set aside entirely the director-focused traditions that have flourished in Iranian cinema studies, but I am inclined to pursue them in coalition with traditions of scholarship that extend back to the period in which the films examined here were made. Not only have director studies been a cornerstone of scholarship considering global new waves (and of world cinema pedagogy), but critics and filmmakers in 1960s–1970s Iran avidly engaged with the global auteurist discourse of that period and provided their own challenges to the canons it formed. So, all the better if an intersectional history can also provide some reflection on these traditions. Such historiographical pairings might help make sense of the careers of those outliers of the new wave who do not fit within a clean narrative of the emergence of a national art cinema. It also helps to position Kimiai's early work with Khachikian's. A history of institutions, interrupted chronologies, and orphaned films could offer some leverage on those directors whose multiplicity of origins make it difficult to categorize their work. In this respect, Kimiai's anomalies open onto an unsettled period in Iranian cinema history. I look to Kimiai at the moment when his work became foundational for critics and audiences within Iran, but from the vantage points of two collaborative compromises that have been largely orphaned in the story.

YEAR OF *THE HEROES*

To examine the nostalgic and the unwanted in constellation, let me begin with Kimiai's work before he became a celebrated director, from this period across which *Eastern Boy* looks back. While *Eastern Boy* is a film of uncertain heritage, the Iranian-US collaboration *Qahremanan* (*The Heroes*, or *The Invincible Six* in its American release; Negulesco, 1969), on which Kimiai worked as a young assistant director, is an orphan film that no one has wanted to claim. The film's significance, or the significance of its absence in discussions of Iranian media history, has to do with the year in which it was completed. The year spanning 1969 to 1970 is known as a year of transformation for Iranian cinema because of the release of two films, Dariush Mehrjui's *Gav* (*The Cow*) and Kimiai's *Qeysar*. In the contemporaneous film criticism in Iran, a tradition that has informed many of the histories written since, these two releases designated a sea change in production and audience. They were held up in heroic contrast to many of the films in recent memory. The suspicion of *filmfarsi*, discussed at length in the last chapter and still common today, found particular urgency in the film culture of the 1960s and 1970s as a way to lump together what was, in reality, a diverse lot of films. Intellectual publications continued to express a kind of embarrassment about *filmfarsi* and the need to find and promote alternatives. *The Cow* marked a new kind of viability for modernist cinema, and *Qeysar* showed that a reflexive social problem film could attract status as well as crowds. Their styles were very different, but together they have presented a milestone used by many critics to reference the complicated shifts toward prestige cinema and the new wave.

Looking back on the polemics of these debates during the rise of the new wave, many current scholars have worked to reconfigure their Manichean categorizations. Hamid Naficy describes the new wave as a "moment" and not a "movement." He highlights the atomization of new wave filmmakers and the tendency among many of them (Kimiai included) to alternate between highbrow and commercial modes.[2] Negar Mottahedeh has recently been exploring the films made earlier in the 1960s by Ebrahim Golestan's company as a way to revise this history.

Rather than working solely on Golestan and his works, she situates the documentaries and fiction features within the politics of oil production in Iran.[3] Working in Iran, critics such as Hassan Hosseini have also pushed against the historiography of a decisive shift around this time. Hosseini takes issue with the very idea of a new wave as a useful category in Iran, let alone its periodization. He calls instead for an expanded historiography of the multiple phases and subgenres of films that have been grouped together as *filmfarsi* to reveal the false oppositions between traits assigned to those maligned melodramas and traits assigned to the films of the new wave.[4] In each of these interventions, the concern is not merely with what we leave out by focusing on a decisive break with tradition but also with the assumptions underlying perfunctory references to the year 1969. Working in conversation with broader shifts in cinema studies such as the interests in global melodrama and sponsored film, they have moved beyond a simplistic notion of heroic iconoclasm to which the discussion of the events of any one year may refer. My intent in considering an odd collaboration from this period is to build on this work and revise the points where the historiography has constricted around certain developments, rather than to reflect on the uses to which critics have put these developments. I attend here to archives pertaining to cinema's circulation, collaborations, and sponsorship in Iran and frame the foundational debates and nostalgic origin stories of 1969 as documents of the architecture of prestige filmmaking in this period.

The Heroes was the most ambitious collaboration of its day, and its story reveals much about the political economy of cinema in Iran at the time.[5] It occupied that period when efforts to globalize the film industry had begun to establish a solid network of recognizable government institutions and offices for foreign film companies. It came about on the eve of the 1970s oil boom and the deregulation of finance capital, before the Tehran International Film Festival, and before the sponsored films of the Center for Intellectual Development of Children and Young Adults (CIDCYA) and the Film Industry Development Company of Iran (FIDCI). Its production was also a major event from which many figures of the commercial cinema and emerging new wave alike received valuable (if not all positive) experience. The film was a curious mix of interests and genres. It was part commercial venture and part sponsored publicity event. It was a genre film, but to which genre it belonged was unclear. It gestured to popular serials from the previous decades with action, pyrotechnics, and hidden treasure. It was partly a jewelry heist film with the kinds of characterization and pacing appropriate to that genre. Most prominently, it was structured like a western in the image of *Rio Bravo* (Hawks, 1959) and *The Magnificent Seven* (Sturges, 1960), both acclaimed by local critics and enormously popular as dubbed films in Iran and throughout the region.[6] A group of six, not seven, heroes defends a small town against a much larger force of outlaws. In retrospect, the film seems obstructed from the start in its design by committee. But the awkward incongruities that would disappoint investors and tangle audience expectations make for a rich text for the cinema historian. This onetime collaboration among so many high-profile figures in the American and Iranian film industries offers a glimpse of globalizing production during a period of rapid transformation and an Iranian film industry on the cusp of the new wave.

The story of the production starts in a different institutional context than many other Hollywood ventures abroad. It was not exactly an instance of Hollywood looking for cheap labor and locations. This more ambitious project originated in the Iranian film industry. Two brothers, Mostafa and Morteza Akhavan, ran a chain of movie theaters that had expanded through the 1960s. Their exhibition business, with headquarters at the Cinema Moulin Rouge, was upscale but not unlike other major Iranian cinema companies in its semi-integrated structure involving production, distribution, dubbing, and exhibition. One of the first dubbing efforts that the Moulin Rouge showcased as a prestige work was *The Great Dictator* (Chaplin, 1940), which premiered during the Iranian New Year celebrations of 1959. In the years that followed, the Moulin Rouge cinema and the Akhavan brothers amassed a sizable surplus from this system of import and dubbing in their multipurpose media hub. They soon reached a point at which it was possible to expand their dubbing operation into a larger studio production space, with all the infrastructural shifts that would require. After producing films such as the successful *Khodahafez Tehran* (*Goodbye Tehran*, Khachikian, 1966), on which Kimiai also worked as an assistant director, they wagered that integrating technology and skilled personnel from abroad was the next step to achieve this goal. They began with a smaller Italian collaboration, *Hashem Khan* (Zarindast, 1967), and soon after began to court American film companies.

By this time, there was already a well-established infrastructure for financing and otherwise supporting deals with foreign business leaders. The government entertained a steady stream of ambitious foreign proposals and was simultaneously on a campaign, which gained momentum in the late 1960s, to localize industrial production of imported goods.

The Heroes film project fit this goal to circulate more production capital, not just products or money capital, across borders. The organization that stepped in to help broker the deal was David Rockefeller's International Executive Services Corps (IESC), an agent of economic liberalism with headquarters in Washington, DC. The IESC saw itself as "the first great public program that [was] entrusted to the private sector of the economy to carry out."[7] It was dubbed the "Paunch Corps" in the regional press for its tendency to send late-career executives to consult on how to move more capital through "sagging" markets around the world.[8] The IESC had just experienced some success at its Tehran branch, wherein retired RKO executive Richard L. Spears helped reorganize the main Iranian private television station and raised its income by half.[9] The IESC representatives were the ones who attracted Paramount and the ever-adaptable studio director Jean Negulesco to the project.

Once contact was made, the contract was negotiated and insured by the Central Bank of Iran, under some scrutiny by Prime Minister Amir-Abbas Hoveyda. It gained the attention of the director of the bank, Mehdi Samii, who personally handled the details of the production pitched by Negulesco and the Akhavans. The contract specified an A-list Hollywood cast, director, and budget to work alongside an Iranian cast and crew.[10] The Akhavans would produce the film but cede creative decisions to Negulesco and his company, Tiga Productions. Both companies would invest money in the production, but the real financial risk would be assumed by the Akhavans and the central bank. In his congratulatory letter upon completion of the contract, Samii wrote, "We wish you success in this venture and know that this project could be the starting point of a successful Iranian international motion picture industry."[11]

The idea was to fund a production with several times the average budget of a spaghetti western, one that would be shot in widescreen Technicolor and would draw talent, technology, and training to the growing Iranian film industry. This production synchronized with the expansion of the Moulin Rouge sound stages and a new film lab. After the Hollywood crew left, these infrastructures would be able to handle more production and postproduction in-country. The producers wanted to promote Iran, as described in Negulesco's reiteration of publicity copy that had appeared elsewhere, "as a tourist center and as a filming site, and to develop a native pool of trained filmmakers."[12] Even before production began, the film project had attracted investment in film production capital. Its backers hoped the release would catalyze commerce, film education, and subsequent ambitious productions. A successful integration of commercial collaboration and government sponsorship could eventually make way for larger projects, including an epic about the life of Cyrus the Great for which the Akhavans already had a draft script.

FAILURES OF *THE HEROES*

The press coverage of *The Heroes*' production process was far reaching and expressed many of the promises of globalization. *Setare-ye Cinema* ran an article praising not so much the production itself but the fact that the news of the project had "echoed through film circles all around the world," including "several pages of the French magazine *Ciné Revue*," whose images it reproduced.[13] Behrouz Vossoughi, Iranian cinema's rising star, compared his role in the film to Omar Sharif's Hollywood break, and the American and British actors discussed their encounters with Iranian culture.[14] As befitting a 1968 production, some of the cast promoted the film as a harbinger of new consumer culture in Iran while others promoted it as leftist allegory.[15] Upon arrival at the Royal Tehran Hilton in the fall of 1968, Negulesco spoke at high-profile banquets alongside heads of industry and state (figure 35).[16] Newspapers published photos of him with Iranian favorites such as Sophia Loren and Angie Dickinson, whom he had directed in Greece and Italy. They touted him as the director to "rescue Farsi films . . . so that hopefully the dream of a good Farsi film [*yek film-e khub-e Farsi*] will become a reality."[17] A cynical journalist might have tried to float the suggestion to the Iranian public, which would not have been entirely untrue, that Negulesco had been taking these foreign assignments because of his second-tier status among veteran Hollywood directors. But these assignments seemed only to enhance his reputation as exactly the kind of multilingual, cosmopolitan director that an ambitious collaborative film like *The Heroes* would require.

The celebrity discourse surrounding the production accompanied in-the-weeds discussions of its financial details and outcomes. The stakes of the production were addressed most clearly in a series of articles written by the Los Angeles–educated filmmaker and writer Bahman Farmanara.[18] He noted how the scale of the project marked a shift, even in its early stages, from the local orientation of previous productions. "They settled on [Michael] Barret's [*sic*] novel [*The Heroes of Yuca*] and acquired its motion picture rights. This in itself was a new step in Iranian filmmaking, because previously everybody borrowed shamelessly

FIGURE 35. Jean Negulesco in front of the Royal Tehran Hilton. From the *Highlights at Hilton* newsletter.

from foreign films. Many producers still do."[19] Farmanara's teasing of local producers gestured to a long legal history of Iran's resistance to international copyright agreements. From clearing a path for wide distribution of this intellectual property to complicated location shooting in Technicolor and with synchronous sound, the scale of this project prompted analysis, reflection, and predictions about its effect on the future of the local film industry. Farmanara and others asked out loud what constituted a global coproduction. How would a production like this best fit the turbulent consumption patterns of the late 1960s? What kinds of combinations of film stars and genres would work, and which combinations of government agencies and local companies would be needed to make it work?

So the production was big business, but it was not business plain and simple. It was tangled in the interests of official institutions, each of which had a different understanding of the film's value. The touristy public relations elements are clear in the haphazard mixture of urban and rural settings and of desert and snowy mountain passes, and in the way chase sequences, staged around major sites such as the ruins of Persepolis, took liberal geographic license. It is not a coincidence that the Royal Tehran Hilton has an important role in the film. This modernist hub for expat entrepreneurs was the IESC headquarters and shared its architect with the Moulin Rouge complex. And when we watch the film and ask what a western is doing in the middle of an urban heist movie, we might ask about the influence of backers like Mehdi Samii, among the major architects of Iran's economic modernization and globalization. The Central Bank, a product of the centralization of Iran's resource extraction and global export economy, guaranteed funding for the film (a territory cautiously avoided by many national banks), and it offered the jewel-encrusted globe housed in its own vault as the item that could plausibly lure a group of jewel thieves to Iran. Everyone involved had agreed that the film was to be a major spectacle that would, as Farmanara noted, put Iran "into [the] world's orbit."[20] But the spectacles of royal sovereignty, of economic globalization, and of transregional genre filmmaking each pulled the film in different directions.

The project worked less like a distinguished $2 million production than like a patchwork of several $250,000 productions. Its synchronous sound production (along with an original Manos Hadjidakis score) was something everyone hoped would give the film more traveling power than the dubbed films made in Iran. But this caused complications in production for many of the scenes shot outside of the studio at Moulin Rouge. Negulesco complained about the days wasted digging holes on location for generators whose noise traveled too easily in the small desert towns.[21] From the start there were disputes on set between the Iranian and the imported crew. Tony Zarindast, who had already directed features for Moulin Rouge (including one in cooperation with Italian producers), resigned from his position as assistant director, which made way for Kimiai to take the job (figure 36). The postproduction,

FIGURE 36. Masoud Kimiai with Stuart Whitman. Private collection.

contracted in Iran as a thrifty alternative to Hollywood facilities, further dispersed managerial responsibilities, although it did help speed along the development of a more capital-intensive film lab in Tehran. The mismatch of networks, intended to aid the prestige and circulation of local productions, wound up entangling *The Heroes* and prohibiting its movement.

The traces of competing interests evident in the film's stylistic choices resulted in a risky bet of a final product. While the goal was to distance this new mode of genre production from *filmfarsi*, the grindhouse effects and displays of hypermasculine violence came a little too close for comfort, despite including Stuart Whitman as well as Robert Mitchum's son in place of the familiar faces of Iranian melodrama. The same is true of the dance sequence. Despite featuring Elke Sommer and Orientalist choreography by Rudolph Nureyev, the scene parallels the dance sequences of local productions. When the film introduces its most famous Iranian actor, Behrouz Vossoughi, it awkwardly presents him as a tragic hero straight out of a *filmfarsi* plot. In a montage sequence, we see that he joins the jewel thieves as a fugitive from the law. He has murdered his wife and her lover in a revenge killing that, like the dance scene and subsequent dance-hall fight sequence, would have been familiar to fans of Iranian muscular melodrama and the intellectuals who denounced it. Instead of seeking prestige by restricting these traditions of popular melodrama, the creators and supporters of the film gambled on hybridization. They comingled actors and production styles of widely varied origin, they derived character motivations from dissonant traditions, and they embellished recognizable formulas of violence and erotic spectacle instead of sidestepping them.

The project did not just bring a season of gloomy returns for the studio; its uncontained risks brought down the entire integrated operation. It began with a blockbuster rollout at major cinemas across Iran but quickly lost momentum.[22] Despite significant efforts to then dub and promote *The Heroes* across Europe and the United States, it never gained traction. Paramount helped initiate the production and might have successfully distributed it as a B movie, but it had moved on. The Iranian stakeholders did not have adequate connections to manage distribution abroad and made a quick deal with Walter Reade's Continental Film Distributors (figure 37). The backers, filmmakers, and distributors had reached for prestige by creating more expensive versions of proven elements of global melodrama. Though not an unreasonable approach, the film's industrial baggage made it unwieldy next to its nimble, low-cost counterparts. It would be the studio's final new production and would lead the owners to sell off much of the business to competitors. Mentions of *The Heroes* lasted in the press but only as the project that sank a studio. In an article a few years later about how "with tight control" of exports Iran could become "as big a market as any on the continent," *Variety* introduced a new major player in distribution, Arsham Yesians, as the beneficiary of this turn of events. "He has more product than the others, having acquired a two-year backlog of UA product from the Akahavan [sic] Bros.—indies who gave up their franchise when they entered big time production on the Jean Negulesco pic *The Heroes*."[23] When *The Heroes* has come up in discussions by historians of Iranian cinema, it has usually been as a necessary final note in an essay about Moulin Rouge's increasingly successful dubbing or exhibition operations: "Contrary to all anticipations, the film did not work in the cinemas, and its failure caused the Akhavans to say goodbye to their ambitions as well as to the production activities of the Moulin Rouge Studio."[24]

Upon recognition of *The Heroes*' missteps, Negulesco implored Prime Minister Hoveyda and the bank director to consider this a stepping-stone

FIGURE 37. Lobby card for *The Heroes* featuring Behrouz Vossoughi and Stuart Whitman (Continental Film Distributors).

for a future series of Hollywood coproductions. Understandably, they met his suggestions with a chilly response. The prime minister, who only a year earlier had been wining and dining the director, described his work in Iran "as an almost total failure and a good, though bitter lesson."[25] Even Cyrus Ghani, the lawyer and film critic who worked pro bono for Negulesco as a friend, advised him to leave the project as a dead end.[26] The film started out with many parents, but its failure to satisfy officials had swiftly rendered it an orphan.

The kind of lesson that Negulesco's orphan film taught, or is capable of teaching, is worthy of sincere consideration. As the continuing work on emergent cinemas has established, grand failed projects, and especially failed experiments in prestige production, mark points of friction and recalibration between cinema institutions with different trajectories. How these failures unfold can reveal the networks and currents undergirding the well-known stories of the hero-directors of a particular national industry. *The Heroes* did not come to Iran at an uneventful time, nor was it a peripheral production. It involved many major political figures as well as people who were or would go on to form the center of the industry in Iran. Several contributors to the film would assume major roles in the development of the Iranian New Wave. This included not only several Iranian actors but also directors and future heads of the film industry. The *Cahiers du cinéma* critic and brother of the prime minister Fereydoun Hoveyda served as a consultant on the production and had a hand in others that would follow. Farmanara went on to direct important films in the 1970s and to head the state-funded FIDCI, where he contributed to several international collaborations. These central figures in 1970s Iranian cinema continued to circulate film investment capital across Iran's borders, but they brought technologies and personnel into Iran with a cautious attention to scale. Later projects linked up not with movie palaces like the Moulin Rouge but with the Tehran International Film Festival and its mode of presenting new and old work. The FIDCI supported, in addition to stand-alone work by local filmmakers such as Kimiai's *Ghazal*, a number of art-house collaborations, including *The Desert of the Tartars* (Zurlini, 1976), which rejected the typical touristic gaze of coproductions by making the fortress at Bam look like a series of de Chirico paintings, and Orson Welles's *F for Fake*, which premiered alongside a Welles retrospective at the festival (figure 38).[27] Looking back at the precursors to this industrial practice, especially the bitter lessons of a year better known for its influential successes, helps provide a context that can counterbalance those nostalgic milestones of the emergence of Iranian cinematic art.

KIMIAI'S FIRST FILM CYCLE

As assistant director on *The Heroes*, Kimiai was the Iranian director with the most to learn, or to forget, from the experience of that production. It was an uncommon experience in any case, and one that marks a banner year for a director whose uncommon education has formed part of his celebrity. Unlike most of his new wave colleagues, Kimiai did not have the opportunity to formally study his craft abroad. Representing his youth in interviews and through his characters, Kimiai suggests that his education came early from participation in neighborhood film fan culture. Even the tough-guy archetypes in his films interrelate with stories of encounters from his childhood.[28] This childhood mythmaking has, over the years, become an important part of the discourse that has framed his films. His experience at Studio Moulin Rouge provides a less romantic, but no less crucial, piece of the story. He was there as assistant director for Studio Moulin Rouge's early hit, the Akhavans produced

FIGURE 38. Advertisement for films sponsored by the Film
Industry Development Company of Iran, *Ghazal* and *F for Fake*.
In *Cinema*, November 27, 1975.

his small first directing effort, and he stayed through the project that
cauterized the studio's growing ambitions. This was the period of professionalization of a filmmaker, outside the sphere of formal education,
that immediately preceded his most influential cycle of films.

Kimiai was still an aspiring filmmaker at work on his first feature
when Negulesco hired him, allowing him to engage with his production
methods firsthand. In an interview I conducted with him in 2014 at
his own creative hub, his studio and film school in downtown Tehran,
Kimiai spoke highly of his time working with Negulesco and said that
Negulesco took some time to join him in the editing room while he
finished his first feature:

I was his first assistant director and was also making my first film at that time. He didn't have anything to do for a few days so he came to look at my work. He told me, about my first film, "This is not your film." It was called *Come Stranger* [*Biganeh Biya*, also produced by the Akhavans]. He told me, "This is not your cinema. Your cinema is [the kind we are making]. I am making a film in Paris after this. Let's go to Paris, and then let's go to Hollywood, where you can make a Western" [laughs]. I love to watch Westerns but that's not the same as making them.[29]

In this moment of looking back late in his career, he describes an experience with a globalized big-budget production and the story of declining an opportunity to work abroad on the eve of his rise to celebrity in Iran. In Kimiai's famous features that followed his work on *The Heroes*, he relayed Hollywood situations and genre conventions as he helped define a new movement in his home industry. These films were rooted in the Tehran neighborhood tough-guy genres, but unlike those films often characterized by a weak authorial presence, they announced the hand of their director and broadcast their allusions to global cinema history. They were authored films that drew from Hollywood action cinema, from film noir, and most prominently from the western. And they employed some of the same Iranian stars and crew from *The Heroes*. To think of his most famous films and his locally trained public persona obliquely, with the recent history of his orphaned work in mind, is to open up the peculiar textures of their many references to other films, which include along with the well-known triumphalism and nostalgia for cinematic canons an equal serving of fascination with the failures of also-ran auteurs.

Qeysar scrambled the codes of the tough-guy genres to produce a peculiar kind of prestige film. It is among the best-known Iranian classic films among Iranians. Unlike the many *filmfarsi* mayflies that remained in cinemas only briefly, *Qeysar*'s endurance on screens caused exhibitors to announce that the industry had reached a turning point.[30] Among critics, the film was long discussed for its revolutionary energy, its violence, and its reception as an allegory for mounting frustrations with the Pahlavi government. The film achieved its uncommon form of prestige by combining Iranian genre tropes with social urgency and by layering its references to both high and low Hollywood. It places Tehran tough guys in situations common in the revenge-plot western of the 1960s. Kimiai took part of his inspiration from *Nevada Smith* (Hathaway, 1966), in which Iranian favorite Steve McQueen plays an antihero who carries out a series of revenge killings. Like Nevada Smith,

Qeysar (Behrouz Vossoughi) uses a blade for his first killing, which he performs in a bathhouse. Hamid Naficy has noted how the rapid cutting and close-ups recall the shower scene in *Psycho*.[31] The location is iconic in two ways. It recalls one of the best-known scenes of violence in Hollywood, and it showcases the space of the hammam, an iconic site often turned into a tourist attraction in historical cities. This relocated auteurist sequence is implanted into a story structure inspired by a Hollywood film that, while certainly watched by dedicated fans of Steve McQueen, was well off the radar of those who would form the Western canons of Hollywood prestige. And yet here is *Nevada Smith*, a lackluster Embassy Pictures production, serving as inspiration for a pivotal prestige film. In their circulation, the film's diverse components encounter a series of realignments of prestige.

Kimiai's next two films, both also starring Behrouz Vossoughi from *Qeysar* and *The Heroes*, explore that same movement between new wave and commercial, and between strata of the archive of Hollywood in Iran. Both *Dash Akol* (1971) and *Reza Motori* (*Reza the Biker*, 1970) end with the genre trope of the tragic death of the noble rogue, or *luti*, but they set this death in reference to Hollywood. In *Dash Akol*, he transposed the basic plot structure of a 1950s western onto nineteenth-century Shiraz. *Dash Akol* reimagines a famous Iranian modernist short story as a western that, like the tragic American western, was set in the nineteenth century at a turning point in its country's engagement with modernity. It mourned the death of a character whose form of masculinity was doomed by the engagement. The final, tragic showdown of that film happens not outside of a watering hole but on a stage, immediately following a *ta'zieh*, a passion-play performance. The action sequences in this film are not the only scenes that walk in close step with *The Heroes*. The staging of the angst-ridden love scene with a dancer, and the camera angle used in the *zurkhaneh* (gymnasium) sequence, appear to borrow directly from his work with Negulesco.

Reza the Biker also centers on a failed *luti* character. Reza's long monologues profess his desire to be a *luti*, but the irretrievable past he longs for is much closer. In this film Kimiai adapted a mistaken-identity plot for the tough-guy genre. Vossoughi played two characters, a motorcycle film deliveryman who becomes a gangster and an absurd, brainy doctor, who were comically opposed in a manner that recalled the plots of imported Indian films. Reza makes an explicit link between his desire to be a *luti* and his longing for the wilder bygone film scene of motorcycle deliverymen who thrived before the expanded corporate management of Tehran screens. Similar to the fate of all the characters from this cycle, the climax of the film is structured around a fated death. In this instance the killing takes place in an outdoor cinema, during which Reza leaves a handprint in blood on the screen. While it is not named, Iranian film fans would have recognized this as the outdoor screen of Cinema Diana—one of the historical downtown cinemas and a hub for import and dubbing.

In each of the three films in this career-defining early cycle, Kimiai's characters are bigger than life. They have outsized plans, but they are almost always at the end of their affective rope. They have exhausted their access to help. Their household or neighborhood economy of care is shattered. They want to return to a type of noble household.[32] They deliver soliloquies about the fantasy of this return to nobility and honor, and they die trying. For Kimiai, these are stories particularly suited to cinema, and they never veer far from a thick texture of citation of the many cinematic crosscurrents alive in 1960s Tehran. It is this fascination with a particular kind of masculine failure, combined with an outsider auteurism built around the fragments of the history of cinema in Iran, that drives the films of this cycle.

By the time Kimiai made the quiet, reflective *Eastern Boy*, he had achieved fame primarily through these three films. This fame, and Kimiai's romantic love of heroic underdog stories, soon landed him on the wrong side of government censors.[33] The CIDCYA, the well-known government organization founded to uplift and educate Iranian youth, had a lower profile than the commercial industry. His colleagues there offered him creative shelter to make *Eastern Boy* and *Asb* (*The Horse*, 1976) while tensions with the government dissipated. *Eastern Boy* is an exceptional Kimiai film in two senses. It stands out as unusual, but it also condenses the elements that had defined his 1970s features. Put another way, this noncommercial return to childhood seems to examine the motifs he had almost compulsively repeated in his commercial narrative features. The look back from *Eastern Boy*, in 1975, to his own formative years as a filmmaker spans this productive period. It is a complicated look back from a film industry that had developed stable systems of sponsorship, a prominent international film festival, and a group of directors with festival ambitions. It is a story of the emergence of this scene, ostensibly set in the present of 1975, but it overlaps with multiple moments in cinema history. It is partly about his childhood in the 1950s and his education through watching serials like *Tarzan* and *Zorro*, but it is also about the growth of urban cinema culture in the

1960s and these cinemas' relay of a heterogeneous spectrum of film that included both scrap footage and prestige films. It incorporates three decades of Iranian cinema history, a history that prominently includes the archive and circulation of films from abroad. It is with this archival history of these crucial years in mind that the orphaned *Eastern Boy* offers its perspective on the institutions of cinema in 1970s Iran.

SPONSORSHIP, NOSTALGIA, AND COLLECTING

What sets *Eastern Boy* apart is its sense of uneasiness with art cinema. It was created in another type of collaborative compromise with the CIDCYA. Thus, it did not rely on commercial infrastructure the way most of Kimiai's other films did. The CIDCYA's film division, operating separately from its successful theater division in its preference for location shooting and untrained actors, is best known as an incubator for the careers of art filmmakers such as Abbas Kiarostami.[34] *Eastern Boy*'s observational style and loose narrative structure do resemble the quasi-neorealist mode of other CIDCYA films. It was a product of the center that nonetheless resisted its ethos of uplifted quality filmmaking and management of media education. Even in this film, made outside his usual commercial sphere of production, the viewer sees the same ambivalent blend of high and low found in the famous features from Kimiai's early cycle. It was a neorealist sponsored film made by a director suspicious of imitating those modes. It was a contemplative film by a master of bravado, which kept the painful clashes of those earlier films within reach. If Kimiai's most successful films can be characterized by ambivalence toward their influences, toward exchanges in cinema history, and toward archetypes of Iranian modernity, *Eastern Boy* translates these concerns in the sphere of sponsored art cinema.

The film turns heavily on nostalgic tropes, but it avoids the recuperative nostalgia common in narrative films about an artist's childhood. It follows a group of boys collecting and trading 35 mm film scraps, playing popular sandlot games while impersonating Tarzan, gambling with their collections in an alley, and flying a homemade kite (emblazoned with its own Zorro mask) from an empty parking structure. Encountering these iconic elements of film-fan nostalgia, a critic might recall Hajir Dariush's claim that *Qeysar* presented iconic scenes of urban Tehran as if looking in on them with a foreign gaze.[35] Such an interpretation might make the link to the thinning of cinema history in nostalgic work by Peter Bogdanovich or later nostalgia films such as *Cinema*

Paradiso (Tornatore, 1988), which trades on similar allusions and arguably reduces history to style. The film does downplay the importance of television, which might have complicated the romantic depictions of the space and material of cinema. But although *Eastern Boy* does look back at a mythologized childhood, it avoids showy landmarks and does not display the sure-footed proprietorship of film history of a polished nostalgia film. Kimiai's ambivalence about the styles and discourses of quality persists here as in his other films, which achieved quality-film status by another route.

The first key to *Eastern Boy*'s untidy relationship to nostalgia is the framing activity of film collecting, itself. It is a trope long familiar in Iranian fan culture and reflects the kinds of cultural adaptations, discussed throughout this book, that emerge in a film scene toward the end of the chain of distribution. An interest in the afterlife of these fragments of film has persisted in fan culture as well as within the most authoritative intellectual institutions of Iranian cinema. They are an important part of the oral history of cinema culture in Iran. In their frequent retelling, these individual stories have become interwoven with the formative accounts of film studies, of museum curating, and of filmmaking. At the Cinema Museum in Tehran, in the center of the exhibit on memorabilia, is featured a similar stack of junk film arranged in front of an album. Darius Khondji, a cinematographer known for his work with Woody Allen, tells stories of "swimming" in celluloid as the child of a Tehran film distributor.[36] Junk celluloid appears in multiple films and publicity materials. It can be found everywhere, from the 1970s Film Bazaar and competition posters at the Tehran International Film Festival to the piles of celluloid being fed to veteran Iranian actor Ezzatollah Entezami in *Naser al-din Shah, Actor-e Cinema* (*Once upon a Time, Cinema*; Makhmalbaf, 1992). This final example is also a reference to 1969 and Entezami's role in *The Cow*. The trope appears, as noted in chapter 1, in recent film scholarship as well. These examples suggest why it is particularly relevant when, in *Eastern Boy*, Kimiai uses this trope to frame the story of his own film education. It is an early iteration of a foundational story of the kind of cinephilia carefully uncovered by Ramin S. Khanjani in his essay on Kimiai's oeuvre.[37] Film here is a forgotten object onto which value has been reassigned. In these scenes, the film reinforces the indication by curators and scholars that this material could be made more visible as an archive.

As a work structured around a reevaluation of secondhand cinema, *Eastern Boy* invites a closer look at the film-historical texture of its assemblages. In chapter 1, I tracked the serial's prominence as an unusual kind of prestige picture in Tehran's late silent era. In *Eastern Boy*, Kimiai extends this history of the inversion of the serial's low-brow status into postwar film culture. Adventure serials feature prominently in Iranian cinema history. Kimiai and Parviz Davaii, the writer who penned the story on which Kimiai based *Eastern Boy*, have helped tell this history throughout their careers when they have revisited their childhood love for Republic serials. *Eastern Boy* is filled with these references. The only time we see any of the junk film projected is after Zorro finds fragments of old films and a silent film projector in the basement that houses all of his father's *ta'zieh* equipment (figures 39a–39c). The clips Zorro mixes and matches in his makeshift basement cinema depict swashbuckling adventures that formed typical plots for midcentury serials, but the most prominent among them is footage from Karel Zeman's *Vynález zkázy* (*Invention for Destruction*, 1958). This footage was likely obtained when the CIDCYA sent emissaries, including Davaii, to Prague and Zlín (Gottwaldov) to purchase material. The 1950s Czech animation comingles with autobiographical references to Republic serials, by way of the CIDCYA. The most prominent reference to serials in the film is, of course, its main emblem. Zorro stories were continually recycled in film serials made after the silent era. Not only does the mask remain on the boy's face throughout the film, but the boys also affix it to a kite made of the same cellulose diacetate material as film frames in their albums. The closest the viewer gets to seeing one of these frames illuminated is when sunlight is transmitted through the boys' Zorro kite, which renders the mask and the faces of the boys behind the kite as images on celluloid (figures 40a, 40b).

UNDER THE SIGN OF *RIO BRAVO*

The film's other major references center, as noted earlier, on Kimiai's favorite genre, but even these scenes foreground the object lives of the films. The film engages less in imitation of western character types than in reflection on the circulation of specific westerns in Iran. *Eastern Boy* does not stage boys playing cowboy like Shapur Gharib's *Hafttir-ha-ye Chubi* (*Wooden Sixshooters*), another CIDCYA film released that same year. Instead, it stages one of the most important scenes, the only scene that comes close to Kimiai's trademark hero monologue from the early cycle of films, in front of a cinema displaying a billboard for *Rio Bravo*. The film choice fits. It is a slow-burn meditation on what constitutes

FIGURES 39A–39C. Zorro projecting film for a paying audience in a basement in *Pesar-e Sharqi / Eastern Boy* (Masoud Kimiai, 1975).

FIGURES 40A, 40B. Sunlight transmitting actors' faces through an album made of film frames and through a kite made of celluloid in *Pesar-e Sharqi / Eastern Boy* (Masoud Kimiai, 1975).

honorable masculinity. The plot of *The Heroes* borrows liberally from it, and one can observe many similarities between its stubborn, diminished characters and those of Kimiai's films. But the physical history of this film is just as important to understanding its position in *Eastern Boy*. The Warner Bros. archive reveals that it was exported to Iran two years after the initial release date in the United States. In late summer of 1961, two used positive prints were shipped from the Warner office in Cairo to the owners of Cinema Rex on Lalezar Avenue.[38] The lag time was minimal and suggests special treatment of a prestige import. The affidavit of destruction was requested in 1964, but some prints survived the ax and the film persisted on screens for more than a decade afterward, when the dubbed version was shown in double features with local productions in second-run cinemas on Lalezar Avenue.[39]

Prints were not the only component of this circulation history, and *Eastern Boy*'s treatment of graphic and audio material is also noteworthy. Distributors' packages included publicity kits and dubbing aids so the material could be adapted for Iranian audiences. Before the prints of *Rio Bravo* arrived in 1961, dialogue scripts were sent to Tehran so that dubbing translation work could begin immediately. The posters shipped for the initial release in Iran came from Italy.[40] They used designs from the Warner office in Rome, and the Italian title, *Un dollaro d'onore*, is listed on the English-language invoice. Kimiai manipulated both image and sound from the *Rio Bravo* kit as he incorporated it into his film. The billboard in *Eastern Boy*, which Kimiai says he had painted for the film, was a mélange of poster designs and used the American release title, *Rio Bravo*. Likewise, since the Warner records indicate that this film was immediately dubbed, it is revealing that the boys in Kimiai's film listen to original English dialogue over the loudspeaker. While this dialogue would have been recognizable to the attentive western fan as belonging to *The True Story of Jesse James* (Ray, 1957), it was structured, diegetically, as dialogue from the print of *Rio Bravo* playing inside. In each of these examples, the fragments and peripheral materials rewarded viewers who knew the many allusions, particularly those of Kimiai's and Davaii's generation. A color Cinemascope print of *Jesse James* premiered in Tehran as part of the New Year holiday program in late March 1959 at Cinema Radio City.[41] At the time of this premiere, Kimiai was about five years older than the boys in *Eastern Boy*, and Davaii was in his mid-twenties.

No one knew these references better than the critics and the readership of auteurist publications in Iran, for whom *Rio Bravo* was foundational. In the intervening years between the Tehran release of *Rio Bravo* and Kimiai's autobiographical film, *Rio Bravo* in Iran underwent a transformation. Auteurists in Iran engaged in conversation with the writers of the French new wave and the British journals *Sight & Sound* and *Movie. Cahiers du cinéma* critics, including Fereydoun Hoveyda, singled out Hawks as among the preeminent auteurs and included *Rio Bravo* on many of their canonizing lists. During this time the editors of *Movie* published their famous special issue on Hawks, which included Robin Wood's influential essay on *Rio Bravo*. These publications circulated among film intellectuals in Iran in English, in French, and in Persian translation. One of the most respected critics working in this vein in 1960s Iran was none other than Parviz Davaii. Davaii's body of work for film journals, and his translations of books such as François Truffaut's *Hitchcock* and Joseph McBride's *Howard Hawks*, cemented auteurism as a critical position from which to structure practices of prestige. In a 1963 issue of *Film va Zendegi*, Davaii published both a review of *Rio Bravo* and a Persian translation of the *Sight & Sound* critic Peter John Dyer's influential essay on Hawks.[42] The *Rio Bravo* reference in *Eastern Boy* thus also nodded to the critical writings of the author who wrote its original story, the same critic who had helped canonize *Rio Bravo* in Iran and had encouraged the intellectual reception of the western. When *Eastern Boy* looks back, it looks back across the period of increasing Iranian engagement with European auteur theory about Hollywood directors such as Howard Hawks and Nicholas Ray.

Taken together, the distribution, publicity, and intellectual histories of *Rio Bravo* in Iran draw attention to the disjointed chronology of the reference to this film within the film. *Eastern Boy* is a film set in contemporary 1975 but is loosely based on the early 1950s childhood of the director. But this film was shipped in 1961 and "destroyed" at least once in 1964, ten years before *Eastern Boy* was made and when the director was in a different formative stage in his early twenties. In this film about his childhood, he was showcasing a western that was in first-run theaters during his formative moments, not as a preadolescent film fan but as an aspiring professional filmmaker. The film's creators gather historical periods and offer a collage of iconic images and sounds from this film within the film. The film looks back to multiple pasts, prints, posters, and the organizations that circulated them. Serials popular from the silent era ripple through later decades. There are traces of a cinephilic childhood in the late 1950s culture of circulation, when Hollywood copyright owners still largely failed to see through the layers of intermediaries that relayed films through the region. In the same references there is a reflection of the auteurist culture from the 1960s. And finally, the film reflects the realities of the sponsored cinema of the 1970s. In this act of layering different moments in cinema history, sometimes a single reference resonates in multiple time frames.

This additive treatment of history calls critical attention to a body of work that had often explored nostalgia and its discourses of durability and obsolescence. Typical nostalgia films craft a marketable form of prestige through palatable historical stylization and a narrowing of history into a romantic narrative of artistic heritage. Kimiai's nostalgia follows these forms to a degree but then seems to take pride in their inversion. Zorro screens junk prints, dresses like Republic Picture serials, and reenacts adventure films. These acts of reevaluating scraps create an uneasy nostalgia. They look back in order to mourn failures as much as to rewrite the origin stories of a successful new wave. They provide an oblique relation to heroic histories of cinema. The boys cannot get inside to see *Rio Bravo*, they are bullied by peers and patriarchs, and their kite string breaks in the final scene. If the film is a kind of artistic autobiography, it seems to take pride in its inversion of nostalgic canons of influence and its resistance to catharsis. The film relays fragmented B melodramas alongside Howard Hawks films, and its main characters never emerge from feeling marginal or backward.

Eastern Boy's inversions complicate its auteurism. Through the film's juxtapositions, there is a kind of shuffling of the prestige of specific directors. Kimiai is in conversation with these traditions, citing Hitchcock, Hawks, and Ray, but he is also continually taking alternative positions in his curating of auteurs. He was perhaps more populist than Davaii in this respect. *Qeysar* is based on a film by Henry Hathaway. *Rio Bravo* is an emblem in *Eastern Boy*, but so is the recycling of its plot by Negulesco at Moulin Rouge in *The Heroes*. And the Hollywood director that Kimiai seems to champion most conspicuously is Vincent Sherman, "whose name was overshadowed by the bigger names in Hollywood."[43] Neither Negulesco, Hathaway, nor Sherman was considered a major director in the hierarchies of the industry or on the rolls of auteurist critics, but their work is active on this scene. Kimiai seems to interpret their work in a way that resonates with the plots of many of his own films. He sees them as second-tier underdogs in an insurmountable system, and he admires their adaptability within it. This is the kind of reoriented canon formation that is essential to understanding the relationship between these outsiders and prestige filmmaking in pre-revolution Iran. This particular constellation of Hollywood filmmakers does not come to the foreground in histories that take the American film industry or European auteur theory as their vantage point.

By cutting an alternative path through Hollywood genre filmmaking and its auteurs, *Eastern Boy* was able to maintain an outsider's view, too, of the CIDCYA. Hollywood was, of course, not the only globalized point of cinematic reference with which Kimiai's films engaged. He also expressed ambivalence about the influence of European new waves that, though not widely circulated in Iran, were an important reference for filmmakers and critics. The CIDCYA was one of the places that fostered a neorealist style in Iran. This style, and the directors who worked within it, brought Iranian cinema into a very different world orbit than the one imagined by the producers of *The Heroes*. Kimiai, with his commercially tuned prestige films, treated this mode with suspicion. Even now, more than forty years later, this is a point that he emphasizes. He appreciates the "logical and practical art" of commercial filmmaking over an art cinema that risks becoming "an intellectual game." This point is tied, for him, to the history of two different (but equally reflexive) approaches to filmmaking in Iran. He says, "Our cinema was 'movie-theater cinema' not 'film-study cinema.'" The CIDCYA is one of the strong markers of the beginning of what one might call "film-study cinema."[44] To a viewer whose attention has been trained on global art cinema, or more specifically on neorealist productions made in the global south and circulated on the festival market, *Eastern Boy* would probably stand out among all of Kimiai's films as affording the most immediate pleasures of recognition. But like *The Heroes*, its incongruities make it most interesting. Here is Kimiai making a sponsored, neorealist film about the education of youth—inhabiting one of the most prominent incubators of a local neorealist tradition. But it is an allegory for this countercurrent in the emergence of the new wave. His story of movie-theater cinema, with its appropriations of secondhand celluloid and overheard movie dialogue, does not completely merge with the educational mission of the center.[45] The film foregrounds its cultural politics with its title (sometimes translated as *Oriental Boy*), but it does not ultimately lend itself to a cultural criticism that would seek a simple imperial target. Its critical engagement is better understood as embedded in the networks of cinema's circulation that had disintegrated that target in Iran. *Eastern Boy*'s citations from the archive of global film commerce should not be considered separate from its uneasy relation to the CIDCYA bureaucracy and its version of global art cinema.

To pursue an archivally focused history of prestige cinema and circulation of this period in Iran means expanding on the work of film historians who think about false starts, asynchrony, and overlapping chronologies—not as obstacles to writing cinema's aesthetic, business, and technological history but as opportunities. *The Heroes* is one of several spectacular false starts in Iranian cinema history, and *Eastern Boy* is a small and largely forgotten film that reflects on the importance of the false starts of this earlier interaction with Hollywood. These films' ambitions and failures indicate a local cinema history with a tricky chronology, one in which 1950s adventure serials, 1960s auteurism, and

1970s sponsored cinema overlap. Here the boundaries delimiting uplift cinema, global melodrama, and sponsored art film, which have worked so well for categorizing modes of film practice elsewhere, are porous. To describe these volatilities as crises in media formation might seek to define this cinema along historiographical lines that work best for other cinemas of the 1960s and 1970s. The early work of a filmmaker like Kimiai, which derives part of its character from its multiple changes of course within ephemeral motion-picture bureaucracies, might instead remind us not to obfuscate the casual flexibility and enduring experimentation in this period, which indeed thrives on the unpredictability of relay.

This moment in Iranian cinema history continues to resurface in new work. When I interviewed Kimiai in 2014, he was about to release a new film, *Metropole*, and was busy with press engagements and awards events coordinated with the release of the film. The timing was more than appropriate. After fielding several questions about looking back at 1970s commercial cinema, the formation of the Iranian new wave, his work on *The Heroes*, and the history of Hollywood in Iran, Kimiai finally paused the interview and brought me into the editing room to see the trailer, set to the soundtrack of *Johnny Guitar* (Ray, 1954), for the soon-to-be-released film. Kimiai naturally wanted to promote his new film as I asked him to reflect back on his work from the 1970s, but it was no stretch to say that *Metropole*, *Eastern Boy*, and his early cycle of features dwelled in the same preoccupations. *Metropole*, set in the ruin of a famous downtown cinema, imagines that ruin as populated by the ghosts of old Hollywood and Hong Kong productions. The film returns to that same decade of origin of the New Iranian Cinema, and its mise-en-scène bulges with material from the archive of Hollywood in Iran. The projection booth is cluttered with lobby cards, junk celluloid, and obsolete paperwork. Several 35 mm films, including some well-known films like *The Hustler* (Rossen, 1961), and more of the works of underdog auteurs like Vincent Sherman, still run in an auditorium that is now used to hang laundry and store motorcycles.[46] Many of the most dramatic scenes inside the cinema include prominent displays of posters for films including *One Eyed Jacks* (Brando, 1961), *The Devil's Disciple* (Hamilton, 1959), and *Killers on Wheels* (Kuei, 1976), which represent the kinds of workhorse action films that Kimiai cited in the 1970s. The new film presents the historic Metropole cinema as a space of collection of curiosities, and it features the most extensive use of found footage of his career. It intercuts between the unfolding gangster drama of disputed inheritance and dubbed scenes of 1960s westerns, including, most prominently, one featuring Kirk Douglas in *Lonely Are the Brave* (Miller, 1962). The stubborn, fate-driven cowboy film is full of quintessential Kimiai pathos, signaled best by its alternate title in its global circulation, *The Last Hero*.

Coda

The curiosity rewarded by histories of relay is one that dwells in odd encounters. These encounters point out the mismatches between small-scale phenomena and broad, seemingly irreversible, trends. They favor the pleasures of adding to explanations rather than the desire to exhaust or complete explanations, and they highlight what is made possible by accidents of being in the right place at the right time. Circulation follows pathways defined as much by obstructions as by opportunities, both of which are often arbitrary. Equally contingent are the obstructions and opportunities encountered by researchers when trying to access material in collections located so far apart.

During my two-year teaching assignment in Qatar, I had the opportunity both to travel easily to archives in Iran and to work out many of this project's questions in the classroom. In Cinemas of the Middle East, during my first year in Doha, the class was discussing the contrasting scales of cinema as it circulates. The incongruities between large sponsored film events and everyday circulation resonated with the students in the course. They appreciated the way a film could exist as a representative of a globally dominant film industry while its cultural life also persisted in informal collections and aging dog-eared magazines. During the course, a Saudi student drew my attention to a local etymology that she believed encapsulated this incongruity. *Wanet*, in Saudi Arabic, refers to a small pickup truck. The term is said to have its origins in the towns where ARAMCO had a strong presence. She told me that the term also has been used to refer, beyond the trucks themselves, to supplies brought in on those trucks, including imported items of popular culture such as magazines and films. Linguists who have discussed the term believe it to be an approximation of the English pronunciation of "one eight," a number somehow associated with American trucks used in the oil towns.[1] Writing this conclusion, now in another contingent location within the orbit of Detroit, has made me curious enough about automotive minutiae to learn that Ford Motor Company used the digits 1 and 8 as a prefix in its serial numbering system of the 1930s to designate a regular (1), eighty-five horsepower, eight-cylinder (8) engine for its pickup trucks. The company archives that detail this also possess information about how many of these vehicles were built in Michigan factories by workers whose native or familial language was Arabic.

What was compelling in our classroom discussion of the Saudi usage was the idea that films and fan magazines could be referenced with a term of small-scale circulation somewhat at odds with the large-scale rhetoric and global reach of the distribution offices and publishers associated with major Hollywood studios.[2] An everyday maintenance vehicle of oil towns could serve as a metonym for the products of a global entertainment industry. The cargo capacity of a small vehicle, as a vector, reminds one of the value in considering the micromovements of objects, no matter how vast the systems of global circulation. Sometimes, one small handoff in the relay of an object through a larger network is enough to consider, even if copies of that object exist elsewhere. From the end of the silent period through the 1960s, a great deal of reimagining and recontextualization took place in these small exchanges. An archive of circulation need not exclusively direct one to macro systems of global circulation during the time of the American century. It might also reveal the modest relays at numerous points within that system. Local maintenance practices, affidavits of destruction, and worries over torn sprocket damage constitute the texture of this history. Moving in closer to small and ephemeral exchanges reveals a wide flexibility and varied forms of labor during this period when media content was globalizing but when media objects still took considerable time and effort to move around.

Conclusions often widen the scope of a project as they address what comes after. What comes after the many encounters at midcentury, the 1970s cinema in Iran, is surely a decade in which distributors, art filmmakers, festival organizers, and Omnimax enthusiasts went big.[3] But even the most high-profile projects have their failures, microhistories, and unfamiliar networks that can be revealed through interarchival investigation. The 1970s included several overlaps of government spectacle and commercial cinema, perhaps the most ambitious of these being the attempt to find a major Hollywood director to make a film about Cyrus the Great. The Akhavans at Moulin Rouge had a script in the 1960s, but it was the energy leading up to a major government spectacle, the 2,500-year celebration in the fall of 1971, that ramped up discussion of this project. Such an effort, this time bringing Hollywood directors to Tehran to pitch the idea, bears a kind of symmetry with the press discussion of Griffith's *Fall of Babylon* in the 1920s. Hollywood's capacity to spectacularize Cyrus the Great was revisited almost fifty years after Griffith's film had ironically served as a pretext for nationalist advertisements in *Ettela'at* back in the 1920s. In an exchange brokered by Arsham Yesians, the importer-exhibitor then serving as the United Artists representative, Joseph Mankiewicz was invited to the project.[4] The idea at this point was to possibly include footage of the events at Persepolis. "The visit [by Mankiewicz] must come before the 2500 years Monarchy celebrations which is commencing from October 12 to 21. Maybe Mr. Mankiewitz [*sic*] will suggest a special cameramen [*sic*] to come over during the celebrations and film part of the historical pageantry which later can be used in the picture."[5] David Chasman, an executive at UA, and Mankiewicz appear to have taken the proposal seriously. They concluded their discussion with a casting suggestion. "Do you think Kirk Douglas is too old to play Cyrus the Great?"[6] The production of this epic did not ultimately work out, but it was during these years that major Hollywood directors found themselves in Iran for a number of projects. Although the Cyrus project was another ambitious dead end of Hollywood encounters in the 1970s, the Tehran International Film Festival took up some of that momentum and endured throughout the decade. It was for the events of 1971 that several filmmakers were invited to Iran, but it was during the years of the festival that major Hollywood directors visited with regularity.

William Wyler first encountered this hospitality in the fall of 1971, when he saw *The Cow*, was gifted a carpet by Fardin, and was "treated royally by various organizations of the film industry" (figure 41).[7] He returned in 1974 for the festival, following the model of Frank Capra, who came in 1973 for a retrospective of his own work while he served on the jury. I am drawn to Capra's and, especially, Wyler's interactions with the festival, but not because they were necessarily the most significant guests of the festival. There is another book to be written about

قالی «فردین» برای «ویلیام وایلر»

● «ویلیام وایلر» که برای دیدار از فیلم «گاو» به‌فردین فیلم رفته بود، وقتی باقالی‌های خوش‌رنگ وفرم دفتر فرودین فیلم رو پروبشد، یادش رفت که اصلا برای چه به آنجا آمده است و همه حواسش متوجه قالی‌ها بود، تا وقتیکه «فردین» متوجه وضع شد ویکی ازقالی‌های دفترش را به او هدیه‌کرد، و آنوقت «وایلر» به صرافت‌فیلم «گاو» افتاد ودرباره‌اش به‌سئوالات اطرافیانش که نظر اوراخواستار بودند، پاسخ داد!! ودرپایان نیز ازفردین خواست که بـا او عکسی به یادگاری برروی قالی بردارد و نتیجه‌اش تصویر بالا شد، ببینید «وایلر» چقدر شادست، انگار بزرگترین و با ارزش‌ترین هدیه طول عمرش را‌گرفته است!

FIGURE 41. Fardin gifts a carpet from his office to William Wyler during a screening of *Gav / The Cow* (Dariush Mehrjui, 1969).

a guest list that included Satyajit Ray and Lina Wertmuller as well as a roster that included Eastern European and Asian films in a different type of triangulation than other festivals at the time. The archives reveal the controversies and opportunities created by critics such as Molly Haskell, both in her home press in New York as well as in the universities of Iran, where she spoke with students alongside Joan Shigekawa and Eleanor Perry.[8] What the exchanges of Capra and Wyler highlight are the differing scales of circulation as well as the linkages between festival and commercial exhibition. They help to place some of these developments of the 1970s in the frame of the earlier configurations traced in this book. Somewhat surprisingly, they also open up to micro-histories of maintenance and care, even at events that took place at this level of official scrutiny and sponsorship. From the sourcing of prints to the appeal to audience, it is the points of intersection among small histories of circulation and large-scale public events that open up avenues for analysis across subfields in cinema history.

The festival itself is a story of several institutional collaborations. As the festival was taking shape, Michael Kutza, the founder of the Chicago International Film Festival, was brought in as its United States chairman. When I interviewed Kutza in 2017, he explained how it was his involvement with juries and programs of young American directors at the Spoleto, Taormina, and Venice Film Festivals when he was in his late twenties that put him on the radar of festival organizers in Tehran. He acknowledged that the event was framed as an outgrowth of the Persepolis celebration, mentioning that he worked with Farah Pahlavi on the details and that the goal was to bring high-profile Hollywood names from the start. He brought long-career stars including Claudette Colbert and emerging critics including Roger Ebert to the festival in its first season. Frank Capra came in the second season, and Wyler returned to Iran in the third. Records in the Wyler papers indicate that Kutza extended the invitation for Wyler to be a guest of the festival only six months after his 1971 visit to Iran. Wyler's friend Melville Shavelson, who was also planning to attend, encouraged him to consider: "An invitation will be sent to you, probably via flying carpet."[9]

Kutza's initial and favored contact in Iran was neither someone at the Ministry of Culture and Art nor the director of the festival, but "this wonderful little blustery guy who reminded [him] of Edward G. Robinson."[10] Nureddin Ashtiany's work as a commercial exhibitor and importer has appeared throughout this book, including my opening example of the premiere of Khachikian's *The Strike*, but it was revealing that he was the point of contact between festival directors. The work of figures like Kavousi and Dariush on the festival is better documented. Ashtiany's involvement as its initial operations officer is less so. It is worth considering the ways that commercial exhibition infrastructure played into the shaping of festival decisions in its early years, despite it being primarily an effort driven by high-level government sponsorship and control. The points of continuity can be seen even in the choice to bring out the main lights of the festival in the early years. Capra and Wyler served on the jury and participated in critics' retrospectives of their work, but they also represented the films that had brought in some of the highest returns in Tehran theaters at the time when Ashtiany was a leader in the lucrative midcentury film trade. Kutza remembers that

FIGURE 42. Advertisement for *Funny Girl* (William Wyler, 1968). Courtesy of Ehsan Khoshbakht.

Ashtiany pushed to bring Barbra Streisand as a guest of the inaugural festival.[11] His hopes to bring Streisand (and Wyler) must have been influenced by the success of *Funny Girl*, which had premiered in Tehran in December 1969, only a few months after its United States release date (figure 42).[12] *Ben Hur* was among the most popular and discussed Persian dubs and played extensively throughout the 1960s. These histories intermingled with the ones that brought Satyajit Ray to serve on the jury in the first year. Capra was on the jury that awarded one of the first statues received by the great Iranian neorealist director Sohrab Shahid Saless. The first festival was being planned during the year that *The Cow* was receiving awards at Venice and at Kutza's festival in Chicago.

The Wyler and Capra festival retrospectives had significant overlap, not only because of their status as evergreen box office drivers but also because they were directors of frequently adapted films. Khachikian had remade Wyler's *The Desperate Hours* (1955) as *Osyan* (*Rebellion*) in 1966. Fardin had adapted *Pocketful of Miracles* (Capra, 1961) as *Gedayan-e Tehran* (*Tehran Beggars*, 1966). *Vasvaseh* (*Temptation*, Raf'at, 1965) was a Tehran adaptation of the Hindi film *Chori Chori* (Thakur, 1956), itself an adaptation of *It Happened One Night* (Capra, 1934).[13] In some ways, this shared terrain of commercial exhibition, remakes, and festival retrospectives returns to Kavousi's harsh criticism in his attempt to call out Azhir Film for counterfeiting *Gilda* with *The Midnight Cry*. Kavousi's main evidence was that he wanted to show the film in his own club in 1960: "About a year ago I visited the owners of the print of *Gilda* to inquire about showing it in a program at the ciné club. They told me that it was with Missaghieh. When I asked if it would be possible to show it the following week, they said no, for now it stays there. . . . They did not want simply to steal the scenario of *Gilda*, but to copy directly from the print itself."[14] Concerns over counterfeit aside, this anecdote illustrates the tug of war between institutions that is a recurring theme in the history of relayed cinema in midcentury Iran. A single print of a celebrated film noir was being held by a producer interested in making an ambitious commercial studio film. It was also pursued by a ciné club for the kind of work that ciné clubs do. This kind of intellectual attention aligned with the festivals in Venice and Locarno, at least more than it aligned with the daily business of filling seats in urban theaters.

But, as with many of these examples of tension, the line between competition and cooperation is not always so easy to draw. The ciné club programs are a clear precursor to the glitzy events of the Tehran International Film Festival of the 1970s, but in fact Ashtiany's festival involvement goes back to this period as well. The retrospective programs of 1337–1339 (1958–1961) indicate several negotiations in which Ashtiany's A.Sh.N.A. company owned some of the films and even put on a competing festival to Kavousi's juried program. They agreed to join efforts in subsequent years and worked together to bring recent films from several countries.[15] They exhibited, and awarded prizes to, some films that had also been through a commercial run in Iran, including *Mother India* (Khan, 1957), *Julius Caesar* (Mankiewicz, 1953), *Gaslight* (Cukor, 1944), *Rear Window* (Hitchcock, 1954), and *Lost Horizon* (Capra, 1937). Much of the discussion in the press was attentive to the task of separating out the commercial films that played in the festivals from proper festival fare. The *Setare-ye Cinema* critic and editor Parviz Nouri was among them when he lamented, in his review of the festival in January 1961, that "the films shown in this festival are not being presented by the countries that made them but are being chosen from among the films imported by movie theaters in the capital city. . . . They chose movies that had been sitting in the inventory for seven or eight years."[16] It was found footage indeed. While a thread of the history of relaying cinema in midcentury Iran has been the recycling of film material—the points of overlap between junk prints and classics, between the maintenance of film and prestige cinema, between the practical uses of found audio and the sonic imaginary of global cinema—it is worth remembering Ken Jacobs's statement that "a lot of film is perfect left alone."[17] Recycled cinema includes film physically transformed but also that which is simply transplanted, or "grafted," to use Ali Behdad's metaphor.[18] Film prints found and presented, particularly when that finding and presentation involves work with reels that were rendered invisible through a convoluted global relay system, can mark a perfect intervention. This overlooked intellectual labor is something to keep in mind when considering the threads that link an earlier history of commercial cinema with the age of festivals and new waves.

To generate a multifaceted historiography of globalized Iranian cinema means improving access, periodizing the enthusiasm for certain films, and exploring methodologies that produce knowledge from what remains. While the largest share of the scholarship on Iranian cinema positions it in a framework of global art cinema, a circulation-focused history can address familiar questions even as it engages with these later types of work. It can emphasize the orphaned projects and odd collaborations in the efforts to globalize. The informal distribution of prints from abroad and mobile Hollywood capital shaped constructions of quality cinema according to different formations of media's political economy than the one that initially circulated Iranian art cinema around the world. This approach, focused as it is on the construction of value, does not seek to reevaluate the great Iranian directors of the 1950s through the 1970s, let alone position Hollywood in Iran as a determining factor in their worth. Instead, it draws from historical Iranian film criticism and theory, much of it auteurist in orientation, and uses methods borrowed from other areas of cinema history to reconstruct some of that orientation. Bringing the archives, institutions, and their processes into the foreground can help locate the work of great directors in unfamiliar contexts. To this end, we might carry over from studies of emergent cinemas a curiosity for the histories of glorious disasters and small victories. This is not to periodize midcentury cinema in Iran as a kind of early cinema analogous to other early cinemas, and it is certainly not to suggest that the cinema of this period was somehow incomplete. The issue is rather how some of the features of the scholarship on early cinema, itself one of the most prominent rejections of infantilizing rhetorics of primitive versus developed cinema industries and aesthetics, might prove advantageous for those watchful of a narrowing historiography. And such watchfulness is well advised considering that a narrowed historiography could itself imply that the Iranian films of a certain period are underdeveloped in comparison to the handful that later achieved worldwide recognition (in part because of these later films' resemblance to work made abroad). The use of *film-farsi* has long intertwined substantive critiques with assumptions that such films are on the wrong side of progress. With a mixed historio-graphical approach, it is easier to suspend the impulse to prioritize the rise of a singular and definite national cinema, to study the geographies of auteurism while bracketing its evaluative mandate, and consequently to engage with the ways in which the discipline has historically posi-tioned cinemas of the Middle East.

The scene of film circulation in the mid-1970s, with its local studio representatives and high-profile international festival, is, for the most part, a different world than that of secondhand circulation and affida-vits of destruction. And yet, archives and oral histories tell us something about the small labors of moving and maintaining even these prints. Let me end with a final exchange that follows the object lives of a hand-ful of films within the noise surrounding the guests of the fest. Wyler's films in Iran were characterized by a tension that should by now be familiar: a simultaneous durability and fragility as they traveled these circuits. Durable in their afterlives, his commercial prints were able to be used for famous dubs and as reference screenings for Iranian film-makers. These off-the-grid prints operated in a separate sphere from festival prints. Even Jack Valenti, during all the conflict over the price of Hollywood films in Iran, agreed. When Wyler was preparing to send his films to Iran for the festival, he confirmed with Valenti, himself a guest of the festival, and was assured, "Jack advises strongly that there really is no problem getting these prints."[19] But the provenance of one of these prints reveals that this separation of categories was not always maintained. The film collector Ahmad Jurghanian, legendary among archivists for his collection of films and print material kept in basements and storehouses around Tehran, recounted meeting Wyler over a print he happened to have of *Roman Holiday* (1953). According to Jurgha-nian, the 1974 festival was not able to secure a print of this film. It was Jurghanian's own private collection, amassed largely from prints that had survived the affidavit of destruction, that made it possible for *Roman Holiday* to be included in the festival.[20] My research in the Wyler papers confirms both the importance of *Roman Holiday* for the 1974 program and its absence from the list of films sent from Los Angeles. In August of that year, Dariush discussed with Wyler the first-choice films for the retrospective.[21] The shipping receipt indicates that each of the first-choice films was sent from Paul Kohner's art-deco office on Sunset Boulevard in October, except for *Roman Holiday*.[22] That film played to acclaim at the festival, with the director as guest of honor, thanks to the labors of a collector and a durable print that had been officially destroyed years earlier.

While an old print of *Roman Holiday* was notable for its durability, it was the fragility of the rest of the films in the program that animated the postfestival correspondence. Upon return of the prints to the Goldwyn offices, general manager Jack Foreman wrote a letter detailing the "deplorable condition" of the returned reels: "We have been the custodian of your prints for a number of years. . . . It is impossible for us to understand how these prints could have been so mistreated."[23] The letter, which Wyler forwarded directly to the head of the Ministry of Culture and Art, listed film by film the torn sprocket holes, scratches, and sequences removed and "put back into the print via scotch tape and out of sequence."[24] Minister Pahlbod, a member of the royal family, settled the issue directly with Wyler while noting that "the films had been received by the festival in un-proper conditions."[25] The record suggests some truth to both positions.[26]

This exchange affirms something that any film programmer must learn: prints are expensive, but conversations about print conditions are never solely about their exchange value. The emotional labor of communicating another kind of value, from one maintainer to another, is part of the job. These objects were important enough for Jurghanian, the archivist, to lend a personal copy back to the director, enough for Foreman the studio executive to refer to himself as their "custodian," and enough for Wyler to tell Pahlbod, "The prints of these films . . . mean a great deal to me, much more than just their financial value."[27] Here, in the quiet months following the spectacle of a festival that drew celebrities to Iran with the promise of caviar and lavish accommodation, a modest and relatively common encounter is made strange by its incongruities of scale. A studio head, an Iranian royal, and a director of some of the most globally recognizable films at midcentury document specific emulsion scratches and torn celluloid perforations in a thirteen-month-long correspondence about the maintenance of secondhand prints.

Notes

1. The stages of production, from the découpage to the construction of sets ("an attraction for the eyes" in themselves on the studio backlot), were detailed in the press as the filmmakers announced that they were making *The Strike* "with the intention of certainly showing it in foreign countries." *Post Tehran Cinema'i*, 13 Khordad 1342 (June 3, 1963), reprinted in *Filmnameh: Zarbat (Screenplay: The Strike)* (Tehran: Museum of Cinema, 1381/2002), 82.

2. The magazine *Film va Honar* (*Film and Art*) printed a response from several filmmakers on 3 Ordibehesht 1343 (April 23, 1964) debating the ethics of this simultaneous release and who was to blame. Reprinted in *Filmnameh: Zarbat*, 82–84.

3. Jamal Omid describes the premiere at the Universal cinema in Tehran as an event that was even attended by the shah's sister. Jamal Omid, *Tarikh-e Cinema-ye Iran 1289–1375* (*History of Iranian Cinema, 1289–1375*) (Tehran: Entesharat-e Rowzaneh, 1374/1995), 360.

4. For an important recent resource to this end, see Massoud Mehrabi, *Sad-o-panj Sal E'lan va Poster-e Film dar Iran* (*One Hundred and Five Years of Film Advertisements and Film Posters in Iran*) (Tehran: Nazar Art Publishing, 1393/2014).

5. Recent scholarship on the design of film materials in the following decades in Iran includes that of the participants of a symposium on poster art in Iran at Northwestern University's Block Museum, particularly Shiva Balaghi, "Tracing History: Iranian Film Posters from the 1960s and 1970s" (paper presented

at *Lucid Figurations: Iranian Movie Poster Art and Film Art*, Evanston, IL, November 2016).

6. The pictorial considerations of his later work are still far less frequently discussed than his reflexive meditations on cinema's engagement with reality.

7. Between his early work for *Film va Zendegi* and his long career as a designer and professor of design in Tehran, Barirani spent some time in Bloomington, where he earned a graduate degree in design from Indiana University.

8. Iain R. Smith, *The Hollywood Meme: Transnational Adaptations in World Cinema* (Edinburgh, UK: Edinburgh University Press, 2016).

9. The source image for this hand-painted portrait of Turner is easy to find and makes a salient point of comparison.

10. "At that time, when the profession was not yet established, I used to memorize the color and form from foreign magazines. I would recreate them in my work using different colors and contrasts." Abbas Mazaheri, "Tarikh-e Shafahi-ye Placard-keshi az Zaban-e Abbas Mazaheri: az *Qeysar* ta *Ben Hur*" ("From the Tongue of Abbas Mazaheri: An Oral History of the Movie Placard from *Qeysar* to *Ben Hur*"), interviewed by Iranian Student News Agency on 31 Tir 1382 (July 22, 2003), last accessed July 17, 2020, www.isna.ir/news/8204 -13687/.

11. Gholam Heydari, *Samuel Khachikian: Yek Goftogu* (*Samuel Khachikian: A Conversation*) (Tehran: Entesharat-e Negah, 1381/2002), 29.

12. The message presented in the opening title sequence of the film, signed by Khachikian, frames the film as a social melodrama before the sequence switches into codes of film noir and gothic thriller. It says, "It is my wish that the story of this film will help to lift the shadow of despair and pessimism from the lives of those who are estranged from hope."

13. *F for Fake* and *The Other Side of the Wind* were produced with the help of institutions that received funding from the government. *And Then There Were None* (Collinson, 1974) was a British production that collapsed historical sites separated by hundreds of miles into one imaginary location. It was shot primarily at the Shah Abbas Hotel in Isfahan with scenes at Persepolis and the Bam Citadel.

14. Such frictions also reveal this sequence's affinity with earlier strains of modernist collage that fed into the commercialization of modern design at midcentury.

15. Bernhard Siegert, *Relays: Literature as an Epoch of the Postal System*, trans. Keving Repp (Stanford, CA: Stanford University Press, 1999), 12. It is worth pointing out that this influential work of media theory begins with the transformations in what Siegert defines as the first postal relay system in ancient Iran during the Achaemenid period.

16. Brian Edwards, *After the American Century: The Ends of U.S. Culture in the Middle East* (New York: Columbia University Press, 2015). Ramon Lobato, *Shadow Economies of Cinema: Mapping Informal Film Distribution* (London: British Film Institute Publishing, 2012).

17. With these specific examples of digital appropriations, I am referencing chapters from Lobato's and Edwards' books. Current work on the mobility and materiality of contemporary media has also informed my conception of the long

history of cinema's mobilities. See Kuhu Tanvir, "Breaking Bollywood: Moving Pictures on Mobile Screens," NECSUS (Spring 2018).

18. Iran received only a brief paragraph in Kristin Thompson, *Exporting Entertainment: America in the World Film Market, 1907–34* (London: British Film Institute, 1985).

19. Such approaches also share affinities with the recent emphasis on maintenance and repair in science and technology studies, which is a connection I take up most extensively in the second chapter.

20. See, for example, Rob King, "Discourses of Art in Early Film, or, Why Not Rancière?," in *A Companion to Early Cinema*, ed. André Gaudreault, Nicolas Dulac, and Santiago Hidalgo, (Oxford: Wiley, 2012), 141–62. I address institutional formations of prestige in my first book, and that question informs some of the work I am doing here despite the projects having no overlapping content. Kaveh Askari, *Making Movies into Art: Picture Craft from the Magic Lantern to Early Hollywood* (London: British Film Institute Publishing, 2014).

21. See Neepa Majumdar, Sudhir Mahadevan, Anupama Kapse, and Ramesh Kumar, "Early Cinema in South Asia: The Problem of the Archive," *Framework* 54:2 (Fall 2013), 134–57. Ana Lopez, "Early Cinema and Modernity in Latin America," *Cinema Journal* 40:1 (Fall 2000), 48–78.

22. Jennifer Bean, "Introduction," in *Silent Cinema and the Politics of Space*, ed. Jennifer Bean, Anupama Kapse, and Laura Horak (Bloomington: Indiana University Press, 2014), 8.

23. Ravi Vasudevan, "In the Centrifuge of History," *Cinema Journal* 50:1 (2010), 135–40. Hatim El-Hibri, "Media Studies, The Spatial Turn, and The Middle East," *Middle East Journal of Culture and Communication* 10 (2017), 27–48.

24. Hansen's analogies using rhetorical topoi date back to her early work on Rudolph Valentino. For a discussion in one of her essays on vernacular modernism, see Miriam Bratu Hansen, "Fallen Women, Rising Stars, New Horizons: Shanghai Silent Film as Vernacular Modernism," *Film Quarterly* 54:1 (2000), 17–19.

25. For Hansen's discussion of the connotations of idiom, discourse, and dialect, see "The Mass Production of the Senses: Classical Cinema as Vernacular Modernism," *Modernism/Modernity* 6:2 (1999), 61. In my evocation of relay's links to analogies of speech in transcultural cinema studies, I also have in mind, of course, Hamid Naficy, *An Accented Cinema: Exilic and Diasporic Filmmaking* (Princeton, NJ: Princeton University Press, 2001).

26. Blake Atwood, "Cassette Tape Histories: Rethinking Media in Iran" (paper presented at the Iranian Revolution and Its Disciplinary Aftereffects Symposium, Ann Arbor, MI, February 2019).

27. Dudley Andrew, "An Atlas of World Cinema," *Framework* 45:2 (2004), 12.

28. Claire Cooley, "Soundscape of a National Cinema Industry: Filmfarsi and Its Sonic Connections with Egyptian and Indian Cinemas, 1940s–1960s," *Film History* 32:2 (2020), 43–74.

29. Negar Taymoorzadeh, "Melodramatic Responses to Modernization across Turkey's Yesilçam and Iran's FilmFarsi" (PhD diss., New York University, forthcoming).

30. Babak Tabarraee, "Iranian Cult Cinema: An Introduction," in *The Routledge Companion to Cult Cinema*, ed. Ernest Mathijs and Jamie Sexton (London: Routledge, 2020), 98–104.

31. For a compelling discussion of circulation after 1979, see Mahsa Salamati, "Transnational Film Circulation in the Iranian Context: From Conjunctural Crisis to Discursive Heterotopia" (PhD diss., University of New South Wales, 2019).

32. Nolwenn Mingant, *Hollywood in North Africa and the Middle East: A History of Circulation* (Albany: SUNY Press, forthcoming).

33. Daniel Steinhardt, *Runaway Hollywood: Internationalizing Postwar Production and Location Shooting* (Berkeley: University of California Press, 2019). Ross Melnick, "Hollywood's Muddle East: Political Change in Egypt and Israel and the Consequences for Hollywood's Middle Eastern Movie Theaters," *Historical Journal of Film, Radio and Television* 37:2 (2017), 272–94. Nitin Govil, *Orienting Hollywood: A Century of Film Culture between Los Angeles and Bombay* (New York: NYU Press, 2015).

34. New designs indicated not just revivals but enduring runs. They engage in a practice that has been most formalized in India, where cinemas commission silver and gold jubilee posters for evergreen films. The Warner records for *Rebel without a Cause* in Iran indicate not only the years in which prints of the film were shipped, 1957 and 1966, but also the year in which new publicity material was requested to reframe the film, 1962. The owners of Cinema Rex had specifically requested an early version of the poster from the New York office, not the Rome office, to shape this film as a prestige film. They made this special request as their print of the film, shipped secondhand in 1957, ran through their projectors. Letter from Cinema Rex, Tehran, to Warner New York Office, Warner Bros. Collection, University of Southern California, Iran Sales, box 1, 1962. Two new 35 mm color cinemascope prints of *Rebel* were shipped to Cinema Rex on April 8, 1966. Warner Bros. Collection, University of Southern California, Iran Correspondence, box 2.

35. *Setare-ye Cinema* 110, 18 Ordibehesht 1336 (May 8, 1957), cover image. Novak is also featured with her Golden Globe statue on the inside cover of the following week's issue of *Setare-ye Cinema*.

36. See the cover for issue 5 (1957) of the arts and culture magazine *Film va Zendegi*, which also has a review of the Preminger film featuring a series of illustrations from the animated title sequence. "Yek Film-e Bozorg-e Ejtema'i" ("A Great Social Film"), *Film va Zendegi* 5, 1336 (1957), 12.

37. Amelie Hastie, *Cupboards of Curiosity: Women, Recollection, and Film History* (Durham, NC: Duke University Press, 2007).

38. Lawrence Liang, "Beyond Representation: The Figure of the Pirate," in *Making and Unmaking Intellectual Property*, ed. Mario Biagioli, Peter Jaszi, and Martha Woodmansee (Chicago: University of Chicago Press, 2011), 167–80.

39. Kavousi describes, as another point of origin, a cartoon he used in the magazine *Film va Honar* that depicted a donkey behind a camera and a title that read "filmfarsi." "An Interview with Dr. Houshang Kavousi," in *What Is Filmfarsi? (Filmfarsi Chist?)*, ed. Hossein Moazezinia (Tehran: Saqi Press, 1999), 9.

CHAPTER I. AN AFTERLIFE FOR JUNK PRINTS

1. "Syria's Picture Shows," *Motography* 7:7 (1912).

2. See the William Selig Papers, Margaret Herrick Library Special Collections, Academy of Motion Pictures Arts and Sciences, Beverly Hills, CA. The majority of correspondence about global distribution in the collection comes from London intermediaries such as the New Bioscope Trading Company and J. W. Wright and Son. The collection also contains a few letters from exhibitors in major cities in the Middle East and North Africa hoping to establish direct and more exclusive trade in Selig films.

3. Homer Croy, "Shadows of Asia: The Indian and the Cowboy Are the Only Favorites East of the Suez," *Photoplay* 11:3 (February 1917), 63.

4. "The Cinematograph in Aden," *Near East and India* 32:862 (1927). The exception of Aden is mentioned again in "Arabian Leaders Opposed to Display of Pictures," *Film Daily* 41 (October 30, 1927), 6.

5. "Arabian Leaders Opposed to Display," 6.

6. "Egyptian Picture-Goers," *Near East and India* 30:798 (1926).

7. "Syria's Picture Shows."

8. Valentia Steer, *The Romance of the Cinema: A Short Record of the Development of the Most Popular Form of Amusement of the Day* (London: C. Arthur Pearson, 1913), 40.

9. See Ernst Bloch, "Nonsynchronism and the Obligation to Its Dialectics," *New German Critique* 11 (1977), 22–38.

10. See Nicky Gregson and Louise Crewe, *Second-Hand Cultures* (Oxford: Berg, 2003), and Susan Strasser, *Waste and Want: A Social History of Trash* (New York: Metropolitan Books, 1999).

11. For more on the fantasies of positing one place as the past of another, see Arjun Appadurai, "Disjuncture and Difference in the Global Cultural Economy," *Public Culture* 2:2 (1990), 1–24.

12. Laurent Mannoni, *Le grand art de la lumière et de l'ombre: Archéologie du cinema* (Paris: Nathan, 1995); C. W. Ceram, *Archaeology of the Cinema* (New York: Harcourt Brace, 1965).

13. Michael Shanks, David Platt, and William Rathje, "The Perfume of Garbage: Modernity and the Archaeological," *Modernism/Modernity* 11:1 (2004), 61–83.

14. On modernist dreams of another archaeology, see the introduction to *Modernism/Modernity* 11:1 (2004), 1–16.

15. Shanks et al. remark that humans are one of the only species not attracted to garbage's colors and smells. They derive "the perfume of garbage" from Dominique Laporte's *History of Shit* (Boston: MIT Press, 2000), but a better reference point for a film historian would be the olfactory similarities between garbage and decaying nitrate and acetate.

16. Mohammad Ali Issari, *Cinema in Iran, 1900–1979* (London: Scarecrow Press, 1989).

17. Henry S. Villard, "Film Importers Face Difficulties in Persia," *Commerce Reports* 14 (1931).

18. On Reza Khan's relation to Atatürk, see Erik Touraj and Zürcher Atabaki, *Men of Order: Authoritarian Modernization under Atatürk and Reza Shah* (London: I. B. Tauris, 2004).

19. Michael Smith, "Cinema for the Soviet East: National Fact and Revolutionary Fiction in Early Azerbaijani Film," *Slavic Review* 56:4 (1997), 645.

20. Denise Youngblood, *Movies for the Masses: Popular Cinema and Soviet Society in the 1920s* (Cambridge: Cambridge University Press, 1992).

21. Yuri Tsivian, "Between the Old and the New: Soviet Film Culture in 1918–1924," *Griffithiana* 55/56 (1996), 15–63.

22. On the advantages of "the regional" as a frame for historical analysis, see Hamid Naficy, "For a Theory of Regional Cinemas: Middle Eastern, North African, and Central Asian Cinemas," *Early Popular Visual Culture* 6:2 (2008), 97–102.

23. Nicholas Dulac, "Distribution sérielle et synchronization du spectateur aux premiers temps du cinéma," in *Networks of Entertainment: Early Film Distribution 1895–1915*, ed. Frank Kessler and Nanna Verhoeff (Eastleigh, UK: John Libbey, 2007), 167–79.

24. See Ben Singer, *Melodrama and Modernity: Early Sensational Cinema and Its Contexts* (New York: Columbia University Press, 2001).

25. Jennifer M. Bean, "Technologies of Early Stardom and the Extraordinary Body," *Camera Obscura* 16:3 (2001), 8–57.

26. Weihong Bao, "From Pearl White to White Rose Woo: Tracing the Vernacular Body of *Nüxia* in Chinese Silent Cinema, 1927–1931," *Camera Obscura* 20:3 (2005), 193–231; Rosie Thomas, "Not Quite (Pearl) White: Fearless Nadia, Queen of the Stunts," in *Bollyworld: Popular Indian Cinema through a Transnational Lens*, ed. Raminder Kaur and Ajay Sinha (New Delhi: Sage, 2005), 35–69.

27. Vakili established the Cinema Zartoshtian, or Zoroastrian Cinema, in one of several attempts to provide gender-segregated screening space (a common problem for exhibitors throughout the region). Other solutions included setting up physical divisions in the Grand Cinema space, complete with separate entrances for women and men: one through the main box office and one through the attached Grand Hotel lobby.

28. *Ettela'at*, 27 Mehr 1306 (October 20, 1927).

29. Guy de Téramond, *Le tigre sacré* (Paris: Les Romans Cinéma, 1920).

30. *Ettela'at*, 28 Azar 1306 (December 20, 1927).

31. For a discussion of the ways in which tie-in promotion exceeded narrative clarification in the United States, see Shelly Stamp, *Movie-Struck Girls: Women and Motion Picture Culture after the Nickelodeon* (Princeton, NJ: Princeton University Press, 2000), 102–25.

32. *Ettela'at*, 3 Dey 1306 (December 25, 1927).

33. André Malraux, *Esquisse d'une psychologie du cinéma* (Paris: Gallimard, 1946), 34. Translation mine.

34. *Ettela'at*, 28 Azar 1306 (December 20, 1927).

35. Paul Moore, *Now Playing: Early Moviegoing and the Regulation of Fun* (Albany: SUNY Press, 2008).

36. The advertisement for *Secrets of an Invisible Woman* describes the film as having been "shown in America for three consecutive years." *Ettela'at*, 27 Mehr 1307 (October 20, 1927).

37. *Ettela'at*, 29 Shahrivar 1306 (September 21, 1927).

38. See Issari, *Cinema in Iran*, 64–65; Hamid Reza Sadr, *Iranian Cinema: A Political History* (London: I. B. Tauris, 2006), 12–26. See also Farrokh Ghaffary, "Cinema I: History of Cinema in Persia," *Encyclopedia Iranica Online*, last updated October 20, 2011, https://www.iranicaonline.org/articles/cinema-i; and Farrokh Ghaffary, *Le cinéma en Iran* (Tehran: Conseil de la Culture et des Arts, Centre d'Étude et de la Coordination Culturelle, 1973).

39. *The Brass Bullet* screened at the Grand Cinema three episodes at a time (*Ettela'at*, 5 Shahrivar 1307 [August 25, 1928]). The Cinema Tehran showed *Barrabas* (*Ettela'at*, 27 Farvardin 1309 [April 16, 1930]) and *The Iron Man* (touting Albertini's celebrity). The Cinema Sepah screened *The Fast Express* as *Death Train*, announcing ten episodes (*Ettela'at*, 14 Dey 1309 [January 4, 1931]). The last notice for *Death Train* is listed as the "fourth and final" (*Ettela'at*, 7 Bahman 1309 [January 27, 1931]).

40. *Mauprat* and *The False Verdict* both screened at the Cinema Sepah.

41. *Ettela'at*, 27 Farvardin 1309 (April 16, 1930).

42. *Ettela'at*, 19 Azar 1305 (December 11, 1926).

43. *Ettela'at*, 27 Farvardin 1309 (April 16, 1930).

44. *Ettela'at*, 19 Azar 1305 (December 11, 1926).

45. *Ettela'at*, 28 Esfand 1306 (March 19, 1928).

46. For an intellectual history of this discourse in the nineteenth and early twentieth centuries, see Reza Zia-Ebrahimi, *The Emergence of Iranian Nationalism: Race and the Politics of Dislocation* (New York: Columbia University Press, 2018).

47. My analysis, here and in the chapters to follow, is indebted to Miriam Hansen's conception of 1920s cinema as a global vernacular. The examples of nationalist appropriations of cinema's modernity given here serve to reinforce Hansen's claims about the cinema's role as a modern vernacular while highlighting an extreme local variation in the political uses of discourse surrounding cinema's modernity. See Miriam Bratu Hansen, "The Mass Production of the Senses: Classical Cinema as Vernacular Modernism," *Modernism/Modernity* 6:2 (1999), 59–77, and "Vernacular Modernism: Tracking Cinema on a Global Scale," in *World Cinemas, Transnational Perspectives*, ed. Natasa Ďurovičová and Kathleen Newman (London: Routledge, 2009), 287–314.

48. See Lee Grieveson and Haidee Wasson, eds., *Inventing Film Studies* (Durham, NC: Duke University Press, 2008).

49. Malte Hagener, "Programming Attractions: Avant-Garde Exhibition Practices in the 1920s and 1930s," in *The Cinema of Attractions Reloaded*, ed. Wanda Strauven (Amsterdam: Amsterdam University Press, 2006), 265–79.

50. Hamid Dabashi gives a brief account of his own experience with this practice in the introduction to his book on contemporary Iranian cinema. "We would collect and trade these pairs of slides pretty much as American kids did baseball cards, except that procuring them was far more of an adventure than

paying a visit to a local store. We found hours of pleasure in just sitting and viewing these slides against sunlight or a lamp." Hamid Dabashi, *Close-Up: Iranian Cinema, Past, Present and Future* (New York: Verso, 2001), 40. I can personally relay many similar stories. In one instance, after explaining to me how easy it was to build a makeshift film-still projector out of cardboard and scrap lenses, my father tried to convince me to make such a project the center of a fifth-grade science presentation. The projector's design, based on the ones he recalled having made in Tehran in the early 1950s, was elegant but not entirely functional.

CHAPTER 2. CIRCULATION WORRIES

1. Sarah Keller, *Anxious Cinephilia: Peril and Pleasure at the Movies* (New York: Columbia University Press, 2020).

2. One type of worry that I bracket in this chapter, in order to focus on the material aspects of circulation, is the concern over imitation. That is, before considering the local worries about a stylistically derivative cinema, an anxiety of influence to be discussed in chapter 4, I first pursue the worries of physical circulation.

3. Andrew L. Russell and Lee Vinsel, "Make Maintainers: Engineering Education and an Ethics of Care," in *Does America Need More Innovators?*, ed. Matthew Wisnioski, Eric S. Hintz, and Marie Stettler Kleine (Cambridge: MIT Press, 2019), 227.

4. See David Edgerton, *The Shock of the Old: Technology and Global History since 1900* (Oxford: Oxford University Press, 2011), 75–102.

5. See http://themaintainers.org/.

6. Russell and Vinsel cite, for example, key works by Carol Gilligan and Ruth Schwartz Cowan: Carol Gilligan, *In a Different Voice* (Cambridge: Harvard University Press, 1982); Ruth Schwartz Cowan, *More Work for Mother: The Ironies of Household Technology from the Open Hearth to the Microwave* (New York: Basic Books, 1983). The stakes of such a position are amplified, as Angela Bielefeldt points out, when framing a conception of engineering ethics that is inclusive of women and people of color in engineering pedagogy. Her study showed that these students were much more likely than their counterparts to list an "ethics of care" as a form of engineering ethics closest to their worldview. Angela Bielefeldt, "Ethic of Care and Engineering Ethics Instruction" (paper presented at the American Society for Engineering Education Rocky Mountain Section Conference, 2015), accessed from academia.edu.

7. Steven J. Jackson, "Rethinking Repair," in *Media Technologies: Essays on Communication, Materiality, and Society*, edited by Tarleton Gillespie, Pablo J. Boczkowski, and Kirsten A. Foot (Cambridge: MIT Press, 2014), 228.

8. Museum of Cinema card photographed in June 2016.

9. I use this spelling of Badi's name because this is how it was printed on the sign outside his shop.

10. The documentary *Engineer Badi: Craftsman of the Cinema* highlights these multiple creative roles as well as the overlap between artisanal (often hobbyist) and industrial engagement with film technology. The film even begins

with the trope of childhood invention discussed at length in the first and last chapters of this book. It describes the young Badi's work as an amateur photographer in his childhood home in Basra, where he also built his own 16 mm projector in the moments when he could evade his father's supervision. In the film, Badi's son describes his father's experiments with Pathé Baby 9.5 mm as evidence of his long-standing interest in cinema in the years before he began developing sound technology for the emergent film studios in Iran. Aziz Sa'ati, *Mohandes Badi: San'atgar-e Cinema* (Tehran: Iran Center for Film Industries, Inc., 1387/2008).

11. "Radiosazi Mohsen Badi, Diplome-ye Paris va London," photograph reproduced in the documentary *Engineer Badi: Craftsman of the Cinema.*

12. In addition to the work already mentioned, I am referring to the discussion of the unanticipated reuse of infrastructures in Lisa Parks and Nicole Starosielski, eds., *Signal Traffic: Critical Studies of Media Infrastructures* (Urbana: University of Illinois Press, 2015), and recent work by Lilly Irani on the cultural politics of innovation in the high-tech workplace. Irani's book presents its case studies in a way that speaks across disciplines and, I would argue, across historical periods. Lilly Irani, *Chasing Innovation: Making Entrepreneurial Citizens in Modern India* (Princeton, NJ: Princeton University Press, 2019), 175–204.

13. Douglas Brunger to David O. Selznick, July 17, 1962, Selznick Collection, Harry Ransom Center, University of Texas at Austin.

14. Peter Decherney, *Hollywood's Copyright Wars: From Edison to the Internet* (New York: Columbia University Press, 2012), 4.

15. Martin Fredriksson and James Arvanitakis, eds., *Piracy: Leakages from Modernity* (Sacramento, CA: Litwin Books, 2014).

16. Kavita Philip, "What Is a Technological Author? The Pirate Function and Intellectual Property," *Postcolonial Studies* 8:2 (2005), 199–218. Lawrence Liang, "Beyond Representation: The Figure of the Pirate," in *Making and Unmaking Intellectual Property*, edited by Mario Biagioli, Peter Jaszi, and Martha Woodmansee (Chicago: University of Chicago Press, 2011) 167–80.

17. "Black Book, Persia," series 1F, box 9, folder 1, United Artists Collection, Wisconsin Center for Film and Theater Research.

18. D. J. Makinson, "Copyright in Iran," December 31, 1974, Copyright Law of Iran file, Foreign Office Files for the Middle East, National Archives, London.

19. Brief from the International Federation of the Phonographic Industry, attached to a letter from D. J. Makinson to Peter Williams Esq., May 28, 1974, Copyright Law of Iran file, Foreign Office Files for the Middle East, National Archives, London.

20. Brief from the International Federation of the Phonographic Industry. Discussion of record piracy continued in memorandums throughout the year. "Estimates of record piracy in Iran indicate that it accounts for 95% of the total sales of sound recordings." A. Holt Esq. to Peter Williams Esq., October 21, 1974, Copyright Law of Iran file, Foreign Office Files for the Middle East, National Archives, London.

21. "It has been suggested to me here that if a British publisher were to acquire a 'dummy' publishing house here, and were to imprint a dozen copies of his books with that (Iranian) name . . . a week before the release in London

or elsewhere, this would satisfy the requirements of the Iranian Law—'first published in Iran'—and would give all copies of the work the protection of law." D. J. Makinson to Peter Williams Esq., November 11, 1974, Copyright Law of Iran file, Foreign Office Files for the Middle East, National Archives, London.

22. That year, 1974, was also the year of the famous boycott of Iran by the Hollywood majors. It was spearheaded, as Hamid Naficy details, by Charles Bluhdorn, the chair of Paramount's parent company, Gulf + Western, who resented fixed ticket prices for Hollywood movies in Iran when oil prices had quadrupled. This is an example of copyright linked to broader economics of globalization in the 1970s. It is also a marker of the tension between a conception of film as a commodity no different from oil and a conception of film as a cultural form whose infrastructures of access deserved special protection. Hamid Naficy, *A Social History of Iranian Cinema*, vol. 2, *The Industrializing Years* (Durham, NC: Duke University Press, 2012), 423–25.

23. "The End of Pirating?," *Tehran Journal*, December 26, 1973.

24. This article was translated and circulated through the British Embassy and discussed by the Department of Trade. The quote is from the embassy's translated and excerpted version of the article. Houshang Vaziri, "Copyright All a Loss," *Ayandegan*, April 22, 1974, Copyright Law of Iran file, Foreign Office Files for the Middle East, National Archives, London.

25. Makinson, "Copyright in Iran."

26. Lawrence Lessig, *Remix: Making Art and Commerce Thrive in the Hybrid Economy* (Bloomsbury Academic, 2008), accessed via Creative Commons license.

27. They also imply a spatial corollary to the claim that copyright battles denote periods of innovation. That is, locating ongoing or recurring piracy battles in the global circulation of moving-image, poster, and sound technologies is a good way to mark some of the most creative spaces of media history.

28. Lessig, *Remix*.

29. Liang, "Beyond Representation," 169.

30. Ramon Lobato, *Shadow Economies of Cinema: Mapping Informal Film Distribution* (London: British Film Institute, 2012), 76–80.

31. Philip, "What Is a Technological Author," 207.

32. Foreign Distribution Files, SRO, 1947, BK 683, Selznick Collection, Harry Ransom Center, University of Texas at Austin.

33. Cabled Foreign Reports, 1935–1951, series 10C, United Artists Collection, Wisconsin Center for Film and Theater Research.

34. Information from the National Archives and Records Administration Iraq file, 1950–54, in Nolwenn Mingant, *Hollywood in North Africa and the Middle East: A History of Circulation* (Albany: SUNY Press, forthcoming).

35. "Annual Motion Picture Report," August 18, 1951, series 5F, box 1, folder 11, pp. 1, 7, United Artists Collection, Wisconsin Center for Film and Theater Research. Page 7 of the report lists the seating capacity for Tehran's principal theaters as follows: 1,100 in Metropole; 1,200 in Palace; 1,200 in Diana; 850 in Crystal; 1,200 in Iran; 900 in Alborz; 1,000 in Homa; 1,000 in Rex; 600 in Park; 800 in Mayak; 950 in Atlas; 1,000 in Nov; 600 in Pars; and 400 in Setareh.

36. "Annual Motion Picture Report," 4–5.

37. *Asian Film Directory and Who's Who* (Bombay: Doriswamy, 1952), 59.

38. George Chasanas framed this growth in the number of cinemas as a problem of control. "The present situation in general is very bad, due to the great increase in number of theaters—22 first-run in Teheran [*sic*] and about over 50 subsequent." George Chasanas to Douglas Brunger, December 27, 1962, Selznick Collection, Harry Ransom Center, University of Texas at Austin.

39. There is a politics of disposal and outsourced storage in terms of which countries were seen as destinations for old nitrate and other risk-laden material. The remaining nitrate in US vaults sometimes went to West Africa. It was offered as a suboptimal option for distributors in the Middle East. Discussions about storage conditions in the Middle East and East Africa, as well as comparable conditions in Bombay, Singapore, Jakarta, and Manila, can be found in letters in the Foreign Correspondence and Legal Files, series 2F, box 23, United Artists Collection, Wisconsin Center for Film and Theater Research.

40. A. S. Johnstone, "Syria and Lebanon," letter to E. R. Beaman, April 6, 1956, Harry Ransom Center, University of Texas at Austin.

41. "You are quite correct in your belief that material for this picture [*Spellbound*] exists in Lebanon . . . [where it is] held by Roxy Films Distribution of Beirut. . . . [They have] ignored UA's requests to hand them over." Knowing that SRO was aware that a lawsuit "would be not only costly but a very lengthy process," the Roxy offered affidavits of destruction in lieu of shipping prints off. A. S. Johnstone to Victor Hoare, January 8, 1954, Selznick Collection, Harry Ransom Center, University of Texas at Austin.

42. For a discussion of an encounter with a collector known to recount stories of the afterlife of "axed" prints, see Brian Edwards, *After the American Century: The Ends of U.S. Culture in the Middle East* (New York: Columbia University Press, 2015), 121.

43. In 1958, Joseph Coen, who worked for United Artists in Cairo, advised Brunger at Selznick Releasing to consider returning to outright sales instead of percentages in response to the instability of trade at the time. Joseph Coen to Douglas Brunger, October 14, 1958, Selznick Collection, Harry Ransom Center, University of Texas at Austin.

44. Aizer is the most visible figure in the available American film distribution records before the 1960s, but there were, of course, several others. One important name that appears a few times in the documents is Manuel Gulyan. He was based in New York and was a vice president for Verity films. In 1948, Gulyan brokered a deal between Hollywood distributors and Cinema Diana in Tehran for seventy-seven features. This was Cinema Diana's founding year. It would soon become not only a major cinema in Tehran but also a major studio. "Three Majors Sell 77 Pix. to Iran's Diana Cinema Company," *The Film Daily*, July 12, 1948, 1, 7. In 1949 and 1950, Gulyan corresponded with United Artists on Verity letterhead with a letter signature that included "Repr. S. [Sanasar] Khachatourian, Cinema Diana-Teheran and [sic]." Manuel Gulyan to H. W. Schroeder, January 31, 1950, Foreign Correspondence, series 2F, box 16, United Artists Collection, Wisconsin Center for Film and Theater Research. In one letter, he mentions that eleven of the films purchased for the initial deal with Cinema

Diana came through the Aizers' network. Manuel Gulyan to H. W. Schroeder, October 26, 1948, Foreign Correspondence, series 2F, box 16, United Artists Collection, Wisconsin Center for Film and Theater Research.

45. Leonard Case to Laudy Lawrence, Selznick Releasing Organization, NY Office, November 21, 1947, Harry Ransom Center, University of Texas at Austin.

46. Victor Hoare to F. I. Davis, Selznick Releasing London, December 31, 1952, Harry Ransom Center, University of Texas at Austin.

47. Back cover advertisement for *Duel in the Sun*, *Setare-ye Cinema* 123, 13 Mordad 1336 (August 4, 1957), 39.

48. "*Duel in the Sun*, according to rumors a print is still in circulation—Naim Aizer sold his rights to Mr. N. Ashtiany. . . . I contacted Mr. Ashtiany, He claims to have returned the Print to Daoud Mayer, an associate to Naim Aizer,— I called Daoud Mayer and he claims that he destroyed the print on April 30th 1959." George Chasanas to Douglas Brunger, December 27, 1962. The reference is to Nurredin Ashtiany, head of the Cinema Owners Syndicate, whose insignia for his Ash. N. A. film company appeared on publicity material for imported films as well as Iranian productions. He spoke up in discussion in the press about certain disputes, including his release of Samuel Khachikian's *Strike*.

49. Naim Aizer, telegram to Selznick Releasing, quoted in A. F. Lee to George Mansour, February 6, 1954, Selznick Collection, Harry Ransom Center, University of Texas at Austin. The stakes of this exchange for Selznick were small, in the low four figures, while the total foreign gross of *Spellbound* was $5.5 million.

50. "The buyer had confused our production with a subject called 'Broken Spell.' . . . Meanwhile, my enquiries into the alleged unauthorized showing has stirred up interest in the picture and I have now received an offer from someone else but for 'Spellbound' only." Douglas Brunger to Tom Walker, November 20, 1959, Selznick Collection, Harry Ransom Center, University of Texas at Austin.

51. Aizer's handwritten ledger for *Spellbound* in the UA archive provides details for August 29–September 5, 1949, at the King Ghazi Cinema. He ran two matinees and two evening screenings, and charged varying prices for six classes of seats ranging from 25 fils to 500 fils (0.5 dinars) for select box seats. Daily net sales ranged from 22 to 115 dinars. Naim Aizer, Summary Takings Sheet, *Spellbound*, Foreign Correspondence, series 2F, box 16, United Artists Collection, Wisconsin Center for Film and Theater Research.

52. A. F. Lee to Victor Hoare, April 1954, Selznick Collection, Harry Ransom Center, University of Texas at Austin.

53. These ironies will go on. For a case study of turn-of-the century Afghanistan in which industry rhetoric about losses to piracy belies a practice of informal circulation with benefits and losses that are not so easy to disentangle, see Barbara Klinger, "Contraband Cinema: Piracy, *Titanic*, and Central Asia," *Cinema Journal* 49:2 (2010), 106–24.

54. Letter from C. Edward Wells, US Embassy in Tehran, to US Department of State, December 28, 1950. Thanks to Ehsan Khoshbakht for sharing this item from his personal collection.

55. Letter from C. Edward Wells.

56. The forty-five minute addition to running time was reported by Manny Silverstone, vice president of the international subsidiary at Fox. In this letter, Douglas Brunger is paraphrasing Silverstone's discovery to Selznick in an effort to convince Selznick to insist on policing sales rates for dubbing rights. He had recently learned that dubbing practices were more extensive in Iran than they had assumed. Douglas Brunger to David O. Selznick, June 5, 1962, Selznick Collection, Harry Ransom Center, University of Texas at Austin.

57. See John Belton, "1950s Magnetic Sound: The Frozen Revolution," in *Sound Theory/Sound Practice*, edited by Rick Altman (New York: Routledge, 1992), 154–268.

58. From an interview quoted in Massoud Mehrabi, *Tarikh-e Cinema-ye Iran; Az Aghaz ta 1357 (History of Cinema of Iran: From the Beginning to 1979)* (Tehran: Mo'allef, 1371/1992), 933.

59. Ahmad Zhirafar, *Tarikhche-ye Kamel-e Dubleh be Farsi dar Iran (A Complete History of Dubbing into Persian in Iran)*, vol. 1, 1320–1350 (Tehran: Ketab-e Kooleh Poshti, 1392/2013), 82.

60. For discussion of Radio Jahan's involvement, see Mehrabi, *Tarikh-e Cinema-ye Iran*, 933.

61. For a comprehensive discussion of the USIA film initiatives in Iran in the context of cold war containment, see Hadi Gharabaghi, "'American Mice Grow Big!': The Syracuse Audiovisual Mission in Iran and the Rise of Documentary Diplomacy" (PhD diss., New York University, 2018). Thanks to Gharabaghi for helping me to understand this initiative and for his generosity with USIA material.

62. Details of the 3M lease can be found in the equipment purchasing records, Syracuse folder, January–April 1953, US National Archives, College Park.

63. R. F. Dubbe, *Sound Talk* 33 (3M bulletin). The history and technical specifications of these processes are discussed at length in Charles Westcott and Richard Dubbe, *Tape Recorders: How They Work* (Indianapolis, IN: Howard Sams Co., 1956).

64. These asynchronies were also pronounced in the fields of nonfiction and sponsored filmmaking. Kamran Shirdel has described the availability of technology as factoring into his decision to leave his filmmaking career in Italy in 1965 to make his renowned nonfiction films in Iran. "The ministry [in Iran] was full of equipment. In fact, in Italy we worked with Moviolas from the second world war, but in Iran everything was new out of the box. I hadn't seen a Steenbeck in my life . . . and I had never worked with Arriflex lenses, brand new everything." Kamran Shirdel, "Screening of Kamran Shirdel's Films," Stanford Iranian Studies Program, February 27, 2014. Thanks to Hadi Gharabaghi for mentioning Shirdel's discussion to me.

65. Douglas Brunger to David O. Selznick, June 5, 1962.

66. Douglas Brunger to David O. Selznick, June 5, 1962.

67. "Here they do not require a dupe negative. They . . . dub the Iranian dialogue on tape and the tape is coated over the original sound track. Sometimes they do order the sound and music effect track. Major companies are

doing the same as independent buyers. I have screened a dubbed picture and I must say that the synchronization of the lips was not bad and the music and sound effects satisfactory." George Chasanas to Douglas Brunger, January 6, 1963, Selznick Collection, Harry Ransom Center, University of Texas at Austin. For more context on Chasanas's work for MGM in Cairo, see Ross Melnick, "Hollywood's Muddle East: Political Change in Egypt and Israel and the Consequences for Hollywood's Middle Eastern Movie Theaters," *Historical Journal of Film, Radio, and Television* 37:2 (2017), 272–94.

68. David O. Selznick to Douglas Brunger, June 8, 1962, Selznick Collection, Harry Ransom Center, University of Texas at Austin.

69. Fredriksson and Arvanitakis, *Piracy*, 5.

70. Selznick's stubborn insistence can be seen, for example, in a letter to Brunger. "You must forgive me if I do not accept your absolute conviction that the Iranian dubbed versions have use nowhere else in the Arabian world." David O. Selznick to Douglas Brunger, March 18, 1963, Selznick Collection, Harry Ransom Center, University of Texas at Austin. The expert rejection of Selznick's plan came a week later, on the Persian New Year as it happens, in the form of a mini-lecture from Wendell relayed by Selznick's assistant. Shirley Harden to David O. Selznick, March 21, 1963, Selznick Collection, Harry Ransom Center, University of Texas at Austin.

71. Whereas the available Hollywood distribution material from before the early 1960s mostly addresses Iranian cinemas obliquely through intermediaries in the region, most of the 1960s correspondence related to Iran in the distribution files in the Warner Bros. archives is between Warner offices (in the United States, Egypt, and Italy) and the owners of Cinema Rex in Tehran.

72. Invoice to "Mr. Sherket Sahami, Cinema Rex, Avenue Lalezar, Tehran," September 19, 1961, Warner Bros. Archive, University of Southern California.

73. See John Guillory, "The Memo and Modernity," *Critical Inquiry* 31:1 (Autumn 2004).

74. The distributors/exhibitors in the list of offers included "Abdul Hussein Houmani—Cinema Niagara, Avenue Shah"; "Middle-East Film Distributors—Mr. J. Rawan & G. Minassian"; "Moulin Rouge Cinema Co. Ltd. Mr. Moustafa Akhavan"; and "Mr. M. Muntakheb [*sic*], Cinema Palaza, Ave. Shah Reza." George Chasanas to Douglas Brunger, December 27, 1962.

75. David O. Selznick to Douglas Brunger, February 12, 1963, Selznick Collection, Harry Ransom Center, University of Texas at Austin. A similar calculus can be seen a year later after learning of television broadcasts. "Clearly there have been illegal exhibitions by whomever we dealt with previously [in Iran], or by someone who has pirated prints (and perhaps even negatives), and for all we know may have done the same things through the Middle East. . . . I only hope that we don't encounter similar situations elsewhere in the world. This is of course one of the penalties in dealing with people we know nothing about." David O. Selznick, letter to Douglas Brunger, April 24, 1964, Selznick Collection, Harry Ransom Center, University of Texas at Austin.

76. Selznick distributors lamented in 1949 that in Egypt, "dubbing rules are very strict, with a limit of three films per year. This is due to a wide popular feeling against dubbing as a 'death blow' to the domestic film industry." Selznick

Releasing Organization, 1946–1950, box 606, folder 14, Selznick Collection, Harry Ransom Center, University of Texas at Austin.

77. We see this in several cases in which studios had to recharge after backing box-office failures, such as Houshang Kavousi's *Seventeen Days to Execution* (1956), but it also occurs in response to disruptions like the 40 percent tax on local productions implemented in 1955. Zhirafar, *Tarikhche-ye Kamel-e Dubleh be Farsi dar Iran*, 220.

78. Hamid Naficy makes productive use of a conception of cultural haggling in his monographs and other books that intervene in postcolonial studies and theories of third cinema. See Hamid Naficy, "Theorizing 'Third World' Film Spectatorship: The Case of Iran and Iranian Cinema," in *Rethinking Third Cinema*, edited by Anthony Guneratne and Wimal Dissanayake (New York: Routledge, 2003), 183–201; and Hamid Naficy, "Self-Othering: A Post-Colonial Discourse on Cinematic First Contacts," in *The Pre-occupation of Postcolonial Studies*, edited by Fawiza Afzal-Khan and Kalpana Seshadri-Crooks (Durham, NC: Duke University Press, 2000), 292–310.

79. See Susan Bassnett, "Postcolonialism and/as Translation," in *The Oxford Handbook of Postcolonial Studies*, edited by Graham Huggan (Oxford: Oxford University Press, 2013), 340–58.

80. Mark Nornes, *Cinema Babel: Translating Global Cinema* (Minneapolis: University of Minnesota Press, 2007), 189.

81. See Scott Curtis, "The Sound of Early Warner Bros. Cartoons," in *Sound Theory/Sound Practice*, edited by Rick Altman (New York: Routledge, 1992), 191–203.

82. For an authoritative discussion of the cultural history of dubbing in Iran, including debates among intellectuals about the value of dubbed films during the emergence of a "national" commercial cinema, see Golbarg Rekabtalaei, *Iranian Cosmopolitanism: A Cinematic History* (Cambridge: Cambridge University Press, 2019), 133–66. Also important here are personal works that document encounters with dubbed films, including *Jerry & Me* (produced, written, and directed by Mehrnaz Saeedvafa, 2012). This chapter, which is primarily a history of media technology and trade, works best when read as a modest supplement to this work.

CHAPTER 3. COLLAGE SOUND AS INDUSTRIAL PRACTICE

1. These are approximate numbers in Gregorian years. The figures in the Iranian calendar years cited in Jamal Omid's history are seven commercially released features in 1331, eighteen in 1333, fourteen in 1334, thirteen in 1335, twelve in 1336, sixteen in 1337, and twenty-seven in 1340. Jamal Omid, *Tarikh-e Cinema-ye Iran 1289–1375* (*History of Iranian Cinema, 1289–1375*) (Tehran: Entesharat-e Rowzaneh, 1374/1995), 241. There were also more films in production each year that did not make it to commercial release.

2. For more on provenance as an underexamined link between film archiving and the study of circulation, see Joanne Bernardi, Paolo Cherchi Usai, Tami Williams, and Joshua Yumibe, eds., *Provenance and Early Cinema* (Bloomington: Indiana University Press, 2021). This conception is more established in

art history than it is in cinema and media studies. See Gail Feigenbaum, *Provenance: An Alternate History of Art* (Los Angeles: Getty Publications, 2012).

3. Another reason I focus on music in this chapter is that direct cut-and-paste was much less common with found image footage in commercial cinemas, although prominent examples do exist. Many Iranian films used shots from imported films as stock footage, particularly exterior shots of rain or nondescript landscapes. Other cinemas in the region, such as Yesilçam in Turkey, made a practice of splicing in more recognizable footage from imported films.

4. Each of the audio examples will come from the hundreds of Iranian films that are currently available via streaming. Accessibility is always in flux, but the reader should have the option of listening to most of the audio examples discussed throughout the chapter. Since multiple dubs of films were made, and since information about these multiple dubs is not always readily available even within the archives that hold the material, there may be instances in which I have misattributed a date (if the dub differs from the original release date) or misidentified a redub. The hope is that later research on this topic will revise the location and the chronologies of the many Iranian films quantified in aggregate here. As in other chapters, I will continue to realign archival information about these scores in Iran with the archival record of their distribution, found by comparing Hollywood studio distribution archives and exhibition notices in Iran.

5. Yasami quoted from a 1969 interview with the author in Omid, *Tarikh-e Cinema-ye Iran* (*History of Iranian Cinema*), 227.

6. The review by Toghrol Afshar was generally positive about the scoring and the songs in the film, but it did point out a few moments when the abrupt changes in fragments in the score went too far. Given the overwhelmingly negative tone for most aspects of the film in this review (a common tack for reviews of local productions), the discussion of the sound stands out as a positive assessment. Toghrol Afshar, review of *The Enchantress*, *Jahan-e Cinema*, 10 Esfand 1341 (March 1, 1953), quoted in Omid, *Tarikh-e Cinema-ye Iran*, 227.

7. Hamid Naficy, *A Social History of Iranian Cinema*, vol. 2, *The Industrializing Years* (Durham, NC: Duke University Press, 2012), 265.

8. Naficy, *Social History of Iranian Cinema*, 265–69.

9. Naficy, *Social History of Iranian Cinema*, 326–28.

10. These range from minor edits and relocations of Rózsa's score to instances in which Selznick purchased the rights to Granville's selection of Roy Webb's work from the RKO spy film *The Fallen Sparrow* (1943). Platte argues that this shift changes the inflection of the film to favor Constance at important moments in the film. Nathan Platte, "Music for *Spellbound* (1945): A Contested Collaboration," *Journal of Musicology* 28:4 (Fall 2011), 418–63.

11. Stephen H. Nyman, "Filming in the New Iran," *Movie Makers*, December 12, 1939.

There is some dispute over some of the films shot at this time. Enayatollah Famin, in an interview with Abbas Baharlou/Gholam Heydari, claims to have shot many of the films for which Nyman took credit. Gholam Heydari, *Khaterat va Khatarat-e Filmbardaran-e Cinema-ye Iran* (*The Challenges Faced by Iranian Cinematographers: Past & Present*) (Tehran: Cultural Research Bureau, 1997), 79.

12. Rezai was the son of the first public cinema operator in Iran, Ebrahim Khan Sahhafbashi Tehrani. Omid, *Tarikh-e Cinema-ye Iran*, 840–41.

13. "Musik-e Matn: Rubik Mansuri," *Film* 150 (November 11, 1993), 61.

14. "I started this work in 1955 with a daily wage of three tomans. After three years, my pay was increased to 270 tomans per month, which was equal to nine tomans per day. Then I left Dubbing Cinema Iran and joined Azhir Film for a monthly wage of 500 tomans. After doing my first film there, my wage was raised to 700 tomans. One year after, I was hired by Iran Film for a monthly wage of 1250 tomans. It was a lot of money in 1957–1958. When Missaghieh, Pars Film and Shahin Film studios started up, I worked for them as well. At Missaghieh studio I was receiving 6000 tomans for each Iranian film and 2500 tomans for a foreign film."

Rubik Mansuri, "Mardi keh Sokut-e Filmha ra Mishkanad" ("The Man Who Breaks the Silence of Films"), interview by Massoud Mehrabi, *Film Monthly* 27 (August 1985), 13.

15. Mansuri, "Mardi keh Sokut-e Filmha ra Mishkanad," 13.

16. Mansuri uses the cognate "montage" where I have used it in this quotation as well as in every verb construction I have translated as "cut" or "edit." Mansuri, "Mardi keh Sokut-e Filmha ra Mishkanad," 13.

17. Mansuri, "Mardi keh Sokut-e Filmha ra Mishkanad," 13.

18. For an extended discussion of this coproduction, see Samhita Sunya, *Nuclear Sirens: World Cinema via Bombay* (Berkeley: University of California Press, forthcoming).

19. Steiner's case against familiar music highlights the stark difference in Iranian uses of familiar songs. "I am, therefore, opposed to the use of thematic material that might cause an audience to wonder and whisper and try to recall the title of a particular composition, thereby missing the gist and significance of a whole scene which might be the key to the entire story." Max Steiner, "Scoring the Film," in *We Make the Movies*, ed. Nancy Schaumburg (New York: W. W. Norton, 1937), 219.

20. Kyle S. Barnett, "The Selznick Studio and the Marketing of Film Music," *Music, Sound, and the Moving Image* 4:1 (Spring 2010), 77–98.

21. Jeff Smith, "'The Tunes They Are A-Changing': Moments of Historical Rupture and Reconfiguration in the Production and Commerce of Music in Film," in *The Oxford Handbook of Film Music Studies*, ed. David Neumeyer (Oxford: Oxford University Press, 2014), 277–80.

22. Henry Mancini, *Did They Mention the Music?* (Chicago: Contemporary Books, 1985), 78–93.

23. *Desire under the Elms*'s moody contemporaneity may have been a favorite of Minai and Mansuri because they constructed the scores for these films, or they may have selected it because of Sophia Loren's significant star power in Iran.

24. I encountered the phrase "sonic nametag" in Kenneth LaFave, *Experiencing Film Music: A Listener's Companion* (Lanham, MD: Rowman and Littlefield, 2017), 22. The theme also influenced the scores of remakes of the film in the Middle East and South Asia, including *Safar Barlik* (Barakat, 1967) and Raj Kapoor's breakout success *Barsaat* (1949). *Safar Barlik*'s is close enough to Steiner's score at points to suggest overt citation.

25. "All prints of *Gone with the Wind* should be made with frozen British Pounds in England, and these Technicolor prints should be sent to the rest of the British Empire." David O. Selznick to L. R. Case, February 16, 1940, box 183.6, Selznick Collection, Harry Ransom Center, University of Texas at Austin. Further research might explore the way these currency issues may have influenced the number of these expensive new Technicolor prints in less lucrative markets around the world. This would make the shell game of wartime circulation a factor in the film's global reception. The correspondence among Selznick executives reveals continual discussion, and a sense of humor, about ways to move capital around the world in the 1930s. Among the correspondence from New York sales manager Lowell Calvert to Selznick about the challenges of distributing *The Garden of Allah* (Boleslawski, 1936), Calvert included a clipping from a *New York Herald Tribune* article about Germany making a payment to Standard Oil in the form of forty million harmonicas. Foreign distribution folder, *The Garden of Allah*, box 20.6, Selznick Collection, Harry Ransom Center, University of Texas at Austin.

26. Elizabeth Thompson has uncovered its success in the Middle East and the dramatic divergences in the reception of its premiere in different cities. In Cairo, its reception corresponded with the tension between the Anglophile collaborationists and nationalists. In Beirut, it flourished as a film about elite social rituals with the francophone audience and faltered as a war movie among Arabophone moviegoers. Audiences in Damascus, where the film was not mapped onto political tensions, received it as a kind of feminist motivational epic. Elizabeth Thompson, "Scarlett O'Hara in Damascus: Hollywood, Colonial Politics, and Arab Spectatorship during World War II," in *Globalizing American Studies*, ed. Brian Edwards and Dilip Gaonkar (Chicago: University of Chicago Press, 2010), 184–209.

27. Babak Tabarraee, "'Gone with the Wind' in Iran," lecture at Seminare Reseau Hescale, YouTube video, posted by Groupe Hescale on January 18, 2018, 39:38, www.youtube.com/watch?v=j7bA7_KCWXs.

28. Quoted in Tabarraee, "'Gone with the Wind' in Iran."

29. An even later composition, Rózsa's score for *Ben Hur*, marks the adventure scenes in this redub. Thanks to music scholar Laudan Nooshin for starting a conversation about the anachronistic music in the available version of *The Lor Girl*.

30. "UA to Test New LP Rack for Theaters," *Billboard*, September 19, 1960, 18.

31. Advertisement for *The Apartment*, Moulin Rouge Cinema Group, Tehran, released on October 30, 1963.

32. At the time of this writing, the version of *Delirium* with the Barry score had been removed from YouTube. Uploaded in its place is a version of the film with patches of silence where the Barry Score previously accompanied the action.

33. The score was famously praised by Bernard Hermann but lost the Academy Award to Maurice Jarre's work on *Lawrence of Arabia* that year. It was also used in promotional campaigns. "Radio time will be devoted to the music from the Franz Waxman score, beginning six weeks before the release."

"Taras Bulba Being Given Intensive Buildup for Christmas Start," *Box Office*, October–December, 1962, 1. A few weeks after the film was released, Henry Mancini released the LP *Our Man in Hollywood*, which included versions of recent film themes including *Taras Bulba*. "Best of the Week's New Albums," *Billboard*, January 5, 1963, 25.

34. Anahid Kassabian, *Hearing Film: Tracking Identifications in Contemporary Film Music* (New York: Routledge, 2001), 3.

35. For a discussion of the soundscape of cinema in Iran, see Claire Cooley, "Soundscape of a National Cinema Industry: Filmfarsi and Its Sonic Connections with Egyptian and Indian Cinemas, 1940s–1960s," *Film History* 32:3 (2020), 43–74.

36. The linguistic metaphor is a useful one, and I will talk more about it in relation to narrative and genre in the next chapter. Here I would like to point out that the concept of code switching hovers between electronic signal and utterance. Before the term was taken up by Roman Jacobson for the field of linguistics, it was used by R. M. Fano in his lectures in the electrical engineering department at MIT. The term originally described relayed communication with electronic signals, which is a technological definition that resonates with the production of the collage score, combining the labor of the cross-cultural curator with that of the engineer.

37. Many Iranian films alternate between formal and vernacular speech to mark layers of mediation or degrees of fantasy, a practice somewhat comparable to the way certain formal dialects or accents are more common in American sword-and-sandal films.

38. The most influential text from the early twentieth century is Hassan Moghaddam, *Jafar Khan az Farang Amadeh* (Tehran: Farus Publishing, 1301/1922).

39. Jamshid Vahidi, *Gigolo* (Tehran: Entesharat-e Sepid va Siah, 1957), 96.

40. Several ads for the film appear beginning with this issue: *Setare-ye Cinema* 111, 28 Ordibehesht 1336 (May 19, 1957).

41. "Rock and Roll!" *Setare-ye Cinema* 112, 29 Ordibehesht 1336 (May 19, 1957), 15.

42. The Haley song is followed by another dance to Billy May's big band arrangement of "Uptown Blues," released in 1957.

43. Andrew Jones, *Yellow Music: Media Culture and Colonial Modernity in the Chinese Jazz Age* (Durham, NC: Duke University Press, 2001), 9.

CHAPTER 4. THE ANXIOUS EXUBERANCE OF TEHRAN NOIR

1. The first essay was serialized over eight consecutive weekly issues, beginning with "Aya be Ayande-ye San'at-e Filmbardari-ye Iran Mitavan Omidvar Shod?". ("Is There Hope for the Future of the Iranian Cinema Industry?"), *Setare-ye Cinema* 24, 22 Dey 1333 (January 12, 1955), 14. The second series ran over four consecutive issues, beginning with "In Parde-ye Jandar" ("This Living Screen"), *Setare-ye Cinema* 103, 12 Esfand 1335 (March 3, 1957), 14, 26.

2. The program, *Tehran Noir: The Thrillers of Samuel Khachikian*, premiered in June 2017 at Il Cinema Ritrovato film festival in Bologna. It was

curated by Ehsan Khoshbakht and Behdad Amini. Original film elements were provided by the National Film Archive of Iran. Preservation and restoration work was completed in Tehran and Bologna. I conducted project development through Northwestern University in Qatar and contributed subtitling work for the program. For the first English-language publication about the films shown in this program, see Ehsan Khoshbakht, "Tehran Noir: Samuel Khachikian and the Rise and Fall of Iranian Genre Films," *Sight & Sound*, June 23, 2017, www.bfi.org.uk/news-opinion/sight-sound-magazine/features/tehran-noir-samuel-khachikian-iranian-genre-films.

3. Khachikian, "Aya be Ayande-ye San'at-e Filmbardari-ye Iran Mitavan Omidvar Shod?" (5 of 8), *Setare-ye Cinema* 28, 1 Farvardin 1334 (March 22, 1955), 6.

4. The term used is *harjai*, "a woman from anywhere," which implies an unrooted woman without financial means. The term can euphemistically refer to a sex worker.

5. Khachikian, "In Parde-ye Jandar" (2 of 4), *Setare-ye Cinema* 104, 19 Esfand 1335 (March 10, 1957), 14.

6. Anton Kaes, Nicholas Baer, and Michael Cowan, eds., *The Promise of Cinema: German Film Theory, 1907–1933* (Berkeley: University of California Press, 2016), 1.

7. Lalitha Gopalan, "Bombay Noir," in *A Companion to Film Noir*, ed. Andrew Spicer and Helen Hanson (Hoboken, NJ: Wiley-Blackwell, 2013), 510.

8. Siamak Pourzand, "Samuel Khachikian va Film-e Jadidash, Tufan dar Shahr-e Ma" ("Samuel Khachikian and His New Film, *Storm in Our City*"), *Setare-ye Cinema* 129, 7 Mehr 1336 (September 29, 1957), 10–11. Two years earlier, Pourzand had organized the first festival of films from Iran, during which Khachikian won the Best Director award.

9. Massoud Mehrabi, *Tarikh-e Cinema-ye Iran az Aghaz ta 1357 (History of Cinema of Iran until 1357)*, 11th printing (Tehran: Nazar, 2016), 111.

10. Khosrow Parvizi, a journalist who would go on to direct several films with generic traces of film noir and the western, notes in his discussion of his interview with Khachikian, "When I entered he said, 'Hussein, please bring us two Technicolor teas.' I was taken off guard because I had heard of every type of tea except technicolor tea." Technicolor tea (*chai-ye technicolor*) also reads as a play on the Persian phrase for "strong" tea (*por rang*), which literally means "full color." Khachikian teases Parvizi for getting lost on the way to the new studio by telling him he should consider work as a guide during the Haj—a punchline that turned on Parvizi's poor sense of direction as well as on Khachikian's subject position as an Armenian-Iranian Christian. During the conversation, which included serious discussion of the future of the film industry in Iran, and Khachikian as the "bright face of our cinema" (*Chehre-ye roshan-e cinema-ye ma*), Khachikian and his star actor, Vida Ghahremani, took turns discussing the artistic possibilities of *Storm in our City*, their ambitious upcoming project (one that he still considered among his best at the end of his life) made possible by the institutional possibilities of the new studio. Parvizi also joked about Ghahremani's real-life talent as a sharpshooter. "I told Samuel, 'What luck that your star actor is also a good shot. If you ever want to make a

western [*film-e cowboyi*], Lady Vida can put on blue jeans and a gun belt and ride a horse at full gallop.' Samuel laughed and said 'inshallah.'" The teasing continued through the end of the interview, when Khachikian ironically invited Parvizi to stay for dinner after escorting him out of the studio. The published interview framed the interaction of the director, actor, and journalist as an arch performance of norms of hospitality infused with cinematic puns. "Meeting Khachikian," *Setare-ye Cinema* 123, 13 Mordad 1336 (August 4, 1957), 8.

11. Jennifer Fay and Justus Nieland, *Film Noir: Hard-Boiled Modernity and the Cultures of Globalization* (London: Routledge, 2010), 184.

12. In interviews he downplayed these similarities. For example, he attributes his cameo appearance in *Storm in Our City* to simple necessity. It was a rainy night, and he was concerned about Rufia, the lead actress, getting drenched: "The extra forgot his line so I stepped forward and delivered the line. I didn't think anyone would notice, so I left the scene in the film. It was discovered by curious viewers. Robert Ekhart, the editor of *Setare-ye Cinema*, called me and asked, 'Was it you?' I said, 'Yes.' 'Are you trying to emulate Hitchcock?' I laughed it off." Iraj Saberi, "Khodahafez Samuel: Goftogu-yi Montasher-nashodeh ba Samuel Khachikian" ("Goodbye Samuel: An Unpublished Interview with Samuel Khachikian"), *Film Monthly* 19:278 (November 2001), 47.

13. These worries continue in the work of contemporary critics and artists such as Leila Pazooki, whose neon installation *Moment of Glory* (2012) consists of fifteen multicolored phrases, including "Middle Eastern Louise Bourgeois," "Iranian Jeff Koons," and "Dalí of Bali." The work, as an object of glory, has trouble unsticking itself from a practice of labeling that is almost always unevenly applied.

14. The image of the gestating cameo appears in a translated interview with the director about *I Confess. Setare-ye Cinema* 24, 22 Dey 1333 (January 12, 1955), 12–13. The magic hand of the director appears in an ad for the film's premiere at the Cinema Rex. *Setare-ye Cinema* 148, 20 Bahman 1336 (February 9, 1958), 31. The first appears to have been assembled for the journal, and the second appears to have been an imported illustration (possibly illustrated in Italy, where much of the export publicity to the Middle East was created) selected for the journal and reproduced unaltered.

15. A synopsis of *Rear Window* (or *Window Facing the Courtyard*; there are two different titles used for the film), translated by "Bahram," appears in *Setare-ye Cinema* 34, 31 Khordad 1334 (June 22, 1956), 34–38. A serialized version of excerpts from the *Life* magazine true crime source for *The Wrong Man*, translated into Persian by Jahangir Afshari, appeared in six issues, beginning with "*The Wrong Man (Mard-e Avazi)*," *Setare-ye Cinema* 117, 2 Tir 1336 (June 23, 1957), 28–29. It is a full translation of Herbert Brean, "A Case of Identity" *Life*, June 29, 1953, 97–107.

16. The first issue of the *Vertigo (Sargijeh)* serialization is in *Setare-ye Cinema* 170, 29 Tir 1337 (July 20, 1958), 28–29.

17. "Alfred Hitchcock, Honarmandi keh Ostad-e Mosallam-e Filmha-ye Jenayi Mibashad" ("Alfred Hitchcock, the Artist and Undisputed Master of Crime Films"), *Setare-ye Cinema* 9, 27 Tir 1333 (July 18, 1954), 9.

18. For example, the critic who translated a number of Hitchcock articles on spectatorship, Hajir Dariush, was by the following decade making films associated with the new wave and taking on leadership roles in the Tehran Film Festival and the National Iranian Radio and Television Corporation.

19. "Man Film-e Por-hayajan Misazam, Na Film-e Asrar-amiz" ("I Make Suspense Films, Not Mystery Films"), *Setare-ye Cinema* 24, 22 Dey 1333 (January 12, 1955), 12–13.

20. Advertisement for *Down Three Dark Streets*, *Setare-ye Cinema* 125, 3 Shahrivar 1336 (August 25, 1957), 27.

21. Advertisement for *The Pushover* (as *The Traitor Detective*), *Setare-ye Cinema* 93, 2 Dey 1335 (December 23, 1956). Advertisement for *The Pushover* (as *The Misguided Detective*), *Setare-ye Cinema* 129, 7 Mehr 1336 (September 29, 1957), 77.

22. *Setare-ye Cinema* 93, 2 Dey 1335 (December 23, 1956).

23. The first installment of *Witness to Murder* appeared in *Setare-ye Cinema* 24, 22 Dey 1333 (January 12, 1955), 35–36.

24. Advertisement for *I Confess*, *Setare-ye Cinema* 41, 16 Mehr 1334 (October 9, 1955), 22.

25. Remember that serialized film stories were regular features in some Iranian periodicals dating back to the 1920s, where they were given ample space even in newspapers with a limited total page count.

26. "Ba Nevisande-ye Ketab-e 'Boose-ye Khoonin' Ashena Shavid" ("Get to Know the Author of the Book *The Bloody Kiss* [*Kiss Me Deadly*]"), *Setare-ye Cinema* 33, 17 Khordad 1334 (June 8, 1955), 17.

27. "Cinema va Filmha-ye Polisi: Az Conan Doyle ta Mickey Spillane" ("Cinema and Crime Films: From Conan Doyle to Mickey Spillane"), *Setare-ye Cinema* 81, 8 Mehr 1335 (September 30, 1956), 15. The negative assessments of crime novelists were not common in the pages of this magazine, but it might be useful to point out one strong statement of cultural conservatism that uses Mickey Spillane as an example in a list of American social ills culminating in rock-and-roll music: "Americans who only have time to read on the streetcar to and from work are not able to enjoy Dickens or Balzac. They have to read Mickey Spillane: books designed to fit in a side pocket so one can use them to 'kill time.'" "Rock and Roll!," *Setare-ye Cinema* 112, 29 Ordibehesht 1336 (May 19, 1957), 15.

28. "Démodé" is the term used in the original Persian text. "*Cinema va Filmha-ye Polisi*," *Setare-ye Cinema* 81, 8 Mehr 1335 (September 30, 1956), 15.

29. "Ostadan-e Jenayat" ("Masters of Crime"). This excerpted translation of Gordon Gow's essay was serialized over three consecutive issues, beginning with *Setare-ye Cinema* 184, 11 Aban 1337 (November 2, 1958), 20. The quotation included here is a translation of the Persian text, not Gow's original text.

30. *Setare-ye Cinema* 90, 11 Azar 1335 (December 2, 1956), 12.

31. *Setare-ye Cinema* 90, 13.

32. The first issue of the magazine was published, with funds from Galestian book kiosk and a publication license from *Asar* newspaper, as a special issue of *Asar* on 28 Bahman 1332 (February 17, 1954).

33. This is in acknowledgment that these patterns are not fully representative of audience taste, critical interest, or programming choices in Iran (as if such elements could ever be homogenous). The coverage of American, British, and French noir writers, directors, and actors is revealing for how it frames these films and stories. But it is also revealing for what it does not admit: the popularity of crime films from India, Egypt, and other countries that were not as frequently covered in the pages of the magazine. These regional forces were often mentioned by filmmakers who wrote about their production process and competition, but there are few reviews or advertisements for regional crime films in the magazine. The institutional separation of the film press from industrial pressures and everyday urban viewing practices is always something to take into account when working with archival material, and in this case there were extensive separations that may seem unexpected to someone trained to examine fan press published in Hollywood. A couple of exceptions proving this rule are the full-page ads for a Mexican film titled *Bloodthirsty* (not a regional film, but one outside of the magazine's typical coverage) and *House No. 44* (Burman, 1955), which stars Dev Anand, a dandy figure and one of the most prominent stars of Bombay crime films. Advertisement for *Bloodthirsty* at Cinema Tehran, *Setare-ye Cinema* 190, 23 Azar 1337 (December 14, 1958), 31. The advertisement for the Bombay film highlights Dev Anand as the star and compares his performance to Raj Kapoor. Advertisement for *House No. 44* at Cinema Park, *Setare-ye Cinema* 120, 23 Tir 1336 (July 14, 1957), 33.

34. The passage comes from the conclusion to Houshang Kavousi's review of *The Midnight Cry* in *Honar va Cinema* 12, 5 Shahrivar 1340 (August 27, 1961). Reprinted in Jamal Omid, *Tarikh-e Cinema-ye Iran 1289–1375* (*History of Iranian Cinema, 1289–1375*) (Tehran: Entesharat-e Rowzaneh, 1374/1995), 335. Kavousi repeated this sentiment in other magazines. See Houshang Kavousi, "Faryad-e Nime-shab, Yek Film-e Taqallobi" ("*The Midnight Cry*: A Counterfeit Film"), *Ferdowsi* 7506, Shahrivar 1340 (September 1961).

35. *Desires of the Emperor* is the Iranian release title for *Quo Vadis* (LeRoy, 1951). Khachikian, "Aya be Ayande-ye San'at-e Filmbardari-ye Iran Mitavan Omidvar Shod?" (8 of 8), *Setare-ye Cinema* 31, 20 Ordibehesht 1334 (May 11, 1955), 6.

36. *Setare-ye Cinema* 332, 2 Khordad 1341 (May 23, 1962). Reprinted in Omid, *Tarikh-e Cinema-ye Iran*, 343.

37. One of the revelations in working through film publications in Iran is the frequency with which these publications rely on the form of the public feud. Polarizing reviews and responses to critics can be attributed to some personalities more than others, but the pattern in the 1950s and 1960s exceeds the idiosyncrasies of any one writer. If we see the work being done on the pages of newspapers like *Ettela'at* and film magazines like *Setare-ye Cinema* as part of the intellectual labor of defining the institutions and audience for a growing film industry, then the form of the feud constitutes an important genre of audience management.

38. Discussion of the two working at the same institution can be found in an article on the very first years of Diana Film studio. They are mentioned alongside

other Diana directors including Sardar Saker (Sager), who had recently moved to Tehran from Bombay, where he had worked as a music director for films. "Studio Diana Film: Mojahaztarin Estudio-i keh Hanuz Yek Film-e Khub Natavanesteh Ast Tahieh Konad" ("Studio Diana Film: The Best-Equipped Studio Has Yet to Produce a Good Film"), *Setare-ye Cinema* 3, 26 Bahman 1332 (February 15, 1954), 20–21.

39. These comments are compiled from a series of earlier interviews with the director in Gholam Heydari, "Hala Digar Dastam Milarzad . . . Samuel Khachikian, Nokhostin, Sabetqadamtarin, va Mobtakertarin Kargardan-e Film-e Jenayi" ("Now My Hands Are Shaking . . . Samuel Khachikian, First, Most Steadfast, and Most Inventive Director of Crime Films), *Mahname-ye Cinemayi-e Film* 278:19 (Aban 1380/November 2001), 40–42.

40. In *Honar va Cinema* 12, 5 Shahrivar 1340/August 27, 1961. Reprinted in Omid, *Tarikh-e Cinema-ye Iran*, 334.

41. Advertisement for *A Cry in the Night*, *Setare-ye Cinema* 180, 13 Mehr 1337 (October 5, 1958), 37.

42. The plot of *A Cry in the Night* bears some relation not to Khachikian's film of the same name but to *Storm in Our City*, which was released later that year and plays on a similar terror of a mentally ill and violent man menacing a young woman in a remote building.

43. Heydari, "Hala Digar Dastam Milarzad," 41.

44. Frances Nevins, *Cornell Woolrich: First You Dream, Then You Die* (New York: Mysterious Press, 1988), 569–75.

45. Examples of journal publications of the poster mentioning Woolrich include *Modern Screen*, September 1954, 5; and *Photoplay*, December 1954, 5.

46. "Panjere-ye Roobehayat" ("The Window Facing the Courtyard"), trans. Bahram, *Setare-ye Cinema* 34, 31 Khordad 1334 (June 22, 1955), 34–38.

47. "Enteghad bar Filmhaye Hafte: *Hefdah Ruz be E'dam*" ("Critique of Films of the Week: *Seventeen Days to Execution*"), *Setare-ye Cinema* 94, 9 Dey 1335 (December 30, 1956), 8–9.

48. "Enteghad bar Filmhaye Hafte," 9.

49. "Enteghad bar Filmhaye Hafte," 9.

50. For a discussion of these various theories, see Ahmad Amini, *Sad Film-e Tarikh-e Cinema-ye Iran* (*One Hundred Selected Films of the Iranian Cinema*) (Tehran: Sheida, 1372/1993), 38. One final point of speculation about this feud: one of the essay's strongest terms of criticism, *ideological spasm* (*sektehaye idiologique*), was an unusual term that Khachikian used in his own writing. It is not impossible that he had a hand in writing the essay or at least was in conversation with those who did. For Khachikian's use of *ideological spasm*, see *Setare-ye Cinema* 29, 23 Farvardin 1334 (April 13, 1955), 6.

51. The credit, for more than eighty issues, did not include a name and instead said "in cooperation with our colleague." Robert Ekhart discussed running into trouble over the fact that someone had reported his disqualifying age to the Ministry of the Interior in "Shahr-e Farang," *Setare-ye Cinema* 101, 28 Bahman 1335 (February 17, 1957), 10–11. Kavousi was only one possible suspect, since others were feuding with the magazine's leadership at the time.

52. "Said Neyvandi Bara-ye Tahie-ye Yek Film-e 5 Daghighei az Khachikian va Doktor Kavousi Da'vat Mikonad" ("Said Neyvandi Invites Khachikian and Doctor Kavousi to Each Create a Five-Minute Film"), *Setare-ye Cinema* 166, 1 Tir 1337 (June 22, 1958), 5.

53. "Said Neyvandi Bara-ye Tahie-ye Yek Film-e 5 Daghighei az Khachikian va Doktor Kavousi Da'vat Mikonad," 5.

54. "Dorober-e Studio-ha-ye Iran" ("Around the Iranian Studios"), *Setare-ye Cinema* 169, 23 Tir 1337 (July 14, 1958), 7.

55. Khachikian, "In Parde-ye Jandar" (1 of 4), *Setare-ye Cinema* 103, 12 Esfand 1335 (March 3, 1957), 14.

56. Samuel Khachikian, "Sharayet-e Kar-e Ma Hatta Charlie Chaplin-ha va De Sica-ha ra Ham Be Zanu Dar Miavarad" ("Our Working Conditions Would Bring Even Charlie Chaplins and De Sicas to Their Knees"), *Setare-ye Cinema* 196, 5 Bahman 1337 (January 25, 1959), 8–9, 40.

57. Khachikian, "In Parde-ye Jandar," 14.

58. Khachikian, "Sharayet-e Kar-e Ma Hatta Charlie Chaplin-ha va De Sica-ha ra Ham Be Zanu Dar Miavarad," 9.

59. Khosrow Parvizi, "Mardi keh Cinema-ye Iran ra az Ebtezal Nejat Bakhshid" ("The Man Who Saved Iranian Cinema from Banality"), *Setare-ye Cinema* 137, 3 Azar 1336 (November 24, 1957), 6.

60. Khachikian, "Aya be Ayande-ye San'at-e Filmbardari-ye Iran Mitavan Omidvar Shod?" (1 of 8), *Setare-ye Cinema* 24, 22 Dey 1333 (January 12, 1955), 14.

61. Soviet training contributed to the functioning of Diana Film studio. Some of their technical staff came from Russia with training in Moscow, and Khachikian continued to work with Russian film professionals, which is part of the reason his shooting scripts were written in English.

62. Parvizi, "Mardi keh Cinema-ye Iran ra az Ebtezal Nejat Bakhshid," 7.

63. Corey Creekmur, "Indian Film Noir," in *International Noir*, ed. Homer Pettey, Susan White, and R. Barton Palmer (Edinburgh, UK: Edinburgh University Press, 2014), 187.

64. Gholam Heydari, *Samuel Khachikian: Yek Goftogu* (Tehran: Entesharat-e Negah, 1381/2002), 44.

65. For featured discussions of Preminger's film in the press, see *Setare-ye Cinema* 110, 18 Ordibehesht 1336 (May 8, 1957), cover image and 11–13. See also "Yek Film-e Bozorg-e Ejtema'" ("A Great Social Film"), illustrated review of *The Man with the Golden Arm*, *Film va Zendegi* 5, 1336 (1957), 12.

66. Shooting script in the collection of the Museum of Cinema, Tehran. Handwritten English in the original.

67. None of the camera movements uses a zoom lens, which the director would only acquire four years later.

68. Trailers themselves are obviously ways of managing and addressing audiences, but this bears additional significance in an industry in which trailers for Iranian films were a late formation. The shipping records from studios do indicate that Hollywood sent trailers for films along with the prints in the 1950s and '60s. Warner Bros. collection, University of Southern California.

Khachikian had to push to be granted support to create his own trailers for his films. As Laura Fish has noted, his status as the creator of the first Iranian film trailer was a key part of the director's author function. Laura Fish, "Marketing beyond the Masses: Iran's Film Trailers and Popular Cinema History" (paper presented at the Middle East Studies Association annual meeting, New Orleans, 2019).

69. "We cannot base the structure of the film industry of a country on imitation. What we need today is a cinema that can stand on its own feet, an independent cinema." Karim Emami, *Keyhan International*, 13 Esfand 1341 (March 4, 1963). Reprinted in Omid, *Tarikh-e Cinema-ye Iran*, 347.

70. From a portion of the shooting script, reproduced in *Filmnameh: Zarbat* (*Screenplay: The Strike*) (Tehran: Museum of Cinema, 1381/2002), 3.

71. Children in typical film noir are an exception to the rule, but they are more common in these atypical genre films. Because they are an exception, one might expect melodramatic pressure to be put on the fact that they were included, but often their presence had a casual or ambient quality that deviated further from purist expectations.

72. Pedram Partovi, *Popular Iranian Cinema before the Revolution: Family and Nation in Filmfārsī* (London: Routledge, 2017) 87, 105–13. Partovi's analysis of the long Iranian literary and cultural history of this trope, feeding into *filmfarsi*, answers Zhen Zhang's call to seek out the ways that "different film traditions reshape or invent anew this age-old figure [of the orphan] in overlapping or divergent visions of enlightenment or modernity." Zhen Zhang, "Transnational Melodrama, *Wenyi*, and the Orphan Imagination," in *Melodrama Unbound: Across History, Media and National Cultures*, ed. Christine Gledhill and Linda Williams (New York: Columbia University Press, 2018), 84.

73. In addition to the ordinary reviews of the film, see the write-in fan columns on the film in "Darbare-ye Film-e 'Bar Bad Rafteh' Che Nazari Darid?" ("What Do You Think about *Gone with the Wind*?"), *Setare-ye Cinema* 96, 23 Dey 1337 (January 13, 1959), 7.

74. Vida Ghahremani, interview in Bahman Maghsoudlou, *Razor's Edge* (New York: International Film and Video Center, 2016). Ghahremani also notes how Clark Gable influenced elements of her films with Khachikian in costuming and performance. Garsha Raoufi, who played the leader of the wealthy dandies and eventual villain of the film *Storm in Our City*, was styled after Clark Gable. His mustache, grin, and habits of lifting his brow and pushing back his hair are unmistakable (and were audibly acknowledged by the audience at Il Cinema Ritrovato). They demonstrate how such citations were portable in these films. They could just as easily accompany leading roles and villains in these films.

75. Jennifer Fay, *Inhospitable World: Cinema in the Time of the Anthropocene* (Oxford: Oxford University Press, 2018), 121.

76. If the choice of staircase is a nod to *Gilda* as it appears, it need not have come from the film itself. One of the popular lobby cards released along with *Gilda* depicts Rita Hayworth posing on a similar staircase.

77. *Dial M for Murder* (*Pelle-ye Panjom* [*The Fifth Step*]) received a long review by Hajir Dariush in the summer of 1957. *Setare-ye Cinema* 116, 26 Khordad 1336 (June 16, 1957), 10, 30.

78. Khachikian denied having seen the film prior to his own, just as he denied having seen *Gilda* before making *The Midnight Cry*, and he did not personally see a resemblance. But the stories of these films were in the atmosphere. *Les Diaboliques* was in theaters beginning at the Cinema Soheila in late February 1958. It was important enough that its poster image was placed on the glossy back cover of *Setare-ye Cinema* 150, 4 Esfand 1336 (February 23, 1958). Another way that Khachikian responded to accusations of imitation was to outflank his critics with his own knowledge of the history of the genre. "If one says that I have appropriated *Les Diaboliques*, then we should also say that Clouzot has appropriated George Cukor's *Gaslight*, who has appropriated elements from Hitchcock, who has imitated directors making films thirty years before him!!!" Samuel Khachikian in *Film va Honar* (*Film and Art*) 3–4, Farvardin–Ordibehesht 1341 (April 1962), quoted in Omid, *Tarikh-e Cinema-ye Iran*, 347.

79. Jarzombek uses as his illustration of this obligatory fireplace Henry Hill's Tamalpais House. Mark Jarzombek, "'Good-Life Modernism' and Beyond: The American House in the 1950s and 1960s. A Commentary," *Cornell School of Architecture* 4 (Fall 1990), 77. See also Justus Nieland, *Happiness by Design: Modernism and Media in the Eames Era* (Minneapolis: University of Minnesota Press, 2020), 12–15.

80. Paul Guth in *Le Figaro Littéraire*, quoted in Christopher Lloyd, "Eliminating the Detective: Boileau-Narcejac, Clouzot, and Les Diaboliques," in *Crime Scenes: Detective Narratives in European Culture Since 1945*, ed. Annie Mullen and Emer O'Beirne (Amsterdam: Rodopi, 2000), 45.

81. Thom Andersen, *Los Angeles Plays Itself* (Los Angeles: Thom Andersen, 2003).

82. For a discussion of stock masculine character types in the films from this period and later, see Kaveh Bassiri, "Masculinity in Iranian Cinema," in *The Global Encyclopedia of Lesbian, Gay, Bisexual, Transgender, and Queer History* (Detroit: Scribners, 2019), 1018–23. Considering how the living spaces around these characters were stylized and gendered complements Bassiri's analysis of male bodies and performances of masculinity.

83. Andersen, *Los Angeles Plays Itself*.

84. It is worth noting here that Vincent Sherman, the director who marks for Andersen the earliest example of this phenomenon when he used Frank Sinatra's modernist Palm Springs home for his crime boss, is cited by Khachikian's protégé, Masoud Kimiai, as one of the Hollywood directors whom he most admires. I elaborate more on this connection in chapter 5.

85. In an interview with a group of colleagues, including Yasami, the director of *Qarun's Treasure*, and Jalal Moghaddam, Khachikian holds that "one of the duties of the guild is that it should articulate the goals of the national cinema industry and force officials to accept the legal rights of artists." "Pa-ye Sohbat-e Kargardanan" ("Listening to the Directors"), *Setare-ye Cinema* 738, 9 Bahman 1349 (January 29, 1971), 14–15, 30.

86. "Pa-ye Sohbat-e Kargardanan," 15

87. André Bazin, "The Style Is the Genre (*Les Diaboliques*)," in *Bazin at Work: Major Essays and Reviews from the Forties and Fifties*, ed. Burt Cardullo (London: Routledge, 1997), 163–65.

CHAPTER 5. EASTERN BOYS AND FAILED HEROES

1. One boy repeats *"Lokhtet mikonam!"* to the other. This is gambler's slang (literally, "I'll make you naked"), comparable to lines such as "I don't rattle, kid. But just for that, I'm gonna beat you flat" from *The Hustler* (1961). Kimiai's scripts are known for their stylized language and attention to neighborhood vernacular.

2. Hamid Naficy, *A Social History of Iranian Cinema*, vol. 2, *The Industrializing Years* (Durham, NC: Duke University Press, 2012), 352–53.

3. Negar Mottahedeh, "Crude Extractions: The Voice in Iranian Cinema," in *Locating the Voice in Film: Global Practices and Critical Approaches*, ed. Tom Whittaker and Sarah Wright (Oxford: Oxford University Press, 2017).

4. Hassan Hosseini, *Majmu'e-ye Dars-goftarha-ye Cinemayi: Filmfarsi* (*Filmfarsi: A Series of Cinema Lectures*) (Tehran: Saqi, 2013), DVD 1 and 3.

5. A notable earlier collaboration with the American film industry was *The Game of Love* (*Bazi-ye Eshq*, Walter Beaver, 1959). This film was made with a relatively inexperienced Hollywood cast and crew in collaboration with Atlas Film Studio, the Iranian production company of George Ovadiah, who went on to have a prolific career as a director in Israel. There were also a number of collaborations with the Italian and Lebanese film industries, including *Hashem Khan* (Zarindast, 1967), *Storm over Petra* (*Tufan bar faraz-e Petra*, Agrama, 1968), and *And Now . . . Make Your Peace with God* (*Ed ora . . . raccomanda l'anima a Dio!*, Fidani, 1968).

6. *Rio Bravo* distribution files from the Warner Bros. Archives indicate that the film received special and sustained attention from exhibitors in Iran. The popularity of these films in Iran was connected to the popularity of dubbing artists like Iraj Dustdar, who got his start at Studio Moulin Rouge and who performed the voice of John Wayne in many films, including *Rio Bravo*. *The Magnificent Seven* was dubbed into Persian three times, a result of its continuing popularity. For a recent fictional reference to the success of these Persian-dubbed versions in Afghanistan, see Khaled Hosseini, *The Kite Runner* (New York: Riverhead Books, 2003), 26.

7. Thomas F. Brady, "Executives Help in Iran's Growth," *New York Times*, March 18, 1968, 67.

8. "US Executive [*sic*] Help Bolster Sagging Business in World," *Kabul Times*, January 17, 1967, 3–4.

9. Donald Robinson, "The IESC: Global Troubleshooter for Business," *Rotarian* 109:5 (1966), 36–38, 59–62.

10. Full contract in the production file for *The Heroes*, Special Collections, Margaret Herrick Library. In addition to the budget details, the contract lists names of specific actors (misspelling many of them) without confirming their participation. Under "American" it lists "Richard Windmark, Glen Ford, James Coburn, Robert Mitchum, William Holden, or one of the same international value and fame." Under "Foreign Female Stars" it lists "Irene Pappas, Ava Gardner, Kim Novak, Marissa Mell, Lolobrigida, Jayne [sic] Fonda, Sylva Koscina, Dahlia Lavi, or some of same value." Under "Male Iranian Cast" it lists "Behrooz Bossughi [sic], Azman, Anoosh, Homayoon."

11. Mehdi Samii to Jean Negulesco, Jean Negulesco Papers, Special Collections, Margaret Herrick Library.

12. Bahman Farmanara, "Moulin Rouge Puts Iran into World's Orbit," *Tehran Journal*, May 28, 1968, 5.

13. *Setare-ye Cinema* 661, 9 Ordibehesht 1348 (April 29, 1969).

14. "Vossoughi Gets His Big Chance," undated clipping [1968], *Heroes* file, Special Collections, Margaret Herrick Library.

15. Lon Satton took the direction of leftist allegory. Heather Wyatt, "Actor Finds Issues Raised in Heroes," *Tehran Journal*, October 23, 1968.

16. "Five of the world's top international movie stars are currently in Tehran for the shooting of Iran's first international film production." Hilton pictorial promotional brochure, *Heroes* file, Special Collections, Margaret Herrick Library.

17. "Jean Negulesco: Kargardan-e Movvafaq-e Hollywood baraye Behbud-e Film-ha-ye Farsi be Iran Amadeh Ast" ("Jean Negulesco: Accomplished Hollywood Director Has Come to Iran to Rescue Iranian Films"), *Ettela'at* 1269, 30 Dey 1346 (January 20, 1968), 12. Note here that the term used is *film-ha-ye Farsi*, not the more pejorative *filmfarsi*.

18. Bahman Farmanara, "A Director to Boost Iran's Movie Industry: Jean Negulesco Teams Up with the Akhavan Brothers," *Tehran Journal*, January 20, 1968, 5. Farmanara, "Moulin Rouge Puts Iran into World's Orbit," 5.

19. Bahman Farmanara, "Foreign Movie Unit to Shoot in Iran," *Tehran Journal*, October 7, 1968, 10.

20. Farmanara, "Moulin Rouge Puts Iran," 5.

21. Anna Francis, with Jean Negulesco, "Negulesco Met the Challenge and Found It Worth His While," *Tehran Journal*, January 16, 1969, 4.

22. Cinemas listed in an advertisement for the film include Moulin Rouge, Diana, Mahtab, Rex, Shahvand, Neptune, Lido, Rangin Kaman, Zhaleh, Homa, Oscar, Pasargad, Tosca, Charkhofalak, Oranus, and Firoozeh.

23. "Print Piracy, Censorship Problems in Iran: A $3,000,000 Market for US Majors," *Variety* 256:13 (1969), 28.

24. Reza Moghaddam, "Behold the Stars That Have Broken the Dark Night: Moulin Rouge Studio and the Dubbing of *Mother Never Dies* [Mikio Naruse, 1942]" ("Be Setare-ha Negah Kon keh Shab ra Shekaste-and: Studio Moulin Rouge va Duble-ye Film-e Hargez Namir Madar"), *Film Monthly* 32:474 (2014), 93.

25. Office of the Prime Minister of Iran to Jean Negulesco, July 31, 1971, Negulesco Papers, Special Collections, Margaret Herrick Library.

26. Cyrus Ghani to Jean Negulesco, April 20, 1969, Jean Negulesco Papers, Special Collections, Margaret Herrick Library.

27. The FIDCI lists *Ghazal* and *F for Fake* together. The country of origin for Welles's film is listed as "France-Iran." FIDCI advertisement for *Ghazal* and *F for Fake*, *Cinema* 54:3 (1354/1975), front matter.

28. Hamid Naficy reads one of Kimiai's childhood encounters with a famous neighborhood tough guy as a kind of "primal scene" that illuminates his preoccupation with tough-guy masculinity. Naficy, *Social History of Iranian Cinema*, 291–95.

29. Masoud Kimiai, interview with the author, School of the Free Film Workshop (Madrese-ye Kargah-e Azad-e Film), Tehran, May 1, 2014.

30. "[Nureddin] Ashtiany, like the Yank distribs and the Iranian producers, feels that local production has reached a turning point with the influx of new, talented young directors. Even the circuit traditionally showing one Persian film every week was forced by 'popular demand' he said, to hold over 'Caesar.'" "H'wood Take Dips in Iran as Native Films Win Bigger Share of Market," *Variety* 261:4 (1970), 23, 62.

31. Naficy, *Social History of Iranian Cinema*, 298.

32. For a discussion of affect and the noble household, see Melinda Cooper, "The Law of the Household: Foucault, Neoliberalism, and the Iranian Revolution," in *The Government of Life: Foucault, Biopolitics, and Neoliberalism*, ed. Vanessa Lemm and Miguel Vatter (New York: Fordham University Press, 2014), 29–58.

33. *The Deer* (*Gavazn-ha*, Masoud Kimiai, 1974), with its representation of the Shah's police, was prominent among these. He was forced to change the ending and some of the dialogue in the film to erase some of its themes of protest.

34. Iranian actor Ali Pourtash, who was part of the CIDCYA theater group in the 1970s, describes this division: "The theater people [at the CIDCYA] were doing their own schtick, which was theater. But film was film. . . . There was not a crossover. They wouldn't come and use the actors, because they would rather make movies with nonprofessional unknown actors." Ali Pourtash, interview with the author, November 12, 2014.

35. See Zavan Qukasian, ed., *Majmue-ye Maqalat dar Naghd va Barresi-ye Asar-e Masoud Kimiai* (*A Collection of Critical Articles and Reviews of the Works of Masoud Kimiai*) (Tehran: Entesharat-e Agah, 1364/1985), 50–51, 121–25.

36. Nic Wistreich, "Interview with Darius Khondji," *Netribution*, 2001.

37. Ramin Sadegh Khanjani, "The Crime That Has to Be Tried on the Street: The Films of Masoud Kimiai," *Off Screen* 18:9 (2014).

38. Prints and posters were sent to Cinema Rex, Lalezar, for a flat royalty of $2,500. Legal Files, 1961, Warner Bros. Archive, University of Southern California.

39. Copyright expiration for one-way print of *Rio Bravo* was September 6, 1964. Warner Bros. Archive, University of Southern California.

40. Invoice for twenty-four posters sent from Warner Bros.' Rome office to "Mr. Sherket Sahami [*sic*], Cinema Rex, Avenue Lalezar, Tehran," September 19, 1961, Warner Bros. Archive, University of Southern California.

41. "Full-page advertisement for *The True Story of Jesse James*" *Setare-ye Cinema* 204, 1 Farvardin 1338 (March 22, 1959), 39.

42. Parviz Davaii, "The Crimson Pirate, Rio Bravo, Vera Cruz" in *Film va Zendegi* 7 (1342/1963), 69–71; and Peter John Dyer's "Hang the Lights Low" (retitled translation: "Yek Mard, Yek Morur: Howard Hawks"), trans. Parviz Davaii, in *Film va Zendegi* 7 (1342/1963), 42–51.

43. Kimiai gives Sherman and his director of photography credit for elements of genre construction and mise-en-scène for which he says Fritz Lang has received recognition. Kimiai, interview with the author.

44. Kimiai, interview with the author.

45. "When you can watch a film only one time but you're hearing the dialogue and soundtrack several times, you imagine the image; this whole process can train a filmmaker." Kimiai, interview with the author.

46. The Sherman film cited in *Metropole* is his Humphrey Bogart and Conrad Veidt vehicle *All through the Night* (1941).

CODA

1. See Muhammad Raji Zughoul, "Lexical Interference of English in Eastern Province Saudi Arabic," *Anthropological Linguistics* 20:5 (May 1978), 217, 225. This essay proposes either an association with a vehicle number or, alternatively, a reference to the carrying capacity, "one-ton weight," embossed on the vehicles.

2. Persian speakers have long used *vanet*, with the same spelling and referent as the Saudi Arabic term. It is tempting to imagine the term's origin as connected, but perhaps it circulated in another direction. *Vanet* may derive, as it sounds, from an uncommon British diminutive of "van," shortened from "caravan," which has its roots in Persian. Whether as Saudi vernacularization of technical specs of an automotive commodity (whose production demands also circulated workers from the Middle East to the United States), or as a circularity of a Persian term into English and back, such stories about etymologies tend to stick because they speak to a collective imagination about history.

3. Iran's interest in Omnimax appears to have been motivated by a visit to the Ruben H. Fleet Space Theater shortly after it opened in San Diego: "Both Boucheri and Pahlbod have visited the San Diego Space Theatre and Science Center. I made arrangements for their VIP treatment there. They are impressed. They would like to have something like the San Diego set-up in Tehran." Don Weed to James Ramsey, February 28, 1975, Film Effects of Hollywood Papers, Margaret Herrick Library, Academy of Motion Picture Arts and Sciences, Beverly Hills, California. Mehrdad (Mel) Azarmi had worked for Film Effects of Hollywood after studying filmmaking at the University of Southern California. In the 1970s he took a position under Mehrdad Pahlbod at the Ministry of Culture and Art in Tehran. Azarmi was the lead negotiator for the construction of a large-format inflatable dome cinema in Tehran that would have used a competing system, Dynavision, developed by his former employers in Hollywood. Tehran's large-format dreams eventually fell through in the late 1970s, but this business relation contributed to the import of optical printing and effects equipment as well as several 16 mm Cine-View systems. This rare format was intended to combine some of the quality advantages of IMAX by running the film horizontally through the projector. Widescreen image and (especially) sound quality would be improved by the rapid movement of film through the gate, but 16 mm portability would be maintained. Both the large-scale plans for Omnimax and the media archaeology of these many smaller devices were enabled by networks that included Azarmi, members of the royal family who would also have a hand in producing Orson Welles's final works, and Elmo Williams, an established Hollywood editor who would be involved in several

film initiatives in Iran including producing the Anthony Quinn vehicle *Caravans* (1978). Film Effects was also connected to Iran through its work producing prints of Mohammad Reza Pahlavi's coronation film. These business partnerships illustrate the combination of government media commissions, a continuation of midcentury expo culture, and commercial filmmaking infrastructure that are so numerous in this period.

4. David Chasman to Joseph Mankiewicz, August 26, 1971, Joseph Mankiewicz Papers, Margaret Herrick Library, Academy of Motion Picture Arts and Sciences, Beverly Hills, California.

5. Arsham Yessaians to Hy Smith, August 19, 1971, Joseph Mankiewicz Papers, Margaret Herrick Library, Academy of Motion Picture Arts and Sciences, Beverly Hills, California.

6. David Chasman to Joseph Mankiewicz.

7. In Wyler's letter declining participation in the Tehran international Film Festival (he would accept an invitation the following year after conferring with Frank Capra about his experience), he describes this treatment during his visit in 1971. William Wyler to Michael Kutza, March 27, 1972, William Wyler Papers, Margaret Herrick Library, Academy of Motion Picture Arts and Sciences, Beverly Hills, California. Wyler referred to his earlier viewing of *The Cow* in the festival-related press: "The director recalled having seen the Iranian film 'The Cow' on an earlier holiday tour of Iran three years ago and found it 'very good.'" Sajid Rizvi, "William Wyler Lashes Out at 'Show-Offs,'" *Tehran Journal*, December 2, 1974, 3.

8. See Nat Hentoff, "Cultivating Torture with a Touch of Culture," *Village Voice*, April 26, 1976, 18; it is followed by a letter to the editor by Reza Baraheni and Ralph Schoenman submitted on June 22 of that year. For a transcript of Perry's diary of their visit to Iran, see Eleanor Perry, "Notes from the International Women's Film Festival in Iran," Eleanor Perry Papers, Margaret Herrick Library, Academy of Motion Picture Arts and Sciences, Beverly Hills, California.

9. Mel Shavelson to William Wyler, February 28, 1972, William Wyler Papers, Margaret Herrick Library, Academy of Motion Picture Arts and Sciences, Beverly Hills, California.

10. Michael Kutza, interview with the author, Chicago, Illinois, March 2017.

11. Kutza, interview with the author.

12. A newspaper advertisement for *Funny Girl* from 3 Azar 1348 (November 24, 1969) lists the premiere date as 13 Azar 1348 (December 4, 1969).

13. There is work to be done in examining not just remakes but remakes in their circularities: the circuits of a romantic comedy that pass from Hollywood to Bombay to Iran. We might also consider the many remakes of *Awaara* in the Middle East and its profound influence around the Indian Ocean. The tramp character owed to the global success of Chaplin, another featured filmmaker at the Tehran International Film Festival, but the transregional nodes of circulation of this vagabond type had stronger gravity in many film markets in this part of the world. For a discussion of *Awaara* and Hindi cinema's outsized influence in Tanzania despite being outnumbered by Hollywood films, see Laura Fair, *Reel Pleasures: Cinema Audiences and Entrepreneurs in Twentieth-Century Urban Tanzania* (Athens: Ohio University Press, 2018), 113–41.

14. Houshang Kavousi, review of *The Midnight Cry*, *Honar Va Cinema* 12, 5 Shahrivar 1340 (August 27, 1961). Reprinted in Jamal Omid, *Tarikh-e Cinema-ye Iran 1289–1375* (*History of Iranian Cinema, 1289–1375*) (Tehran: Entesharat-e Rowzaneh, 1374/1995), 336.

15. *Setare-ye Cinema* 285, 11 Dey 1339 (January 1, 1961).

16. Parviz Nouri, *Setare-ye Cinema* 288, 2 Bahman 1339 (February 1, 1961). Reprinted in Omid, *Tarikh-e Cinema-ye Iran*, 970.

17. Ken Jacobs, "Perfect Film," *Film-Maker's Cooperative Catalogue* 7 (1989), 272.

18. Ali Behdad, *Camera Orientalis: Reflections on Photography of the Middle East* (Chicago: University of Chicago Press, 2016), 111–14.

19. Henry Rogers to William Wyler, July 22, 1974, William Wyler Papers, Margaret Herrick Library, Academy of Motion Picture Arts and Sciences, Beverly Hills, California.

20. This anecdote is documented in multiple sources. See Brian Edwards, *After the American Century: The Ends of U.S. Culture in the Middle East* (New York: Columbia University Press, 2015), 121. I have also discussed it with Ehsan Khoshbakht, who plans to include video of the anecdote in his forthcoming documentary on Ahmad Jurghanian, tentatively titled "Celluloid Underground."

21. William Wyler to Hajir Dariush, August 6, 1974, p. 3, William Wyler Papers, Margaret Herrick Library, Academy of Motion Picture Arts and Sciences, Beverly Hills, California.

22. Shipping invoice from Paul Kohner, Inc. to the Third Tehran International Film Festival, October 31, 1974, William Wyler Papers, Margaret Herrick Library, Academy of Motion Picture Arts and Sciences, Beverly Hills, California.

23. Jack Foreman to William Wyler, May 19, 1975, William Wyler Papers, Margaret Herrick Library, Academy of Motion Picture Arts and Sciences, Beverly Hills, California.

24. Jack Foreman to William Wyler, 1. Wyler's forwarded letter to the ministry, May 30, 1975, William Wyler Papers, Margaret Herrick Library, Academy of Motion Picture Arts and Sciences, Beverly Hills, California.

25. Mehrdad Pahlbod to William Wyler, June 17, 1975, William Wyler Papers, Margaret Herrick Library, Academy of Motion Picture Arts and Sciences, Beverly Hills, California.

26. The most financially significant claim by Foreman was that *The Best Years of Our Lives* "was returned broken down into nine reels" after being projected. The shipping manifest for this film from Hollywood clearly indicates that it went out on nine reels. Shipping invoice from Paul Kohner, Inc. to the Third Tehran International Film Festival.

27. William Wyler to His Excellency S. E. M. Pahlbod, May 30, 1975, William Wyler Papers, Margaret Herrick Library, Academy of Motion Picture Arts and Sciences, Beverly Hills, California.

Index

Founded in 1893,
UNIVERSITY OF CALIFORNIA PRESS
publishes bold, progressive books and journals
on topics in the arts, humanities, social sciences,
and natural sciences—with a focus on social
justice issues—that inspire thought and action
among readers worldwide.

The UC PRESS FOUNDATION
raises funds to uphold the press's vital role
as an independent, nonprofit publisher, and
receives philanthropic support from a wide
range of individuals and institutions—and from
committed readers like you. To learn more, visit
ucpress.edu/supportus.